MW00988530

# Applicational Grammar

S.K.Shaumyan

---

# Applicational Grammar

## as a Semantic Theory of Natural Language

Translated by
J. E. Miller

*The University of Chicago Press*

The University of Chicago Press, Chicago 60637
Edinburgh University Press, Edinburgh



Published 1977

Printed in Great Britain by
R. & R. Clark Ltd
Edinburgh

*Library of Congress Cataloging in Publication Data*

Shaumian, Sebastian Konstantinovich.
Applicational grammar
Translation of Applikativnaia grammatika kak semanticheskaia teoriia estestvennykh iazykov.
Includes bibliographical references and index.
1. Semantics. 2. Structural linguistics. I. Title.
P325.S4813 1977 415 77-4432
ISBN 0-226-75102-3

**Contents**

## Foreword

In this book a semantic theory of natural language is proposed, based on the formal apparatus of applicational grammar and the genotype language defined by it.

The goal of a semantic theory of natural language is to explain the process of linguistic communication, which consists of an exchange of messages by a speaker and a hearer. In this process one and the same message can be expressed by different sentences and, conversely, one and the same sentence can express different messages.

In order to explain how the speakers of a language are able to recognise one and the same message in different sentences and different messages in one and the same sentence we shall assume that each natural language can be split into two languages: a) a primitive language in which the content of a message is represented unambiguously; b) an expression language into which the expressions of the primitive language are mapped ('expression language' is used here to mean 'a language possessing various means for the expression of one and the same message').

To model this splitting up of a natural language the genotype language is itself divided into a primitive genotype language and an expression genotype language. The latter is derived from the former in that it has new objects added to it by the rules that map into it the sentences of the primitive genotype language. These rules are formulated with the help of special logical operators that, following Curry, we shall call combinators.

The genotype language is a universal semiotic system that models semantic processes, that is, mappings from natural primitive languages into natural expression languages.

A semantic theory of natural languages is complemented by a phenotype grammar, which provides the correspondence rules connecting the genotype language and the phenotype, i.e. natural, languages.

To avoid confusion it must be indicated that there are crucial differences between some of the concepts in the semantic theory presented here and apparently similar concepts to be found in other modern works on semantics.

First of all, a semantic theory of languages should be distinguished from paraphrase theory. Paraphrase theory describes equivalent transformational relations on one single level, whereas a semantic theory deals with equivalent transformations as a generative process, progressing from the simplest objects to the most complex.

The concept of a genotype language should not be confused with that of deep structure, nor that of a phenotype language with that of surface structure. In fact, semantic deep structure corresponds to the primitive genotype language and semantic surface structure corresponds to the expression genotype language. That is, in terms of the distinction between deep and surface structure the genotype language models both semantic deep structure and semantic surface structure, and also the processes by which semantic deep structures are mapped into semantic surface structures.

It should be noted, however, that the correspondence between primitive and expression genotype languages on the one hand and semantic deep and surface structure on the other is valid only for semantic deep structure, since Chomsky and his colleagues work in fact with deep and surface structures that are both syntactic and not comparable to the genotype language. The latter, a universal semiotic system, is a fundamentally new concept that has no counterpart in transformational grammar.

# 1. The Methodological Bases of Applicational Grammar

## 1. The Problem of Meaning

Let us begin with the concept of a sentence. Definitions like the following are widespread: 'A sentence is a thought expressed in words'; or 'A sentence is a complete thought expressed in words'; or 'A sentence is a linguistic unit expressing a thought'.

Strictly speaking, these are not definitions of a sentence but explanations of what we intuitively understand by 'sentence', and they immediately raise the question of what a thought is and how it is embodied in a sentence. The difficulty is that a thought has no independent existence but is always manifested together with a linguistic unit, just as a value has no independent existence but is always manifested as the value of some particular product. Just as the value of a given product is determined with respect to other products of equivalent value, so a thought incorporated in a given sentence can be revealed only through the relationships between that sentence and others expressing the same thought. Just as goods are said to be equivalent in value if they can be exchanged one for the other, so sentences are said to be equivalent if they can be substituted one for the other in a given situation.

Any product can be taken as the value-standard by which the other products are judged, that is, as directly representing the value, and the other products are regarded as embodying the value. In exactly the same way any one out of a given class of sentences can be taken as the thought-standard, i.e. as the sentence that directly represents a thought, and the other sentences have then to be regarded as the formal linguistic expression of the thought. Consider, for example, the following sentences:

(1) *Bol'šaja sobaka ukusila spjaščego malen'kogo mal'čika* (big–dog–bit–sleeping–small–boy)

(2) *Sobaka byla bol'šaja, i ona ukusila spjaščego malen'kogo mal'čika* (dog–was–big–and–it–bit–sleeping–small–boy)

(3) *Spjaščego malen'kogo mal'čika ukusila sobaka, kotoraja byla bol'šaja* (small–sleeping–boy–bit–dog–which–was–big)

(4) *Bol'šaja sobaka ukusila malen'kogo mal'čika, kotoryj spal* (big–dog–bit–small–boy–who–was sleeping)

(5) *Bol'šaja sobaka ukusila spjaščego mal'čika, kotoryj byl malen'kij* (big–dog–bit–sleeping–boy–who–was–small)

(6) *Sobaka ukusila mal'čika, sobaka byla bol'šaja, mal'čik byl malen'kij, mal'čik spal* (dog–bit–boy, dog–was–big, boy–was–small, boy–was sleeping)

Each of these six sentences can be arbitrarily chosen as the thought-standard, i.e. as the direct representation of the thought, and the other five have then to be regarded as linguistic forms expressing the thought.

We can now answer the question of what a thought is and of how it is embodied in a sentence. From a linguistic point of view a thought is any sentence that is taken by convention as being the direct representation of the thought. The embodying of the thought in a sentence is the paraphrasing of the sentence directly representing the thought by any other sentence. Since one and the same sentence can be paraphrased in many ways, we say that one and the same thought can be embodied in many sentences, all serving as its various forms of expression.

Thus, in defining the relation 'being a thought-standard' on the sentences of a language we divide all the sentences of the language into classes, in each of which one sentence is taken as the pure thought and the others as the various forms of expression, the various embodiments of that thought. From now on we will use as synonyms of the term 'thought-standard' the terms 'standard of meaning of a sentence' and 'standard of sense of a sentence'.

The analogy between the concepts of thought and value can be continued. Just as money is a general measure of value, so there must be a general measure of sense, and it is reasonable to suppose that for each language this general measure of sense consists of the grammatically simplest sentences. But which sentences have to be considered the simplest? The answer is, those sentences that are either elementary predicate structures or combinations of elementary predicate structures. Each elementary predicate structure is the conjunction of an *n*-place predicate and one or more arguments. For example, *Mal'čik čitaet* (boy–reads) is a one-place elementary predicate structure, *Brat čitaet knigu* (brother–reads–book) is a two-place elementary predicate structure and *Otec daet den'gi synu* (father–gives–money–to son) is a three-place elementary predicate structure.

Combinations of elementary predicate structures are of two sorts. The first is obtained by joining elementary predicate structures with conjunctions, as, e.g., *Brat čitaet knigu, a sestra pišet pis'mo* (brother–reads–book–and–sister–writes–letter). The second sort is obtained by introducing another elementary predicate structure as one of the arguments of a given elementary predicate structure. Consider the elementary predicate structure *Ja znaju X* (I–know–X), in which the second argument is empty. If we replace X with the word *otca* we obtain the elementary predicate structure *Ja znaju otca* (I–know–father), and if we replace X with the elementary predicate structure *Otec priexal* (father–came) we obtain the sentence *Ja znaju: otec priexal* (I–know: father–came), which is a combination of two elementary predicate structures. This method of obtaining combinations of elementary structures will be called the embedding of one structure in another.

It is precisely such sentences that must be taken as 'thought-standards', as 'standards of meaning of a sentence'. For example, of the six sentences given above the sixth is the simplest grammatically and can be given quite naturally the role of standard.

It must be emphasised that simplicity is relative, since, if the complexity of sentences were measured by the number of clauses, the sixth sentence would be the most complex. What is essential in measuring simplicity is whether a sentence consists of homogeneous units, and in every language such sentences are elementary predicate structures or combinations of such structures. From this point of view the first sentence is the most complex, because it results from the reduction of four elementary predicate structures into one non-elementary predicate structure.

In this way we can establish for each language a primitive sub-language, consisting of the sentences that are grammatically the simplest. The language is split up into this primitive sub-language, which is taken to be a direct representation of thought, and a derived sub-language, which is regarded as expressing the thought, as embodying the thought, in linguistic form.

Stricter measures of simplicity could be applied to the primitive sub-languages of natural languages. For example, we could require that each elementary predicate structure of the sub-language contain no more than two arguments. Other requirements in connection with simplicity will be described later.

Each sentence, then, has a dual nature. Either it is a standard of meaning or it is a linguistic form that embodies the meaning. The same holds for linguistic units that are constituents of a sentence, i.e. words and morphemes. Each linguistic unit can be either a standard of meaning for a given class of linguistic units or a linguistic form embodying the meaning of the linguistic unit.

We have now proceeded far enough to be able to define the meaning of a linguistic unit, which we shall take to be the class of linguistic units that are the translations of the given unit. The concept of meaning is thus reduced to the concept of translatability, since to state the meaning of a linguistic unit is to state the rules that translate it into other linguistic units. Obviously this is not the only approach to the problem of meaning but it is a fruitful one for semantic analysis within the framework of universal grammar, and this book should be seen as demonstrating its usefulness.

## 2. Semantic Analysis of Natural Languages and the Concept of a Genotype Language

Let us now consider what is meant by a semantic theory of language. It is a linguistic theory that has as its aims a) to define the primitive sub-language that is regarded as the direct representation of thought and b) to define the rules mapping the primitive sub-language into the derived language. From now on the latter will be called the expression language, and will be considered to be the form or linguistic embodiment of thought.

From the above definition it follows that each language must have its own semantic theory and that there must be as many direct representations of thought as there are languages.

Let us examine first of all the second consequence of the definition. The same considerations apply to the primitive sub-languages, as direct representations of thought, as applied in the foregoing discussion of sentences in one language that are equivalent in meaning. If from different primitive sub-languages we take sentences that are equivalent in meaning, the problem of the correlation between a thought and its linguistic embodiment appears once more. Compare, for example, the Russian sentence *Ja obučaju detej grammatike* (I–teach–children (accusative case)–grammar (dative case)) with the equivalent Latin sentence *Doceo pueros grammaticam* and the French *J'enseigne la grammaire aux enfants*. Each of these sentences can be chosen arbitrarily as the thought-standard, i.e. as the direct representation of the thought, and the other sentences must be considered to be linguistic forms expressing the thought.

We now have to look for a general way of measuring meaning that can be applied not just within each separate language but also across languages. It is reasonable to suppose that there exists a language, not open to direct observation, whose expressions can serve as a standard of meaning and that the expressions of Russian and other natural languages are to be regarded as various linguistic embodiments of the meaning. I will call this ideal language the genotype language, concrete natural languages being phenotype languages.

The genotype language, being an abstract model of natural languages, must model semantic processes in these languages, and since in each natural language a distinction is drawn between a primitive sub-language (the direct representation of thought) and an expression sub-language (the formal expression or linguistic embodiment of thought) a corresponding distinction will have to be made in the genotype language. In the genotype language, therefore, we shall distinguish between a primitive sub-language and an expression sub-language, and we shall take semantic processes in natural languages to be modelled by the rules that map the former sub-language into the latter.

In the light of the preceding discussion the concept of a semantic theory must be generalised so that a semantic theory of natural languages is one that models semantic processes in these languages by means of a genotype language. The goals of this theory are now a) to define the primitive sub-language in the genotype language, considered as a direct representation of thought, and b) to define the rules that map the primitive sub-language into the expression language of the genotype language. This expression language is regarded as linguistic embodiment of thought.

This definition of a semantic theory is not compatible with the notion that there is a semantic theory for each natural language. Instead it is more sensible to talk of a semantic theory of natural language and the semantic description of each language in accordance with this theory. There must be, so to speak, a two-way relationship between the semantic theory and semantic descriptions, in that the semantic theory is an abstract imitation of concrete semantic descriptions and concrete semantic descriptions in their turn are concrete imitations of the semantic theory. Further research should lead to improvements in both the theory and the descriptions.

Without going into the philosophical aspect of the question, let us note in passing that the genotype language allows us to view the notion of linguistic relativity in a new light. The hypothesis of linguistic relativity that was propounded at one time in linguistics is most clearly formulated in the work of Sapir and Whorf. Its central assertion is that the world is divided up and represented in different ways by different languages. It is indeed indisputable that any one language will give a relative picture of the world but this is only one part of the story. The other part is that each relative picture embodied linguistically in a concrete language must be considered as the projection of an invariant picture of the world, represented by the genotype language. Phenotype languages, being different projections of the genotype language, thus present relative pictures of the world in which there is also something non-relative, something of the invariant, represented by the genotype language.

A semantic theory of natural languages must be deductive.

Since the writer's previous work has shown that this can be achieved with the formal apparatus of applicational grammar, a deductive semantic theory can be provided by an applicational grammar equipped with semantic transformation rules in the genotype language.

The problem posed above and the solution offered lead to a fundamentally important conclusion. If we want to ascend from empirical data to theory we must examine language not on its own but correlated with thought. The problem of this correlation has many facets and has aroused the interest of specialists in different areas, including logicians, psychologists, and philosophers. Linguists too have been attracted by the problem for a long time, though it has occupied a peripheral place in linguistics. Indeed, no matter how interesting discussions of the problem might be, they were considered not part of linguistics proper and were consigned to the philosophy of language. The preceding discussion brings about a radical change in that the correlation of language and thought can be seen not as some philosophical problem but as a central, properly linguistic one, right at the heart of linguistics.

## 3. The Construction of the Genotype Language

The genotype language, being a hypothesis about the general semiotic basis of natural languages, is a system of universal linguistic categories, which raises the question of how we arrive at a set of such categories.

They can be obtained in two ways. The first is to investigate systematically very many languages of the world (ideally, all the languages) and to establish general linguistic categories. The second is to define the basic properties of the object that we are calling a natural language and to deduce all the consequences of that definition.

The first method is widely used in modern linguistics and has yielded interesting results that testify how fruitful it is. However, to construct an abstract linguistic theory we must choose the second method. From the point of view of abstract linguistic theory a system of universal categories is in itself neither true nor false but is simply given by definition. This does not mean that any system of universal linguistic categories will do, as we shall be satisfied only with a system that successfully predicts possible linguistic categories in real languages. Thus, the crucial factor is the predictive power of the system, which, if great enough, enables the system to be an effective tool for the investigation of natural languages.

This way of constructing the genotype language is a partial instance of the hypothetico-deductive method that is used by the modern theoretical sciences. This method is a cyclic procedure that has four stages: 1) The problem is determined; 2) a hypothesis is advanced for solving the problem; 3) the consequences of the hypothesis are deduced; 4) the consequences of the hypothesis are compared with the facts of reality, which allows the degree of probability of the hypothesis to be measured. Let us examine each stage of the hypothetico-deductive method.

1. A problem arises when facts of essential importance are revealed that stand in need of an explanation. As was shown in the previous section, one fact that is of essential importance to linguistics and that needs to be explained is the possibility of translating from one language to another.

2. When a hypothesis is advanced as a solution to a problem, use is made of what is called a thought-experiment. This involves placing the object under investigation in some imaginary, ideal conditions that cannot be obtained in the course of an actual experiment, and that allow the essential features of the object to be revealed in an ideal fashion, unencumbered by extraneous factors. For example, the law of inertia in mechanics is a hypothesis that was formulated with the help of a thought-experiment. Moving bodies were considered under ideal conditions in which all resistance to movement was removed. These conditions cannot be established in the real world, but their simulation by a thought-experiment led to the discovery of one of the fundamental laws of mechanics.

3. The consequences deduced from the hypothesis should not just concern the facts that the hypothesis was formulated to explain in the first place, but should predict new facts, hitherto unknown. Thus each hypothesis is simultaneously a tool for explanation and a tool for prediction; that is, it must have explanatory and predictive power.

4. Comparison of the consequences of a hypothesis with the facts of reality make it possible to verify the hypothesis, correct it, and even reject it in favour of a new, more probable one. Since new problems arise in the course of verification, we go back to the initial stage (but on a new level).

From now on we shall use the term 'hypothesis' to mean both a single hypothesis and a system of hypotheses, and when it is necessary to distinguish these concepts we shall use the terms 'system of hypotheses' or 'hypothetico-deductive system'. These latter terms contrast with the term 'hypothesis', denoting in this case a single hypothesis.

The term 'theory' will be used as a synonym of the terms 'system of hypotheses' or 'hypothetico-deductive system'. Some people reserve 'theory' for a thoroughly tested system of hypotheses. Of course, the term 'theory' can be used in this sense but from a logical point of view there is no essential difference between 'system of hypotheses' and 'theory', as each theory must be subject to constant verification no matter how thoroughly it has already been tested. The history of science shows that theories that seem unshakeable have been overthrown not only by new facts but by the development of new points of view concerning facts already known.

The rapid transformation and turnover of theories in the abstract theoretical sciences may create the impression in the layman that our cognition is shaky and that we are incapable of understanding the area of objective reality that is under investigation. But just the opposite is true, since it is precisely the rapid turnover of theories that testifies to the successes of a flourishing science. And it is the constancy of theories that indicates the science in stagnation, the science in an unfavourable theoretical state. In this connexion the following passage from Einstein is of interest:

> To use a comparison, we could say that creating a new theory is not like destroying an old barn and erecting a skyscraper in its place. It is rather like climbing a mountain, gaining new and wider views, discovering unexpected connections between our starting point and its rich environment. But the point from which we started out still exists and can be seen, although it appears smaller and forms a tiny part of our broad view gained by the mastery of the obstacles on our adventurous way up.[1]

To put forward a system of hypotheses is to construct a network of concepts that are defined simultaneously as elements of a formal system without being directly linked to an empirical science. There are no analytical procedures for deriving a system of hypotheses from the data collected by an empirical science, since the formulation of a system of hypotheses is not connected with any analytical mental activity but with the creative imagination, the creative intuition, of the scientist. This process of formulation can be illustrated with the following example from Einstein:

> Physical concepts are free creations of the human mind, and are not, however it may seem, uniquely determined by the external world. In our endeavor to understand reality we are somewhat like a man trying to understand the mechanism of a closed watch. He sees the face and the moving hands, even hears its ticking, but he has no way of opening the case. If he is ingenious he may form some picture of a mechanism which could be responsible for all the things he observes, but he may never be quite sure his

[1] A. Einstein and L. Infield, *The Evolution of Physics*, pp. 158–9. Simon and Schuster, New York 1938.

picture is the only one which could explain his observations. He will never be able to compare his picture with the real mechanism and he cannot even imagine the possibility or the meaning of such a comparison. But he certainly believes that, as his knowledge increases, his picture of reality will become simpler and simpler and will explain a wider and wider range of his sensuous impressions. He may also believe in the existence of the ideal limit of knowledge and that it is approached by the human mind. He may call this ideal limit the objective truth.[1]

The genotype language is a specified system of linguistic objects that is defined by the mathematical rules for constructing such objects and by the rules for deriving new linguistic objects from the given linguistic objects. These rules are called the grammar of the genotype language or an applicational grammar, since in the construction of objects of the genotype language a crucial role is played by the operation of application, about which more shortly.

When we call a system of linguistic objects specified, we have in mind the possibility of constructing first of all a primitive system of linguistic objects, the system changing in different ways according to a definite set of rules depending on what the investigator wants to do. We shall therefore draw a distinction between the primitive form of the genotype language and various specifications of the genotype language.

## 4. Applicational Grammar as a Formal System

Abstract theories of natural languages can be cast in various mathematical forms, of which the most convenient is without doubt the formal system or calculus. A formal system, as defined in mathematical logic, is a mathematical system that satisfies the following conditions:

1. A set of initial objects, called atoms, is postulated.
2. A finite set of rules is postulated for constructing complex objects from the atoms. The set of atoms and the complex objects constructed out of them are called an inductive class of objects.
3. On the inductive class of objects are defined elementary predicates by means of which statements about the objects are built up.
4. A subset of the set of possible statements about the objects of the inductive class are accepted by convention as being true, and these true statements are called axioms.
5. Rules are postulated for deriving from the axioms other true statements called theorems.

The foregoing points can be exemplified by a formal system that

[1] Einstein and Infield, *op. cit.*, p. 33.

generates the inductive class of natural numbers. In this system the following primitives are postulated:

1. An atom, 1.
2. Rules for constructing the inductive class of natural numbers. These rules take the following form: a) 1 is a natural number; b) if $X$ is a natural number $XS$ is also a natural number.

In rule b), $S$ denotes a one-place function, which has $X$ as its argument and $XS$ as its value. The function $S$ establishes a correspondence between a natural number $X$ and a natural number $XS$ that follows $X$. Using these rules we can generate: 1 (=1); $1S$ (=2); $1SS$ (=3); $1SSS$ (=4); and so on. Also postulated are:

3. One elementary predicate, =. The elementary statements about the natural numbers are of the form $X = Y$.
4. One axiom $1 = 1$.
5. One derivational rule: If $X = Y$, $XS = YS$. This rule generates the theorems $1S = 1S$, $1SS = 1SS$, $1SSS = 1SSS$, and so on.

This formal system shows how the infinite set of natural numbers can be reduced to its simplest constituent elements: the natural number 1 and rules for constructing the inductive class of natural numbers. Moreover we can say that the inductive class of natural numbers is but one interpretation of an abstract class of symbols constructed from some abstract symbol by means of the above construction rules. Using the derivational rule we deduce from the statement $1 = 1$, which is accepted as true, the other true statements about the identity of natural numbers. By representing abstract theories of natural languages in mathematical form, as formal systems, it becomes possible to see how complex linguistic objects can be reduced to their most simple constituent elements, to linguistic atoms. One of the most important tasks of linguistic explanation lies precisely in this process of reducing the complex to the simple.

Semantic theories of natural languages belong to the class of abstract theories, whose goal is to show how complex linguistic objects can be derived from simpler ones. Thus from the point of view of an abstract linguistic theory, to explain a complex linguistic object is to reveal a mechanism for constructing it out of simple linguistic objects. In this respect abstract linguistic theories belong to those explanatory theories of contemporary science that are called construction theories. These theories play an important role in other sciences, for example in physics. According to Einstein:

> We can distinguish various kinds of theories in physics. Most of them are constructive. They attempt to build up a picture of the more complex phenomena out of the materials of a relatively simple formal scheme from which they start out. Thus the kinetic

> theory of gases seeks to reduce mechanical, thermal, and diffusional processes to movements of molecules — i.e., to build them up out of the hypothesis of molecular motion. When we say that we have succeeded in understanding a group of natural processes, we invariably mean that a constructive theory has been found which covers the processes in question.[1]

In the same way, abstract linguistic theories try to reduce the properties inherent in complex linguistic objects to the properties of the linguistic atoms.

It is well-known that the explanatory power of any theory is connected with its power to predict facts that were unknown before, though possible in principle. This applies also to abstract linguistic theories, which do not explain only known linguistic facts but which predict theoretically possible but not yet observed linguistic facts.

## 5. The Two-Level Principle

The philosophy of science distinguishes two sorts of scientific concepts: elementary concepts and constructs. The elementary concepts are those that reflect the immediate data of experience, e.g. white, black, light, heavy, sweet, bitter, stone, wood, horse, etc. Constructs are concepts of which no direct experience is possible, e.g. the electron in physics, the gene in biology and the phoneme in phonology.

Elementary concepts are formed by generalising from the data of direct observation but constructs, not being deducible from direct observation, can not be formed by generalisation. Instead they are introduced into a science by postulates. The formation of elementary concepts by generalisation does not raise us above the level of direct observation, whereas the postulation of constructs enables us to reveal the relationships underlying the observed facts, to penetrate to the essentials.

In addition to the distinction between elementary concepts and constructs the philosophy of science also recognises two levels of abstraction: the level of observation, the empirical basis of science, and the level of constructs. The constructs and the empirical base are connected by correspondence rules.

It should be mentioned that the term 'level of observation' is to be interpreted in a logical, not psychological, sense as denoting the initial facts of a science that are to be given a theoretical explanation. The question as to what we do or do not observe will always be controversial, even if approached from the point of view of psychology. But from the point of view of logic the concept of a level of observation is

[1] A. Einstein, *Ideas and Opinions*, p. 228. Crown Publishers Inc., New York 1954.

absolutely unambiguous, since it consists of those facts that are defined as observed within the framework of a given science and that by definition serve as the empirical basis of that science. This enables us to use the term 'level of observation' or 'the empirical basis of a science'.

The dichotomy that has just been discussed is typical only of highly-developed sciences. In descriptive sciences like botany and zoology there are no constructs, as the method of generalisation used in these sciences does not permit them to rise above the level of direct observation.

When we speak about two levels of abstraction and about the dichotomous structure of a science we must remember that the concept of a 'level of abstraction' can include abstractions of various sorts, which can be distributed among various levels. There are many levels of abstraction but only two in the above sense.

The realisation that abstract sciences have this dichotomous structure enables us to consider the logical properties of scientific laws in a new light. If it is correct that every scientific law should reveal the underlying essentials of observed facts and phenomena, it follows from the dichotomous structure of the abstract sciences that these laws can not be established by generalisation, since the latter does not go beyond the level of direct observation and does not give us access to the essentials.

In order to reveal the relationships underlying observed facts it is not enough that a scientific law be simply a universal proposition. It must be a universal proposition that includes constructs. It follows that scientific laws can not be established by generalisation from the immediate data of experience, but have to be postulated as universal propositions that play an explanatory role in relation to the empirical basis of the science.

Why are abstractions introduced into a science? If a science is to amass knowledge of the real world it must distinguish the essential from the inessential in the facts under investigation and this can only be achieved by abstracting from the inessential details. This leads to the formation of abstract concepts and abstract objects corresponding to them, without which not one generalisation nor one law could be formulated. But in order to connect a generalisation or a law with the data of experience the abstract objects must be replaced by concrete ones, i.e. the abstract objects must be excluded. You can not sit on an abstract chair, only a concrete one. When we say *A dog loves meat* this assertion contains an abstract object 'dog' (for convenience we shall ignore the fact that 'meat' is also an abstract object) and *loves meat* is regarded as a predicate. But an abstract dog can not love meat.

The introduction of an abstract object is valid only if there are rules for excluding it by combining the above assertion with concrete assertions of the sort *Fido is a dog*, therefore *Fido loves meat*; or *Bonzo is a dog*, therefore *Bonzo loves meat*. Thus, associated with each abstract object in a science are rules for its introduction and its exclusion.

Our immediate task is to explain in general terms the rules for introducing and excluding abstract objects. Let us begin with the sort of generalisation that is called a generalising or identifying abstraction (idealisation). This consists in abstracting from the dissimilar properties of concrete objects and simultaneously isolating identical properties of the objects. In connexion with idealisation it is interesting to read Markov's remarks on the concept of an abstract letter. He writes:

> 'The possibility of establishing identity between letters allows us, by way of *abstraction by identification*, to set up the notion of an abstract letter. The application of that abstraction consists in a given case in that we actually speak of two identical letters as of *one and the same letter*. For example, instead of saying that in the word "identical" two letters enter, which are identical with "i", we say the letter "i" enters in the word "identical" twice. Here we have set up the concept of an abstract letter "i" and we consider concrete letters, identical to "i", as representatives of this *one* abstract letter. *Abstract letters* are letters considered with a precision up to identity.'[1]

'Being identical' is a relative property, since what is identical in one respect may be different in another. Markov, in his discussion of the identity of letters, says:

> 'The concept of identity and difference of letters is also conventional. In particular, for the identity of printed letters it is usual to impose more rigid requirements than for the identity of handwritten ones: the identity of the former is closer to a geometric "equivalence" than the identity of the latter. The arbitrariness of the concept of identity is thrown into a particularly sharp relief in establishing the identity of a printed with a handwritten letter.'[2]

Let us now turn to constructs. A good example of a construct is the concept of value, a property that cannot be revealed in concrete objects either by direct observation or with the help of instruments. It might be asked how the power of abstraction permits the construc-

[1] Markov, A. A., *Teorija Algorifmov*, Akademija Nauk, Moscow-Leningrad 1954, pp. 7–8. Translated by J. Schorr-Kon and staff of Israel Program for Scientific Translations and published by the latter organisation under the title *The Theory of Algorithms*, Jerusalem, 1961.

[2] Markov, *op. cit.*, p. 7.

tion of this concept. The answer is that values are arrived at by studying the relations that are established between goods when they are being exchanged, one item being traded either for one other item or for several other items. During this process of exchange an equivalence relation is set up between goods that differ in quality and quantity. We shall use the term 'relational abstraction' for the construction of concepts like that of value, to distinguish it from identifying abstraction.

An interesting analogy can be drawn between the concept of value and the concepts of valeur and the phoneme in theoretical linguistics. This is worthwhile because an analogy is not just an instrument of proof but may play a heuristic role, in that it can elucidate the concepts of one science through the more perspicuous concepts of another.

Since an analogy between the value of goods and the valeur of an expression was made in section 1 of this chapter, I shall concentrate here on an analogy between the concept of value and the concept of the phoneme. To this end we shall examine my law of phonological reducibility, illustrated by examples from the interesting work of the Rumanian linguist Ştirbu.[1]

The law is formulated thus: 'If there is a set of sounds $M_i$, held to be a standard, then for each sound $a_i$ in this set it is possible to find a sound $a_j$ belonging to $M_i$, the difference between the two sounds being reducible to the effect of a positional operator $P_j$'.[2] This law can be illustrated with the following examples.

Let there be in position $P_1$ a set of sounds, taken as a standard, $M_1\{x_1, y_1, z_1\}$. Let us consider the set of sounds $M_2\{x_2, y_2, z_2\}$, that is a transformation of the set $M_1$ by the operator $t_2$ that characterises the position $P_2$ in which $M_1$ occurs.

The law of phonological reducibility gives the mapping

$$\left.\begin{matrix} x_1 \\ y_1 \\ z_1 \end{matrix}\right\} + t_2 \rightarrow \left\{\begin{matrix} x_2 \\ y_2 \\ z_2 \end{matrix}\right.$$

Or, to represent it differently:

$$x_2 = x_1 + t_2$$
$$y_2 = y_1 + t_2$$
$$z_2 = z_1 + t_2$$

If we abstract from $t_2$ as a physical element, from a purely functional point of view the equivalences are

[1] V. Ştirbu. Reducţie şi extensiune. *Cercetări de Linguistica*, anul XIV, 1, Tannarie-Înie, 1969. Editura Academia Republicii Socialiste România.

[2] S. K. Shaumyan. *Problemy teoretičeskoj fonologii*, Moscow 1962, p. 95. English translation *Problems of Theoretical Phonology*, The Hague, Mouton, 1968.

$$x_1 = x_2$$
$$y_1 = y_2$$
$$z_1 = z_2$$

On the basis of this equivalence relation we can postulate the invariants X, Y, Z.

In Rumanian the laminal stops $d^o$, $t^o$, $n^o$, which occur in combination with back vowels, are a positional transformation of the series d, t, n, by the operator $t_{labial}$. We thus obtain the mapping:

$$\left.\begin{matrix} d \\ t \\ n \end{matrix}\right\} + t_{labial} \rightarrow \left\{\begin{matrix} d^o \\ t^o \\ n^o \end{matrix}\right.$$

From this it follows that

$$d^o = d + (^o)$$
$$t^o = t + (^o)$$
$$n^o = n + (^o)$$

Abstracting from labialisation we obtain

$$d^o = d$$
$$t^o = t$$
$$n^o = n$$

What are these invariants X, Y, Z? They are abstract properties that are ascribed to sounds on the basis of their role in keeping words apart and are called phonemes. Phonemes are ideal semiotic elements, ideal semiotic values that have no physical existence, the relationship between phoneme and sound being the same as that between exchange value and use value. Just as not one atom of matter enters into the value of goods, so not one atom of the physical substratum enters into the linguistic value embodied in a sound, that is, in a phoneme.

No matter what instruments we use or what degree of accuracy we attain, a sound, i.e. a phoneme, will always elude us. We can see that the concept of the phoneme is introduced via the same sort of abstraction as the concept of value, which sort was called relational abstraction. Both value and the phoneme are not to be found by direct observation but are abstract concepts.

It was shown above that the invariants X, Y, Z are abstract properties that are ascribed to sounds, but there is a widespread view that phonemes are not properties of sounds but independent objects of some sort. This view is to be explained by the influence of the word 'phoneme', which by its linguistic form is a word that should denote an object. The use of terms denoting objects for the denotation of properties is called reification, and is to be found in situations where it is more convenient to speak about properties than about objects. But we should not forget when we indulge in reification what is concealed by these terms denoting objects. As a construct the phoneme has the status of the property of a sound, just as a value is a property of goods.

The question of distinctive features might be brought up. After all, the phoneme as an object is considered to be a bundle of distinctive features. This question too is caused by the hypnotic influence of the word. We say 'phoneme' and 'distinctive feature' and think that the first word denotes an object, the second a property. In reality both these words correspond to properties, but properties of different orders. A distinctive feature is the simplest semiotic property of a sound and is incapable of further analysis into smaller components, whereas a phoneme is a complex semiotic property of sounds that can be split up into simple semiotic properties—namely, distinctive features.

Reification is also to be found in applicational grammar since, although linguistic functions are relations, they are there looked upon as objects.

Returning to the concept of the phoneme and to other constructs that are introduced via relational abstraction, we can formulate a general rule for excluding these constructs. The rule consists in specifying how to establish equivalence relations between sounds and other empirical objects to which the given constructs correspond.

In linguistic literature, especially in typological studies, a law is identified with a high degree of statistical probability. This conception of a law can be exemplified as follows. Before duck-billed platypuses were discovered in Tasmania zoologists considered the essential feature of mammals to be that they did not lay eggs. Although with this discovery it became clear that mammals can lay eggs, the zoologist's law that mammals do not lay eggs has not lost any of its force, because it is indeed the case that the overwhelming majority of mammals do not lay eggs. With its high degree of statistical probability the proposition that mammals do not lay eggs has remained an important statistical law. Going on the previous description of scientific laws as universal propositions that contain constructs, we shall assume that the high degree of statistical probability associated with a universal proposition does not in itself entitle that universal proposition to be considered a law.

Let us take a bit further the example of duck-billed platypuses. The data on the laying or non-laying of eggs by mammals are obtained by direct observation and therefore the proposition that the overwhelming majority of mammals do not lay eggs can not be considered a law, not even a statistical one. Not even if it had been established that not one mammal lays eggs could the proposition be considered a law, since in both cases we would be dealing not with a law but with a generalisation. The first is a statistical generalisation, i.e. one with a high degree of statistical probability, and the second is a complete generalisation, i.e. one without exceptions. Even if the proposition about the egg-laying of mammals were supported in all cases by the data of direct observation, to be considered a law it would have to be linked without fail to constructs characterising the essence of mammals.

The law of phonological reducibility can serve to illustrate the difference in principle between a generalisation and a law. The basic problem is that of the criteria by which the concrete sounds that can be experienced directly are judged to be the realisation of the same phoneme. In his *Grundzüge der Phonologie* Trubetzkoj made use of the following rule to solve the problem of phonological identity: if two physically related sounds are mutually exclusive in a given position, they are to be considered realisations of the same phoneme.

Can this rule be regarded as a law? The answer is that it can not, because Trubetzkoj established it by simply accumulating data by direct observation. His argument ran approximately like this. In Russian, realisations of the same phoneme are physically related and mutually exclusive in a given position, and the same is found in English, French, German, Italian, etc. Consequently, the essential characteristic of sounds that realise the same phoneme is that they are mutually exclusive in a given position while being physically similar. This rule possesses a high degree of statistical probability but is a generalisation, not a law.

The above law of phonological reducibility was arrived at not via generalisation but by investigating how communication takes place by means of natural language. In principle this investigation can be carried out on the basis of data from any one natural language, but in this case the information was obtained not by sifting through a large number of different languages but by means of a thought-experiment that involved placing the object under investigation into ideal conditions that could not be obtained in a physical experiment but that allow the essential features of the object to be revealed in an ideal fashion, unobscured by circumstantial detail.

If we thus investigate the role played by sounds in communication by means of natural language the essential property of sounds turns out to be their ability to distinguish words. But this does not imply that sounds with the same word-distinguishing ability should be physically similar. Indeed, it becomes clear that the physical relatedness of sounds that often accompanies semiotic relatedness is precisely a circumstantial detail that obscures the essential facts of the matter. The essential facts with respect to the semiotic function of sounds in distinguishing words is that, independently of physical similarity, a one-to-one relationship can be established between sets of sounds in different positions. The law of phonological reducibility can be demonstrated with the following thought-experiment: if from the semiotic point of view what is essential is that sounds that distinguish words should not be confused then we can allow that sounds in position $P_1$, denoted by A, B, and C, change in position $P_2$ so that A becomes a new sound denoted by D, B becomes the sound denoted by A and C becomes the sound denoted by B. The correspondence is shown in the table below.

| $P_1$ | $P_2$ |
|---|---|
| A | D |
| B | A |
| C | B |

This thought-experiment lays bare the essential semiotic properties of sounds so that they can be seen in an ideal pure form. But what we see is that the one-to-one correspondence between the two sets of sounds reveals that physically identical sounds—A in position $P_1$ and A in position $P_2$; B in position $P_1$ and B in position $P_2$—possess different semiotic properties, that is, realise different phonemes, whereas physically different sounds—A in position $P_1$ and D in position $P_2$; B in position $P_1$ and A in position $P_2$; C in position $P_1$ and B in position $P_2$—possess semiotically identical properties, that is, realise the same phonemes.

This experiment relies entirely on investigating the conditions under which communication takes place by means of natural language, and its significance does not depend on whether only one language is taken into account or a thousand languages. From the law of phonological reducibility it is clear that the laws of the structure of a language are established by postulating linguistic constructs, in which task a crucial role is played by thought-experiments.

The preceding discussion strongly suggests that statistical methods are not appropriate in investigations of linguistic structure, but this conclusion would be too hasty. The point is that we should distinguish as clearly as possible between potential and actual linguistic systems. For example, phonological systems with one vowel phoneme are potentially just as possible as phonological systems with several vowel phonemes, but in actual phonological systems there are characteristically several vowel phonemes. It is clear that while statistical methods are no use in the search for the structural laws of potential linguistic systems they are important in investigations of how potential linguistic systems are realised in the linguistic systems of actual languages. Statistical methods only come into their own once constructs have been postulated in order to establish the units and structural laws of potential linguistic systems.

When distinguishing between potential and actual linguistic systems we should also distinguish between immanent and typological laws of linguistic structure, because statistical methods are no use in the search for the immanent laws but are crucially important in the discovery of the typological ones. In this connexion it should be emphasised that the above discussion concerning the confusion of law and generalisation not only does not undermine the concepts behind the typological investigation of languages in terms of universals and quasi-universals but, when taken together with the distinction between the empirical basis and the level of constructs, actually increases their power and significance.

Generalisation is by nature inductive, whereas thought-experiments are deductive, but we should remember that induction and deduction are connected. It is not at all a case of preferring one method of investigation to the other, but merely of specifying the place occupied by different methods in the general strategy of scientific research.

The concept of the genotype language resulted from a thought-experiment. In an investigation of communication by means of natural languages the question arises as to what are the simplest universals without which, by definition, a language would not be a natural language. Abstracting away from all irrelevant details, we can suppose that not one natural language could exist without sentences. We here interpret 'sentence' in the broadest possible sense as an expression denoting a situation or as a communication. Indeed it is hard to imagine a natural language in which the stream of speech was not broken up into definite discrete semiotic elements functioning as sentences in the above sense. Furthermore, it is scarcely possible that there could be natural languages without expressions denoting objects, i.e. nouns in the broad sense, or terms. With sentences and terms as the simplest universal elements, a formal system can be constructed showing how any complex expressions from any natural language can be reduced to these universal elements.

Applicational grammar may seem very complex to the reader but is in fact very simple. This statement might seem paradoxical, but the crux of the matter is that the simpler the initial elements are from a logical point of view, the longer is the deductive chain of derived elements connecting the initial elements with the final results that can be confirmed or refuted experimentally. The paradox is that applicational grammar may seem complex precisely because it is so simple. It may seem so complex and difficult because we have to start from fundamental elements that are very abstract in form, and it takes a long time to move down the deductive chain going from one link to the next until we reach the links that are directly connected with the empirical basis, with the level of observation.

By means of a thought-experiment the genotype language is constructed so that the representation of meanings is free of anything irrelevant and inessential with respect to communication. The genotype language models the universal features of natural languages that enable man to code, transcode and decode messages in these languages. What is essential is that the same message can be coded into different sets of signs and that each set can be transcoded into the other. Thus the genotype language is teleological in that it is constructed for a semantic calculus that shows how man can use natural language for expressing the same message or the same thought in different ways. Since the genotype language is a hypothesis about a universal language base for the languages of the world, the hypothetico-deductive method is used in applicational grammar.[1]

The concepts of identificational abstraction and relational abstraction have already been introduced, but the postulation of a formal system by means of the hypothetico-deductive method brings us to a third type of abstraction, which can be called systemic abstraction.

The first two types of abstraction are first and foremost connected with analysis, being used when we simply want to isolate the essential aspects of objects that are being compared, abstracting away from the irrelevant and inessential, or when we are establishing complex relational links between the objects; that is, when we are isolating the properties that are not directly observable.

As was shown earlier, the hypothetico-deductive method is a cyclic cognitive procedure that is carried out in four stages. What was called above 'systemic abstraction' takes place on the second stage, when theories are advanced as a hypothetico-deductive system.

Systemic abstraction consists in the construction of a whole network of concepts that are given simultaneously as elements of the formal system, without any direct link with the empirical basis of the science. Systemic analysis is connected not with the analytic activity

[1] The suggestion that the hypothetico-deductive method be used as the logical basis for linguistic theory was first put forward in Shaumyan, *op. cit.*

of the scientist but with his creative imagination, his creative intuition.

What is the ontological status of the abstract objects in a hypothetico-deductive system? Or, to put it another way, in what sense do the abstract objects in a hypothetico-deductive system exist? In answering this question a useful analogy can be drawn between a hypothetico-deductive system and a geographical map (not forgetting, of course, that the analogy cannot be complete in all details and that it is valid only from a certain point of view.)

A geographical map exists, but not in the same sense as the geographical territory that it represents. The territory belongs to objective reality and exists independently of the map but the map is a symbolic system, that is, a creation of the human mind that is used to represent a particular aspect of objective reality, a particular territory. A hypothetico-deductive system exists in the same sense as a map exists. It is a symbolic system that serves to represent a particular aspect of reality.

As for a linguistic hypothetico-deductive system, that is a hypothetico-deductive system that represents objective reality of a special sort—natural languages, i.e. natural symbolic systems. Although natural languages are a creation of the human mind, serving as a means of communication and as a tool for finding out about reality, they are here considered as belonging to objective reality.

## 2. The Genotype Language

### 1. The Normal Form of the Genotype Language

In developing the hypothesis of the genotype language a thought-experiment will be performed. If we abstract away from everything in natural languages that is irrelevant to the process of communication between speaker and hearer we have to recognise as essential only three classes of linguistic objects: a) the names of objects; b) the names of situations; and c) transformers. What exactly are these classes of linguistic objects?

Nouns and noun phrases can serve as the names of objects, for example in Russian: *sobaka* (dog), *bol'šaja sobaka* (big dog), *bol'šaja moxnataja sobaka* (big hairy dog), *bol'šaja moxnataja černaja sobaka* (big hairy black dog). The label 'term' will be used to denote the name of an object.

A situation is any whole that is an object and a property (in the broadest sense of the word) that is ascribed to it, or a whole that is several objects and relations which are ascribed to them and which bind them together. Objects that form part of a situation will be called the participants in the situation. The participants may themselves be situations. A distinction will be drawn between simple and complex situations, a simple situation being one whose participants are only objects and a complex situation being one among whose participants there is at least one situation.

A further distinction will be drawn between concrete and abstract situations. Concrete situations are those whose participants are concrete objects to which concrete properties are ascribed; for example *Sobaka est mjaso* (dog–is eating–meat), *Koška p'et moloko* (cat–is drinking–milk), *Mal'čik čitaet knigu* (boy–is reading–book), *Otec pišet pis'mo* (father–is writing–letter). Abstract situations are those in which we abstract away from the participants, properties and relations of concrete situations. For instance, corresponding to the above examples of concrete situations is one abstract situation: *X soveršaet nekotoroe dejstvie nad Y* (X–is carrying out–some–action–on–Y).

The names of situations are sentences and the names of properties and relations are predicates, with the names of the participants in the situation being arguments of a predicate.

From the preceding definition of a predicate it is obvious that the linguistic concept of a predicate differs from the logical one, since in logic predicates are not simply properties or relations but those properties or relations that are held to be true or false.

Transformers are objects that convert the objects of one class either into objects of another class or into objects of the same class. If terms and sentences are taken to be initial classes of linguistic objects, then in addition to these two classes we obtain four more: a) objects that transform terms into sentences; b) objects that transform sentences into terms; c) objects that transform terms into terms; and d) objects that transform sentences into sentences.

These classes can be represented as follows. A term will be denoted by $\alpha$ and a sentence by $\beta$. The word 'transformer' will be denoted by $\Delta$, and by convention the formula $\Delta$xy will be read thus: 'the transformer of x into y'. We now have the following six formulae:

$\alpha$ 'term'
$\beta$ 'sentence'
$\Delta\alpha\beta$ 'transformer of a term into a sentence'
$\Delta\beta\alpha$ 'transformer of a sentence into a term'
$\Delta\alpha\alpha$ 'transformer of a term into a term'
$\Delta\beta\beta$ 'transformer of a sentence into a sentence'.

These formulae, which can serve as the names of classes of linguistic objects, will be regarded as objects of the genotype language. We shall now introduce a notation for linguistic objects belonging to some class or other. The general notation for these objects takes the form eX, and is to be read thus: linguistic object X belongs to the class e of linguistic objects.

Different linguistic objects, regarded as linguistic constants, will be denoted either by different capital letters of the Roman alphabet or by the same Roman letter with different indices: for example, A, B, C, . . ., or $A^1$, $A^2$, . . ., $B^1$, $B^2$, . . ., $C^1$, $C^2$, and so on.

Let us examine some concrete examples of the notation for individual linguistic objects (or simply 'objects' for short). Suppose there are the formulae $\alpha$A, $\alpha$B, $\alpha$C, or $\alpha A^1$, $\alpha A^2$, $\alpha A^3$. These formulae are read thus: 'object A belonging to the class of terms', 'object B belonging to the class of terms', and so on.

Other formulae are $\Delta\alpha\beta A^1$, $\Delta\alpha\beta A^2$, which are read: 'object $A^1$ belonging to the class of transformers of terms into sentences', 'object $A^2$ belonging to the class of transformers of terms into sentences', etc.

Before examining other objects of the genotype language, let us consider how these objects are to be interpreted. Two types of interpretation will be distinguished, abstract and empirical. Abstract interpretation is determined exclusively by the rules for constructing objects. For instance, the interpretation of the objects $\Delta\alpha\beta$, $\Delta\beta\alpha$, $\Delta\alpha\alpha$, $\Delta\beta\beta$ is determined by the rules for constructing them out of the objects $\alpha$, $\beta$ with a given interpretation. Thus, if we assign $\alpha$ the value of a term, $\beta$ the value of a sentence, and $\Delta$ the value of a transformer, it follows that, for example, $\Delta\alpha\beta$ must be interpreted as 'transformer of a term into a sentence'. It is thus necessary to distinguish between given and derived abstract interpretations.

To explain what is meant by the empirical interpretation of objects in the genotype language we must examine first the concept of isomorphism (identity of structure), which is crucial to an understanding of empirical interpretation.

A classic example of a description that involves isomorphism is the theory of vibration. There are various sorts of physical vibrations: mechanical vibrations, acoustic vibrations, electromagnetic vibrations, physiological vibrations in live tissues, and so on. But vibration theory is the study of vibration independently of the physical nature of the objects subject to the vibration. Thus for vibration theory the objects being studied are characterised not by their physical nature but by a definite network of relations expressed in the form of mathematical equations. Since there is an identity of structure (an isomorphism) holding between the various sorts of physical vibration, one type of vibration can be transformed into another. For example, the mechanical vibration of a gramophone needle is transformed into the acoustic vibration of particles of air, and the acoustic vibration of particles of air is transformed into the physiological vibration of the eardrum. For these reasons it can be maintained that there is an identity of structure holding between the surface of the gramophone record, the music produced by the record-player and the aural sensations of the person who perceives the music.

We can now proceed to the following definition of isomorphism: a class X, ordered by the relations $R_1, \ldots, R_n$, has the same structure as class Y, ordered by the relations $R_1', \ldots, R_n'$, if the elements of class X can be associated with the elements of class Y and vice-versa, so that if the elements $a_1, a_2, \ldots, a_n$ belonging to class X are associated with the elements $b_1, b_2, \ldots, b_m$ belonging to class Y, and if $R_i$ connects $a_1, a_2, \ldots, a_n$ (in that order) then $R_i'$ connects $b_1, b_2, \ldots, b_m$ (in that order), and vice-versa.

It is obvious that on this definition isomorphism is a very abstract concept, and indeed objects that are physically very different can be related by isomorphism. Isomorphism is of fundamental importance for any abstract empirical science, since such a science gives an exact definition of the empirical objects within its sphere up to isomorphism.

Let us illustrate isomorphism with respect to the description of a language. Compare the Russian phrase *malen'kij dom* (small–house) and the Russian word *domik* (small house). The adjective *malen'kij* (small) transforms the noun phrase *dom* (house) into a new noun phrase. (A noun in a natural language is a partial instance of a noun phrase.) Exactly the same is done by the suffix *-ik*, which transforms the noun phrase *dom* into a new noun phrase, *domik*. Thus if we set up two classes of noun phrase—a) *malen'kij dom* (class X); b) *domik* (class Y)—the first class is ordered by the relation *dom*→*malen'kij dom* (R), the second by the relation *dom*→*domik* (R′). We see that the elements of class X can be associated with the elements of class Y (*dom*=*dom*, *malen'kij dom*=*domik*) and vice-versa. If the elements of the first class *dom* and *malen'kij dom* are connected by a relation of diminution (R) and are then put in correspondence with the elements of the second class *dom* and *domik*, then the elements of the second class, *dom* and *domik* (in that order), will be connected by a relation of diminution (R′). This means that there is a relation of isomorphism between the two classes of noun phrases, i.e. we can say that class X, ordered by the relation R, has the same structure as class Y, ordered by the relation R′, and this enables us to consider the classes identical.

With the notion of isomorphism we can now set about explaining empirical interpretation, beginning with some concrete examples.

The object $\Delta\alpha\alpha$ of the genotype language is interpreted on the abstract level as the transformer of a term into a term. To obtain an empirical interpretation for it we must find an object in a natural language that resembles it (is identical with it up to isomorphism). For instance, if one term $\alpha$ is interpreted as the noun *stol* (table) and a second term $\alpha$ is interpreted as the noun *stolik* (small table) then the suffix *-ik* can be regarded as the transformer of the noun *stol* into the noun *stolik*. That is to say, with respect to the Russian nouns *stol* and *stolik* the suffix *-ik* plays the same role as does $\Delta\alpha\alpha$ with respect to the objects $\alpha$ and $\alpha$ in the genotype language and can be considered an empirical interpretation of the object $\Delta\alpha\alpha$.

Similarly, an adjective can be taken as an empirical interpretation of the object $\Delta\alpha\alpha$ (the adjective *malen'kij* transforms the noun phrase *dom* into a new noun phrase just as the suffix *-ik* transforms the noun phrase *dom* into the noun phrase *domik*). This example shows that in Russian there is an isomorphism between the class of noun phrases consisting of an adjective and a noun and the class of derived nouns consisting of a simple root and a derivational suffix.

This does not exhaust the possibilities, as the transformer of a term into a term can be interpreted in Russian as a participle (cf. *gorjaščij dom*, burning–house), as the genitive case form of a noun (cf. *dom otca*, house–of father), as a noun preceded by a preposition (cf. *dom na beregu*, house–on–bank), and as any other oblique case form of a noun, which we shall ignore for the moment. The empirical interpretation of the object $\Delta\alpha\alpha$ thus reveals an isomorphism between various types of noun phrase and derived nouns. Similar results can be obtained in, e.g., English for the interpretation of $\Delta\alpha\alpha$, but since English has no cases the isomorphism holds between noun phrases and various types of prepositional constructions. The empirical interpretation of $\Delta\alpha\alpha$ also allows an isomorphism to be established between various types of noun phrase in different languages, e.g. between the Russian *dom otca* and the English *the house of the father*.

The empirical interpretation of $\Delta\alpha\alpha$ reveals two traits characteristic of this process: a) empirical interpretation specifies exactly, up to isomorphism, the empirical objects corresponding to the abstract objects; b) unlike abstract interpretation, which is deductive in nature (as was shown above, the abstract interpretation of arbitrary abstract objects is derived by deduction from the interpretation of the initial simple abstract objects), empirical interpretation is given in the form of definite correspondences between abstract and empirical objects. These correspondences are called rules of correspondence.

Moreover empirical interpretation, as we shall see shortly, is incomplete, since not every abstract object has a corresponding empirical object. There are abstract objects that have meaning only as elements of deductive systems.

Let us consider the interpretation of the other objects in the genotype language. $\Delta\alpha\beta$ is interpreted as a one-place predicate, such a predicate having exactly the function of transforming a noun phrase into a sentence. This reveals an isomorphism not just between sets of Russian sentences like *Mal'čik guljaet* (boy–walks), *Otec—učitel'* (father–(is a) teacher), and *Den' xolodnyj* (day–(is) cold) but also between these sentences and nominative sentences like *Noč'* (night). In nominative sentences there is an implicit predicate that is expressed by the appropriate intonation.

The object $\Delta\beta\beta$ is interpreted on the empirical level as sentence adverbs, the negation of a sentence, devices for transforming declarative sentences into interrogative ones and in general every grammatical device for transforming one sentence into another. From this point of view the classes exemplified by the following sentences are isomorphic: *On zabyl ob ètom* (he–forgot–about–this); *Kstati, on zabyl ob ètom* (by the way–he–forgot–about–this); *Nepravda, čto on zabyl ob ètom* (not true–that–he–forgot–about–this); *Zabyl on ob ètom?* (forgot–he–about–this?).

The object $\Delta\beta\alpha$ is interpreted on the empirical level as a device for transforming sentences into noun phrases, i.e. as subordinating conjunctions (cf. *mal'čik guljaet*, boy–is walking; and *čto mal'čik guljaet*, that–boy–is walking).

As we can see, the object $\alpha$ is interpreted on the empirical level as a noun phrase of any degree of complexity, and the object $\beta$ is interpreted as a simple or complex sentence. In fact, what is presented here as the empirical interpretation of the objects $\alpha$ and $\beta$ was the starting point in the construction of the genotype language (cf. the data at the beginning of this chapter).

I will turn now to the objects of the genotype language on the abstract level. As the initial elements we took $\alpha$ and $\beta$, and then the notion of a transformer was introduced, denoted by $\Delta$. Since every object in a given class can be transformed either into an object in another class or into an object in the same class, the four new classes $\Delta\alpha\beta$, $\Delta\beta\alpha$, $\Delta\alpha\alpha$, $\Delta\beta\beta$, were constructed. Altogether there are six classes of objects, which themselves can be regarded as abstract objects, and having these six classes we can transform the objects of any one class either into objects of the same class or into objects of any of the other five classes. In this way another 32 classes of transformers are obtained, and having 38 classes of objects altogether we can transform an object of any one class either into an object of the same class or into an object of any of the other 37 classes, and so on.

A formal description can now be given of the calculus that generates the classes of objects in the genotype language. In the calculus there are:

1. The atoms $\alpha$, $\beta$, called elementary episemions. The object $\Delta$, called a deriver of episemions.
2. The rules for construction of the objects called episemions: a) the elementary episemions $\alpha$, $\beta$ are episemions; b) if p and q are episemions, $\Delta$pq is also an episemion.

Rule b) can be written in the form of the schema below, called a tree diagram:

$$\frac{p \quad q}{\Delta pq}$$

The horizontal line is to be read as 'is constructed from', i.e. $\Delta$pq is constructed from p and q by adding the symbol $\Delta$ to p and q.

There are various stages in the construction of episemions. The first stage yields the episemions $\alpha$ and $\beta$, the second stage the episemions $\Delta\alpha\alpha$, $\Delta\beta\beta$, $\Delta\alpha\beta$, $\Delta\beta\alpha$. The third stage yields the episemions constructed out of the episemions obtained on the first two stages, and so on. On each stage episemions are constructed out of the episemions obtained on the preceding stages.

The set of episemions that can be constructed using the above two rules will be called the system of episemions.

All episemions except $\alpha$ and $\beta$ are transformers. The notion of a transformer is relative, since any transformer can function as the element that is being transformed by another transformer. From now on transformers will be called operators and the elements that are transformed will be called operands.

Let us introduce the following rule into the system of episemions: the application of the operator $\Delta$pq to the operand p yields q; that is, the episemion q follows from the episemion $\Delta$pq and the episemion p. This rule, called the application of an operator to an operand can be represented by means of the tree diagram:

$$\frac{\Delta pq \qquad p}{q}$$

The diagram below shows a concrete instance of application:

$$\frac{\Delta\alpha\beta \qquad \alpha}{\beta}$$

This instance can be interpreted empirically as the transformation of a noun phrase into a sentence by a one-place predicate.

The calculus of episemions can be regarded as a tool for describing the languages of the world, a tool that enables us to state many universal and essential features of these languages. However, the fact that the episemions are classes and that these classes are discussed as though they were independently existing objects, with no attempt to explore any possible differences between the elements of these classes, leads to a fundamental difficulty, as the following example illustrates.

With respect to Russian the episemion $\Delta\alpha\alpha$ is interpreted on the empirical level as a suffix *-ik*; as an adjective, *malen'kij*; as a participle, *gorjaščij*; as a noun in the genitive case, *otca*; as a prepositional phrase, *na beregu*; and so on. That is to say, the words *malen'kij, gorjaščij, otca*, the phrase *na beregu* and the suffix *-ik* are regarded simply as grammatically identical elements belonging to the same class. It is clear, however, that, although the words *malen'kij*, *otca* and *gorjaščij* all function as modifiers of *dom* in the examples given earlier, this function has a different status for each of them. For *malen'kij* the role of modifier is primary and inherent, whereas for *otca* and *gorjaščij* this role is secondary. *Otca* is a noun and *gorjaščij* is a verb to which has been assigned the role of adjective. We can now see the elements belonging to the class $\Delta\alpha\alpha$ are not only identical but are organised into a definite hierarchy, the investigation of which holds great interest for the linguist. The elements of each of the other classes are organised hierarchically and this hierarchy is crucially important to linguistic structure. The fundamental difficulty that arises when the calculus of episemions is applied in the description of languages is that it cannot be used to investigate the hierarchy.

To overcome this difficulty we have to move down a level, to the level of elements belonging to each episemion, and we have to construct a calculus for these elements, which will be called semions.

In the semion calculus are postulated:

1. Atoms, called elementary semions. These are divided into two groups: a) basic elementary semions A and B; b) elementary operators, each one being denoted by $\phi$, to which can be added the symbol for any episemion except $\alpha$ and $\beta$: $\phi_{\Delta\alpha\beta}$, $\phi_{\Delta\alpha\alpha}$, $\phi_{\Delta\beta\alpha}$, $\phi_{\Delta\beta\beta}$, $\phi_{\Delta\Delta\alpha\beta\Delta\alpha\beta}$, $\phi_{\Delta\alpha\Delta\alpha\beta}$.

2. Rules for constructing semions: a) elementary semions are semions; b) if X is a semion belonging to the episemion $\Delta$pq, and if Y is a semion belonging to the episemion p then XY is a semion belonging to the episemion q.

Rule 2b) can be set out in a tree diagram, as shown below:

$$\frac{\Delta pqX \qquad pY}{qXY}$$

All the semions constructed in accordance with rule 2b) are not elementary but are derived from elementary semions. X is an operator, Y an operand and XY the result of applying X to Y. Rule 2b) itself is the rule of application of semions.

There are many instances of each elementary semion. Instances of the same elementary semion will be distinguished from each other by indices, for example A, $A^1$, $A^2$, . . ., B, $B^1$, $B^2$, . . ., $\phi_{\Delta\alpha\beta}$, ${\phi^1}_{\Delta\alpha\beta}$, ${\phi^2}_{\Delta\alpha\beta}$, . . ., $\phi_{\Delta\alpha\alpha}$, ${\phi^1}_{\Delta\alpha\alpha}$, ${\phi^2}_{\Delta\alpha\alpha}$, . . ., and so on.

It is quite clear to which episemion each elementary semion belongs. In the case of operators this is shown by the lower index assigned to them, and of the semions A and B, A belongs to the episemion $\alpha$, B to $\beta$.

With respect to the operation of application all elementary semions can be divided into three groups: 1) absolute operands, that is, A and B; 2) primary operators, that is, operators whose operands are semions belonging to the episemions $\alpha$ or $\beta$; 3) secondary operators, that is, operators whose operands are other operators. These groups are exemplified below:

1. Absolute operands: A, B.
2. Primary operators: $\phi_{\Delta\alpha\beta}$, $\phi_{\Delta\alpha\alpha}$, $\phi_{\Delta\beta\beta}$, $\phi_{\Delta\beta\alpha}$, $\phi_{\Delta\alpha\Delta\alpha\beta}$, $\phi_{\Delta\alpha\Delta\alpha\alpha}$, $\phi_{\Delta\alpha\Delta\beta\alpha}$, $\phi_{\Delta\beta\Delta\alpha\alpha}$, and so on.

3. Secondary operators: $\phi_{\Delta\alpha\alpha\Delta\alpha\beta}$, $\phi_{\Delta\alpha\beta\Delta\alpha\beta}$, $\phi_{\Delta\Delta\alpha\beta\alpha}$, etc.

The construction of semions takes place in stages. On the first stage elementary semions are obtained; on the second stage, semions consisting of two elementary semions; on the third, semions consisting of three or four elementary semions; and so on. The set of all the semions that can be constructed is called the genotype language.

I will now provide an empirical interpretation of some elementary semions using Russian data. If semion A is taken to be a noun in Russian or its equivalent in a sentence (the equivalent can also be called a noun), and if the semion B is taken to be a sentence, then the operator $\phi_{\Delta\alpha\alpha}$ can be regarded as the transformer of a noun into a noun, the operator $\phi_{\Delta\alpha\beta}$ as the transformer of a noun into a sentence, the operator $\phi_{\Delta\beta\beta}$ as the transformer of a sentence into a sentence and the operator $\phi_{\Delta\beta\alpha}$ as the transformer of a sentence into a noun.

The question now arises as to what data in Russian can be regarded as the interpretation of these four operators. Let us begin with the transformer $\phi_{\Delta\alpha\alpha}$. Taking 'noun' in the sense mentioned in the preceding paragraph we can see that the devices for transforming a noun into a noun fall into groups: morphological, i.e. operating within a word, and syntactic, i.e. those that form word groups. The morphological group contains various suffixes (for example, the suffix *-nik* that transforms the noun *ključ*, key, into the noun *ključnik*, steward); prefixes (e.g. *anti-*, which transforms the noun *mir*, world, into the noun *antimir*, antiworld); circumfixes (e.g. the combination of the prefix *anti-* and the suffix *-in* which transforms the noun *gripp*, influenza, into the noun *antigrippin*, anti-flu drug); inflections (e.g. the inflection *-a*, which transforms the noun *suprug*, spouse, into the noun *supruga*, of–spouse).

Using the accepted terminology we can say that the most common syntactic transformers of nouns into nouns in Russian are adjectives (for example, the addition of the adjective *belyj*, white, to the noun *stol*, table, yields the combination *belyj stol*, which is equivalent to a noun—*belyj* transforms *stol* into a noun), numerals, participles and possessive pronouns. All these words can be regarded as interpreting the operator $\phi_{\Delta\alpha\alpha}$. Word groups consisting of a noun and a preposition perform the same function as adjectives: for example, the word group *k knigam* (to–books) can be considered as transforming the noun *interes* (interest) into the noun *interes k knigam* (interest–in–books), and the word group *na dva santimetra* (of–two–centimetres) transforms the noun *rost* (growth) into the noun *rost na dva santimetra* (growth–of–two–centimetres). As many of these word groups answer the question 'What?' or 'Which?' and can be transformed into adjectives (*iz dereva*, from–wood→*derevjannyj*, wooden) they can be regarded as the syntactic equivalent of adjectives. A noun in the genitive or instrumental case also functions syntactically like an adjective (*stol brata*, table–of brother; *rabota šoferom*, work–as chauffeur), and so do adverbs (*rabota doma*, work–at home). All these examples are interpretations of the operator $\phi_{\Delta\alpha\alpha}$.

In the above examples the transformation of a noun into a noun is achieved by the formation of word groups in which one of the constituents is subordinate to and modifies the other. The categorial status of the head constituent does not change, the head merely being specified in more detail by the modifier. There are other transformations in Russian which preserve the categorial status of the noun, but in other ways; for instance in the transformation of *devočka* (girl) into *devočka-pionerka* (girl-pioneer), *devočka i mal'čik* (girl–and–boy), *devočka s mal'čikom* (girl–with–boy). The constituents that are combined are associated with the same set of grammatical categories and this set (associated with each individual constituent and with them both together) is the invariant that allows the term 'noun' to be applied both to *devočka* and *devočka-pionerka*.

Let us pass on now to the interpretation of the semion $\phi_{\Delta\alpha\beta}$. To transform a Russian noun or a noun phrase equivalent to it into a sentence it is sufficient to add to the noun a finite form of a one-place verb or the short form of an adjective. For example, the addition of the verb form *svetit* (shines) to the noun *solnce* (sun) transforms this noun into the sentence *Solnce svetit* (sun–shines), and similarly the short-form adjective *opasen* (dangerous) transforms the noun *put'* (road) into the sentence *Put' opasen* (road–(is) dangerous). If nominative sentences like *Fonar'* (lamp), *Okno* (window) and *Apteka* (chemist's shop) are analysed as sentences from which a present tense form of the copula *byt'* (be) has been omitted, then the formation of nominative sentences can be looked on as resulting from the transformation of a noun into a sentence by the addition of a null copula. In some instances the copula is equivalent to a suprasegmental unit of predicative intonation. Thus the copula, like finite verb forms and short forms of adjectives, is a transformer of nouns into sentences, i.e. an interpretation of the semion $\phi_{\Delta\alpha\beta}$.

In Russian, interpretations of the operator $\phi_{\Delta\beta\alpha}$, which transforms a sentence into a noun (in the broadest sense of the term 'noun'), are to be found in various subordinating conjunctions. If to the sentence *Solnce svetit* (sun shines) the conjunction *čto* (that) is added, the word group *čto solnce svetit* (that–sun–shines) is obtained. This word group is not a sentence but functions syntactically like a noun, as in the sentence *Ja znaju, čto solnce svetit* (I–know–that–sun–shines).

The interpretation of the operator $\phi_{\Delta\beta\beta}$ can be exemplified in Russian by various sentence adverbs. For instance, to the sentence *Solnce svetit* can be added *po-vidimomu* (apparently), giving the sentence *Po-vidimomu, solnce svetit* (apparently–sun–shines). The same function belongs to adverbs of place and time that modify a whole sentence, e.g. *doma* (at–home), *segodnja* (today).

Since an interpretation system must be isomorphic with that of which it is an interpretation, all the correlations between operators and operands in the semion calculus must be preserved in the interpretation system. In the semion calculus each operator can be an operand and as such can be transformed into another element. Correspondingly, in the interpretation system the analogues of these operators must function sometimes as operators and sometimes as operands. For example, a numeral, which is an analogue of the operator $\phi_{\Delta\alpha\alpha}$, must be described sometimes as an operator, which was how it was described above, and sometimes as an operand, that is, as an element that can be transformed into another element (e.g. a noun) by a transformer that is the analogue of the operator $\phi_{\Delta\Delta\alpha\alpha\alpha}$. An example of this transformer in Russian is the suffix *-ada*, which can be added to the numeral *tri* (three; described above as an interpretation of the semion $\phi_{\Delta\alpha\alpha}$) to yield the noun *triada* (triad), which is an interpretation of the semion A. It follows that the suffix *-ada* is an interpretation of the semion $\phi_{\Delta\Delta\alpha\alpha\alpha}$.

In Russian there are processes that are the reverse of the ones we have been examining. One such process is the transformation of an analogue of the semion A (a noun) into an analogue of the semion $\phi_{\Delta\alpha\alpha}$ (an adjective). Examples of transformers of nouns into adjectives are the suffixes *-ov* and *-in*, and also the suffixes *-ov-*, *-n-*, *-in-*, *-cat-*, *-ansk-*, *-ovat-*, *-ovit-*, *-ist-*, etc. together with inflections. For instance the suffix *-ov* transforms the noun *ded* (grandfather) into the adjective *dedov* (grandfather's) and the suffix *-in-* together with the nominative masculine singular inflection *-ij* transforms the noun *zver'* into the adjective *zverinij* (of wild animals). All these formatives, then, can be regarded as interpretations of the operator $\phi_{\Delta\alpha\Delta\alpha\alpha}$. Another interpretation of this operator is to be found in the oblique case endings of nouns, with or without a preposition.

Another operator is $\phi_{\Delta\Delta\alpha\alpha\Delta\alpha\alpha}$, which can be interpreted as affixes that form adjectives from adjectives, e.g. the prefixes *a-*, *anti-*, *arxi-*, *bez-*, *do-*, *za-*, *kvazi-*, *nai-*, *ne-*, *pere-*, *pre-*, *pred-*, *pri-*, *protivo-*, *psevdo-*, *raz-*, *sverx-*, *super-*, *ul'tra-*. Thus the affix *a-* transforms the adjective *logičnyj* (logical), which is an interpretation of the operator $\phi_{\Delta\alpha\alpha}$, into the adjective *alogičnyj* (alogical), which is an interpretation of the same operator.

A suffix and an inflection transform the adverb *doma* (at home) and similar adverbs (it is one of a class of adverbs that interpret the operator $\phi_{\Delta\beta\beta}$, since they can modify a whole sentence) into adjectives, in the case of *doma* the adjective being *domašnij* (domestic). This means that the suffix and the inflection together are an interpretation of the operator $\phi_{\Delta\Delta\beta\beta\Delta\alpha\alpha}$.

If the suffix *-om* is added to the noun *večer* (evening) the adverb *večerom* (in the evening) is obtained, which, like *doma*, is an interpretation of the semion $\phi_{\Delta\beta\beta}$. Thus the suffix *-om* functions here as an analogue of the operator $\phi_{\Delta\alpha\Delta\beta\beta}$.

It is not difficult to establish an interpretation for the operator $\phi_{\Delta\beta\Delta\beta\beta}$, since its analogue is subordinating conjunctions that join two sentences.

Let us look at the interpretation of operators derived from the semion $\phi_{\Delta\alpha\beta}$, that is, derived from operators whose analogues transform nouns into sentences. It was mentioned above that analogues of this operator in Russian are the finite forms of one-place verbs. As equivalents of one-place verbs we can recognise two-place verbs, one of whose arguments is a complement, or three-place verbs, two of whose arguments are complements. For instance, *čitaju knigu* (read–book) is a transformer that transforms the noun *ja* (I) into the sentence *Ja čitaju knigu* (I–am reading–(a) book). The word group *čitaju knigu* is an interpretation of the operator $\phi_{\Delta\alpha\beta}$, and the verb *čitaju* itself is an interpretation of the operator $\phi_{\Delta\alpha\Delta\alpha\beta}$: the conjoining of *čitaju* ($\phi_{\Delta\alpha\Delta\alpha\beta}$) and the noun *knigu* (A) yields the word group *čitaju knigu*, which functions as an operator ($\phi_{\Delta\alpha\beta}$), the application of this operator to the noun *ja* giving the sentence *Ja čitaju knigu* (B). A three-place verb, e.g. *daju* (give: present tense, first person singular), can be regarded as an interpretation of the operator $\phi_{\Delta\alpha\Delta\alpha\Delta\alpha\beta}$.

To make it easier to set out the interpretations that we still have to deal with, the operators $\phi_{\Delta\alpha\beta}$, $\phi_{\Delta\alpha\Delta\alpha\beta}$ and $\phi_{\Delta\alpha\Delta\alpha\Delta\alpha\beta}$ will be combined into one class of operators $\phi_{\Delta\pi\beta}$. Let us now see what transformations the Russian analogues of these operators are subject to; what elements they are transformed into and what transformations they themselves are the output of.

The effect of the operator $\phi_{\Delta\Delta\pi\beta\alpha}$ can be interpreted as the transformation of a verb or the short form of an adjective into a noun, e.g. the transformation of the verb *žit'* (live) into the noun *žitel'* (inhabitant) or the transformation of the short adjective *velik* (great) into the noun *velikan* (giant). The effect of the operator $\phi_{\Delta\Delta\pi\beta\Delta\pi\beta}$ can be interpreted as the transformation of verbs into verbs. For example, the infix *-a-* transforms the verb *stegnut'* (lash) into the verb *steganut'*; the infix *-yv-* transforms the verb *perepisat'* (rewrite: perfective aspect) into the verb *perepisyvat'* (rewrite: imperfective aspect); the suffix *-sja* transforms the verb *videt'* (see) into the verb *videt'sja* (see one another); and the prefix *pere-* transforms the verb *pisat'* (write) into the verb *perepisat'* (rewrite). All these Russian affixes are analogues of the operators $\phi_{\Delta\Delta\pi\beta\alpha}$ and $\phi_{\Delta\Delta\pi\beta\Delta\pi\beta}$.

The formation of verbs from nouns and personal pronouns (analogues of the semion A) can be regarded as the effect of the operator $\phi_{\Delta\alpha\Delta\pi\beta}$. Thus, from the noun *xlam* is formed the verb *zaxlamit'* (fill with rubbish) by the addition of the prefix *za-* and the suffix *-it'*, the noun *partizan* is transformed into the verb *partizanit'* (be a partisan), and the pronoun *vy* (you: plural and polite form) is transformed into the verb *vykat'* (address as *vy*). These formatives can therefore be considered the interpretation of the operator $\phi_{\Delta\alpha\Delta\pi\beta}$.

Let us now return to the interpretation of the episemions $\Delta\alpha\alpha$ and $\Delta\alpha\beta$. Using these examples we shall show how the semion calculus makes possible a more insightful classification of the facts of natural languages. As was shown above the following interpretations are possible for these episemions:

| $\Delta\alpha\alpha$ | $\Delta\alpha\beta$ |
|---|---|
| *-ik* (as in *dom-ik*, house-let) | *guljaet* (cf. *mal'čik guljaet*, boy–walks) |
| *malen'kij* (cf. *malen'kij dom*, small–house) | *byl učitel'* (was–teacher; cf. *otec byl učitel'*, father–was teacher) |
| *otca* (of father; cf. *dom otca*, house–of father) | *učitel'stvuet* (teaches; cf. *otec učitel'stvuet*, father–teaches) |
| *na beregu* (on bank; cf. *dom na beregu*, house–on–bank) | *byl xolodnyj* (was cold; cf. *den' byl xolodnyj*, day–was–cold) |
| *gorjaščij* (cf. *gorjaščij dom*, burning–house) | predicative intonation in nominative sentences like *noč'* (night) |

Let us consider once again the episemion α, which can be interpreted as:

| | |
|---|---|
| *dom* (house) | *dom na beregu* (house–on–bank) |
| *dom-ik* (house-let) | *gorjaščij dom* (burning–house) |
| *malen'kij dom* (small–house) | *guljanie* (walking: deverbal noun) |
| *dom otca* (house–of father) | *belizna* (whiteness: deadjectival noun) |

On the level of episemions the interpretations of each of these episemions were considered as equal in status but on the level of semions these interpretations can be organised into a hierarchy. Among the interpretations of the episemion $\Delta\alpha\alpha$, for instance, the suffix *-ik* and the adjective *malen'kij* (small) correspond to the elementary semion $\phi_{\Delta\alpha\alpha}$. The participle *gorjaščij* (burning) corresponds to the tree

$$\frac{\phi_{\Delta\Delta\alpha\beta\Delta\alpha\alpha} \qquad \phi_{\Delta\alpha\beta}}{\Delta\alpha\alpha\phi_{\Delta\Delta\alpha\beta\Delta\alpha\alpha}\phi_{\Delta\alpha\beta}}$$

Since the lower index of each elementary semion distinguishes that semion from all the others, in that it shows unambiguously what episemion that semion belongs to, in future the derivational characteristic (the episemions written on the left) will be omitted from the elementary semions in the tree diagrams. Since the derivational characteristics of the elementary semions A and B are also unambiguously defined they can be omitted as well. It goes without saying that the derivational characteristic of elementary semions is left out only to simplify the notation and that it must be understood to be there.

*Otca* (of father) and *na beregu* (on–bank) correspond to the tree

$$\frac{\phi_{\Delta\alpha\Delta\alpha\alpha} \qquad A}{\Delta\alpha\alpha\phi_{\Delta\alpha\Delta\alpha\alpha}A}$$

Let us move on now to the interpretations of the episemion $\Delta\alpha\beta$. The finite forms of *guljaet* (walks) or the predicative intonation will correspond to an elementary semion. The word group *byl učitel'* (was–teacher) or the derived finite verb form *učitel'stvuet* (teaches; derived from the noun *učitel'*, teacher) correspond to the tree

$$\frac{\phi_{\Delta\alpha\Delta\alpha\beta} \qquad A}{\Delta\alpha\beta\phi_{\Delta\alpha\Delta\alpha\beta}A}$$

The word group *byl xolodnyj* (was–cold) corresponds to the tree

$$\frac{\phi_{\Delta\Delta\alpha\alpha\Delta\alpha\beta} \qquad \phi_{\Delta\alpha\alpha}}{\Delta\alpha\beta\phi_{\Delta\alpha\alpha\Delta\alpha\beta}\phi_{\Delta\alpha\alpha}}$$

Consider the interpretations of the episemion $\alpha$. *Dom* (house) corresponds to the semion A. *Domik* (houselet) and the word group *malen'kij dom* (small–house) correspond to the tree

$$\frac{\phi_{\Delta\alpha\alpha} \qquad A}{\alpha\phi_{\Delta\alpha\alpha}A}$$

*Guljanie* (walking) corresponds to the tree

$$\frac{\phi_{\Delta\Delta\alpha\beta\alpha} \qquad \phi_{\Delta\alpha\beta}}{\alpha\phi_{\Delta\Delta\alpha\beta\alpha}\phi_{\Delta\alpha\beta}}$$

*Belizna* (whiteness) corresponds to the tree

$$\frac{\phi_{\Delta\Delta\alpha\alpha\alpha} \qquad \phi_{\Delta\alpha\alpha}}{\alpha\phi_{\Delta\Delta\alpha\alpha\alpha}\phi_{\Delta\alpha\alpha}}$$

The word group *gorjaščij dom* (burning–house) corresponds to the tree

$$\dfrac{\dfrac{\phi_{\Delta\Delta\alpha\beta\Delta\alpha\alpha} \qquad \phi_{\Delta\alpha\beta}}{\Delta\alpha\alpha\phi_{\Delta\Delta\alpha\beta\Delta\alpha\alpha}\phi_{\Delta\alpha\beta}} \qquad \mathrm{A}}{\alpha\phi_{\Delta\Delta\alpha\beta\Delta\alpha\alpha}\phi_{\Delta\alpha\beta}\mathrm{A}}$$

The word groups *dom otca* (house–of father) and *dom na beregu* (house–on–bank) correspond to the tree

$$\dfrac{\dfrac{\phi_{\Delta\alpha\Delta\alpha\alpha} \qquad \mathrm{A}^1}{\Delta\alpha\alpha\phi_{\Delta\alpha\Delta\alpha\alpha}\mathrm{A}^1} \qquad \mathrm{A}^2}{\alpha\phi_{\Delta\alpha\Delta\alpha\alpha}}$$

These examples show that with the semion calculus one can formalise the distinction between simple and derived words and the associated distinction between the primary and secondary roles of words, not to mention the distinction between words and word groups. For example, *guljat'* (to walk) is a simple word (i.e. contains a simple root) but *guljanie* (walking) is a derived word (i.e. contains a complex root) and this difference is reflected in the different formulae. Moreover the primary role of *guljaet* (walks) is that of predicate, whereas the role of noun that is associated with *guljanie* is one of the secondary roles of *guljaet*. Similarly, a difference of formula distinguishes the simple word *dom* (house) from the derived word *domik* (house-let) and from the word groups *malen'kij dom* (small–house) and *dom otca* (house–of father).

The following important observation must be made with respect to these formular differences. If necessary this distinction can be made relative. For instance, when investigating the syntax of a natural language linguists have to ignore, at least partly, the morphology, and in this case derived words can be treated like simple ones. In correspondence with the elementary semion $\phi_{\Delta\alpha\beta}$ could be put not only the simple word *guljaet* (walks) but the derived words *proguljaet* (will be absent from work), *otguljaet* (will take time off), etc. When investigating grammatical functions like subject and object the linguist can treat the word group *malen'kij dom* (small–house) like a simple constituent and put it in correspondence with the elementary semion A. Thus the distinction between simple and derived constituents is absolute if a language is being investigated in its entirety but relative if one particular level of structure is under analysis. One essential feature of the semion calculus is that it allows us both to draw the distinction and to make it relative.

It has been shown that each semion consisting of several semions is represented by a tree diagram. However, tree diagrams, though easily read, can be unwieldy and inconvenient and to achieve a compact notation we shall have to find a way of representing trees linearly. To demonstrate how this can be done rule b) for the construction of semions will be formulated with brackets. In tree form this rule is

$$\frac{\Delta pqX \qquad pY}{qXY}$$

The above tree can be replaced with the linear formula (XY).

Taking as an example the tree corresponding to the word group *gorjaščij dom* (burning–house), we shall show how the use of brackets allows us to replace the tree with a linear formula. With the introduction of brackets the tree has the form

$$\frac{\dfrac{\phi_{\Delta\Delta\alpha\beta\Delta\alpha\alpha} \qquad \phi_{\Delta\alpha\beta}}{\Delta\alpha\alpha(\phi_{\Delta\Delta\alpha\beta\Delta\alpha\alpha}\phi_{\Delta\alpha\beta})} \qquad A}{\alpha((\phi_{\Delta\Delta\alpha\beta\Delta\alpha\alpha}\phi_{\Delta\alpha\beta})A)}$$

This tree can be replaced with the linear formula $((\phi_{\Delta\Delta\alpha\beta\Delta\alpha\beta}\phi_{\Delta\alpha\beta})A)$. It is not difficult to see that this formula enables us to reconstruct the tree by applying rule b).

If in the linear notation a semion is of the form $(\ldots((XY^1)Y^2)\ldots Y^n)$, the brackets can be left out in accordance with the principle of left-wards grouping and the semion will be written $XY^1Y^2\ldots Y^n$. Applying this convention to the semion representing *gorjaščij dom* we get $\phi_{\Delta\Delta\alpha\beta\Delta\alpha\alpha}\phi_{\Delta\alpha\beta}A$.

The fact that semions can be represented both as trees and as linear formulae brings us to an abstract concept of the semion that does not depend on how the semion is represented. As an abstract object a semion is the invariant relative to the transformation of a tree representation into a linear representation and vice-versa.

Further remarks are now in order concerning the formal interpretation of episemions. Each episemion $\Delta$pq is an abstract object consisting of a left-hand component p and a right-hand component q. An episemion is interpreted as a one-place function whose argument is denoted by the left-hand component p and whose value is denoted by the right-hand component q.

The requirements of linguistic analysis make it desirable to introduce a new level of formal interpretation for the episemion $\Delta$pq on which it can be interpreted as a many-place function by the following formal rule: let the episemion $\Delta$pq be decomposed into its components, p and q, which in turn are episemions. If the right-hand component q is equivalent to $\alpha$ or $\beta$ no further decomposition takes place, but if q is a new episemion $\Delta p'q'$ it is also decomposed—into a left-hand component p′ and a right-hand component q′. If the right-hand component q′ is equivalent to $\alpha$ or $\beta$ the process of decomposition stops, but if it is a new episemion $\Delta pq$ the decomposing continues until the right-hand component of one of the episemions obtained during the decomposition of the initial episemion $\Delta pq$ is equal to $\alpha$ or $\beta$. This completes the decomposition. If the decomposition of an episemion $\Delta pq$ takes place in *n* steps, the episemion $\Delta pq$ is interpreted as an *n*-place function.

Here are some examples of how the rule applies. The decomposition of the episemions $\Delta\alpha\beta$, $\Delta\beta\beta$, $\Delta\beta\alpha$, takes place in one step and they can only be interpreted as one-place functions. The episemion $\Delta\alpha\Delta\alpha\Delta\alpha\beta$ on the other hand, decomposes first of all into a left-hand component $\alpha$ and a right-hand component $\Delta\alpha\Delta\alpha\beta$. In the second stage the right-hand component is decomposed in turn into a left-hand component $\alpha$ and a right-hand component $\Delta\alpha\beta$. In the third stage the latter component is decomposed into a left-hand component $\alpha$ and a right-hand component $\beta$. Since the decomposition takes place in three stages, this episemion must be interpreted as a three-place function.

The episemion $\Delta\Delta\alpha\beta\Delta\alpha\beta$ is decomposed in the first stage into a left-hand component $\Delta\alpha\beta$ and a right-hand component $\Delta\alpha\beta$, and in the second stage this right-hand component in turn is decomposed into a left-hand component $\alpha$ and a right-hand component $\beta$. Since the episemion is decomposed in two stages it must be interpreted as a two-place function.

Semions too can be interpreted in accordance with the above formal interpretation of episemions. If a semion X belongs to an episemion Y which is interpreted as an *n*-place function then that semion X must be interpreted as an *n*-place function.

Of special interest are those episemions in the decomposition of which the last stage is performed on the episemion $\Delta\alpha\beta$ and the first stage on an episemion whose left-hand component is a term, i.e. the episemion $\alpha$. Examples of such episemions are $\Delta\alpha\beta$, $\Delta\alpha\Delta\alpha\beta$, $\Delta\alpha\Delta\alpha\Delta\alpha\beta$, etc. From now on episemions of this type will be called predicates, and terms will be called their arguments. Depending on the number of steps in the decomposition of a predicate we shall talk about a one-place predicate ($\Delta\alpha\beta$), a two-place predicate ($\Delta\alpha\Delta\alpha\beta$), and so on.

## 2. A Model of a Situation and the Relator Genotype Language

The preceding section deals with the normal form of the genotype language, which can be defined as the genotype language without any restrictions on the choice of episemions or semions. That is, the genotype language included all the episemions that were generated and with which some set of semions could be put in correspondence. Of course, interpretations can be found in natural languages only for those episemions and their corresponding semions that are obtained during the first stages of the generative process. But episemions and semions are considered objects of the genotype language whether they have an interpretation in a natural language or not.

Although the normal form of the genotype language is a sufficiently powerful tool for the description of natural language, there are many essential features of natural languages that it fails to capture. For greater depth of analysis the genotype language must have defined on it a model of a situation that will make it possible to predict natural language structures involving casual relations.

Let us begin with the analysis of concrete situations, such as that described by the sentence:

(1) *Poezd idet iz Moskvy v Tallin čerez Leningrad* (train–goes–from–Moscow–to–Tallin–through–Leningrad).

In this situation there are four participants: i) a moving point—*poezd* (train); ii) a starting point—*Moskva* (Moscow); iii) a finishing point —*Tallin*; iv) a point on the path of the movement—*Leningrad.* This situation can be considered one of the concrete manifestations of the situation-model that will be defined on the genotype language. A situation-model is a space consisting of one moving point and three motionless points with respect to which the moving point is located— the starting point of the movement, the finishing point of the movement and a point in the path of the movement. The points in the space are the roles played by the participants. Granted that the names of these roles are cases, four cases can be introduced: i) objective—the name of the moving point—to be denoted by $o$; ii) ablative—the name of the starting point—to be denoted by $a$; iii) allative—the name of the finishing point—to be denoted by $l$; iv) prolative—the name of the point on the path of the movement—to be denoted by $p$. The situation-model can be represented as a labelled tree as in figure 1.

The situation-model can be broken down into its component parts. The first component is the whole model, which will be called an improper component of the situation-model. In addition six components can be distinguished, which will be called proper components of the situation-model and which are shown in figures 2–7. The individual components are manifested in the following sentences, with corresponding numbers:

(2) *Poezd idet iz Moskvy v Tallin* (train–goes–from–Moscow–to–Tallin)

(3) *Poezd idet iz Moskvy čerez Leningrad* (train–goes–from–Moscow–through–Leningrad)
(4) *Poezd idet v Tallin čerez Leningrad* (train–goes–to–Tallin–through–Leningrad)
(5) *Poezd idet iz Moskvy* (train–goes–from–Moscow)
(6) *Poezd idet čerez Leningrad* (train–goes–through–Leningrad)
(7) a) *Poezd pribyl v Tallin* (train–arrived–in–Tallin)
b) *Poezd v Talline* (train (is) in–Tallin)

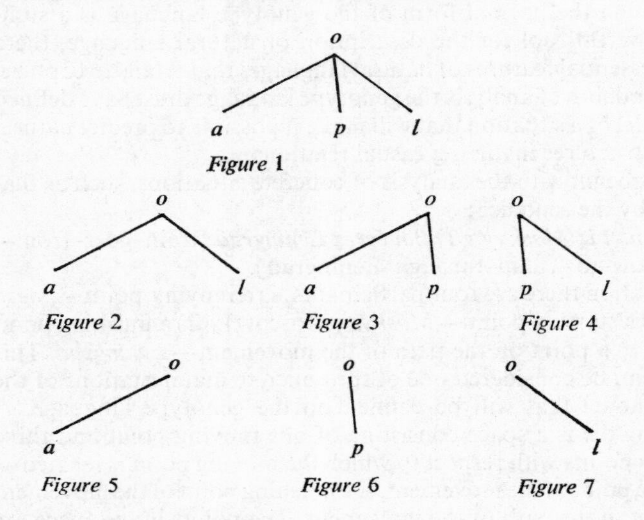


Figure 1

Figure 2

Figure 3

Figure 4

Figure 5

Figure 6

Figure 7

It is worthwhile taking a closer look at the situation-model (henceforth SM). In the component in figure 7, *l* is interpreted not just as the finishing point of the movement but as the place where the object corresponding to the point is located. This comes about through the fact that, in the SM, *l* can be interpreted as the finishing point of a movement only if it contrasts with the points *a* and *p*. If there is no such contrast the finishing point of a movement is reinterpreted as a point of location, as exemplified in 7b. When *l* was considered the name of the finishing point it was called an allative, but as the name of a point of location it will be called a locative.

Granted the validity of this reinterpretation, the allative and the locative are simply variants of the same case, which will be called a locative (in the broadest sense of the word) and will be denoted by *l*. The interpretation of the allative and the locative as variants of the same case is supported by the facts of natural language. For instance, French has a locative, in the broad sense, that can be understood depending on the context as an allative or as a locative in the narrow sense (cf. *aller en Angleterre* and *vivre en Angleterre*).

The prolative is a complex case, being a combination of the allative and the ablative. The prolative denotes a point *p* that a moving point *o* approaches and then moves away from. This means that 6 can be broken down into two sentences:

(8) a) *Poezd idet v Leningrad* (train–goes–to–Leningrad)
  b) *Poezd idet iz Leningrada* (train–goes–from–Leningrad)

It should be mentioned that from an empirical point of view the point *p* must be understood as a space that is traversed and in the limiting case this space may lie along the entire path of the movement of point *o* from point *a* to point *l*. This is obvious from sentences like:

(9) a) *On idet v derevnju čerez les* (he–goes–to–village–through–wood)
  b) *On šel v derevnju vdol' dorogi* (he–went–to–village–along–road)
  c) *On šel domoj po glavnoj ulice* (he–went–home–along–main–street)

Any component of the SM must be considered an instance of the degeneration of the SM. If the component of the SM is not proper it is considered to be an instance of the null degeneration of the SM. The above examples show that each degeneration of the SM can be manifested in grammatically correct sentences, but the SM need not always have a complete interpretation. Often it is possible to find an interpretation for some degeneration of the SM when it is not possible to find an interpretation for the whole SM that would include the interpretation of that particular degeneration. Examples will be given below.

Since an isomorphism can be established between spatial and temporal relations, the model can be given a temporal interpretation. For instance, the component in figure 2 can be interpreted as:

(10) *Poezd šel s utra do večera* (train–travelled–from–morning–till–evening)

The component in figure 6 can be interpreted as:

(11) *Poezd šel pjat' časov* (train–travelled–five–hours)

There is also an isomorphism between, on the one hand, spatial relations and, on the other hand, the relations between the active participant in the situation, the participants on which the active one acts, and the instrument with which the action is carried out. With respect to these relations, the ablative can be interpreted as the acting participant (the acting participant and the starting point of a movement can be subsumed under a general notion of starting point), the locative as the indirect object of the action, the objective as the direct object of the action and the prolative as the instrument. The complete SM can be interpreted by such sentences as the following:

(12) a) *Pomošč' prišla ot Ivana k Petru čerez tovarišča* (help–came–from–Ivan–to–Peter–through–friend)

b) *Ivan okazal pomošč' Petru čerez tovarišča* (Ivan–gave–help–to Peter–through–friend)

c) *Ivan nanes ranu Petru nožom* (Ivan–dealt–wound–to Peter–with knife)

Compressed versions of these sentences are:

(13) a) *Ivan pomog Petru čerez tovarišča* (Ivan–helped–to Peter–through–friend)

b) *Ivan ranil Petra nožom* (Ivan–wounded–Peter–with knife)

Consider now:

(14) *Ivan ispugal Petra* (Ivan–frightened–Peter)

This sentence has two interpretations, corresponding to:

(15) a) *Ivan namerenno ispugal Petra* (Ivan–on purpose–frightened–Peter)

b) *Vid Ivana ispugal Petra* (appearance–of Ivan–frightened–Peter)

In 15a *Ivan* is an active acting participant, but in 15b he is an inactive acting participant. Inactive acting participants are also found in sentences like:

(16) a) *Mne slyšitsja pesnja* (to me–hears itself–song)

b) *Mne viden dom* (to me–visible–house)

(17) a) *Ja slyšu pesnju* (I–hear–song)

b) *Ja vižu dom* (I–see–house)

Here the inactive acting participants are denoted by *pesnja* (song), *pesnju* (song: accusative) and *dom* (house). *Mne* (to me: dative) and *ja* (I) denote the participants that are subjected to the action. These participants are also inactive. That is to say, in these sentences two sorts of inactive participants must be distinguished—acting and non-acting. The former are interpreted as ablatives, the latter as locatives, and both types occur with verbs denoting mental processes—*slyšu* (I hear), *vižu* (I see), *čuvstvuju* (I feel), *nravitsja* (pleases), *ogorčajus'* (I am distressed), *vozmuščajus'* (I am indignant), etc.

Cases are roles played by participants in a situation, but a particular case is not always associated with the same participant. Since in the genotype language the participants in simple situations (i.e., situations none of whose participants are situations) are denoted by terms, cases must be considered primarily as the characteristics of terms.

In the SM there are only terms, since predicates are not expressed directly but are defined by the various arrays of cases represented by the components of the SM. Sentences that manifest the SM contain predicates, but these predicates have no directly corresponding elements among the nodes of the SM trees and must be regarded as relations defined either by a simple array of cases, as in 1 with the simple predicate *idet* (goes), or by an array of cases in combination with a term, as in 12, with the compound predicates *pomošč' prišla* (help–came), *okazal pomošč'* (gave–help), *nanes ranu* (inflicted–wound). Among the nodes of the SM tree there are no elements corresponding directly to these predicates but there are elements corresponding to the words *pomošč'* and *ranu*. In 13 *pomog* (helped) is a compressed form of *okazal pomošč'* and *ranil* (wounded) is a compressed form of *nanes ranu*.

Let us now turn our attention to the construction of an interpretation system for the SM. The interpretation system (henceforth IS) must contain semantic features that are assigned to specific cases, and it must have two components: 1) a set of semantic features, and 2) rules for assigning semantic features to cases (rules of interpretation). Let us examine each of these components.

1. In the IS five semantic features are postulated: place (Pl), time (T), activity (A), inactivity (I), process (P). 'Process' includes actions and states. 'Activity' can be defined in various ways, but for present purposes it is convenient to take as the necessary condition for assigning this feature to an object that the object be performing an action intentionally. Of course, only animate objects (or personified inanimate objects in, e.g., fairy tales) can perform an action on purpose.

2. The rules of interpretation consist of restrictions on the table of semantic features (table 1). The crosses indicate which features can be assigned to which cases. An empty cell indicates that a particular feature cannot be assigned to a particular case.

*Table* 1

| | case | | | |
|---|---|---|---|---|
| feature | *o* | *a* | *p* | *l* |
| Pl | | + | + | + |
| T | | + | + | + |
| A | + | + | | |
| I | + | + | + | + |
| P | + | + | + | + |

The assigning of semantic features to cases is to be understood in the following way. The definitions of the cases involve movement, which can be movement in space, movement in time, or abstract movement, i.e. an action being performed on one participant by another. It is this aspect that is captured by the interpretation table. For example, if the ablative is assigned the feature Pl, this means that the starting point of the movement is taken to be a place, but if the ablative is assigned the feature T the starting point of the movement is taken to be a starting point in time. If the ablative is assigned the feature A or I the starting point of the movement is taken to be an active or an inactive object, and if the ablative is assigned the feature P the starting point is taken to be a process that affects some object.

These remarks apply to the assignment of semantic features to the other cases. If the locative is marked Pl the finishing point of the movement is taken to be a place, but if it is marked I the finishing point is taken to be an inactive object that is subjected to an action, and so on. The following restrictions are placed on the use of table 1: a) the objective and the locative can not both be marked P; b) if the ablative is marked A, the objective must be marked I or P.

It is now time to present some Russian interpretations of the SM. The SM is represented by means of labelled trees, and a complete tree has a root labelled *o*, a leftmost lower node labelled *a*, a middle lower node labelled *p* and a rightmost lower node labelled *l*. Incomplete SM trees are subtrees of the complete tree. When the SM trees are being interpreted the case labels will be replaced with the labels of semantic features so that the interpretation of a tree may look like figure 8.

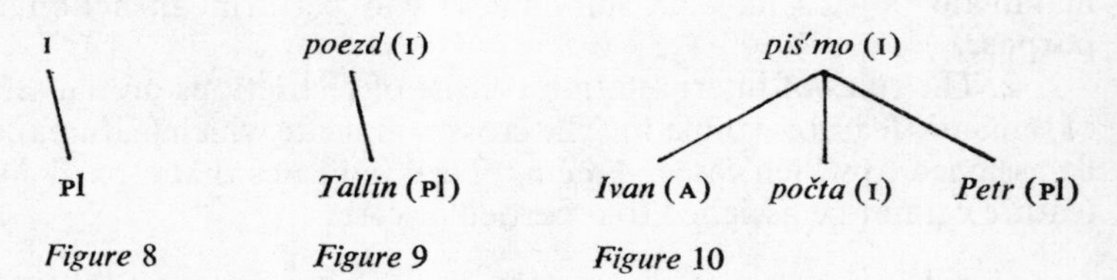


*Figure* 8 *Figure* 9 *Figure* 10

To show what lexical correspondences are possible, nouns in their dictionary form will be attached to the nodes and the symbols for semantic features will be written at the side in brackets. Thus, on the level where lexical items are inserted the tree of figure 8 may be shown as in figure 9, which represents:

(18) *Poezd v Talline* (train–(is) in–Tallin)

Figure 10 represents both 19 and 20:

(19) *Pis'mo prišlo ot Ivana k Petru po počte* (letter–came–from–Ivan–to–Peter–by–post)

(20) a) *Ivan poslal pis'mo Petru po počte* (Ivan–sent–letter–to Peter–by–post)

b) *Petr polučil pis'mo ot Ivana po počte* (Peter–received–letter–from–Ivan–by–post)

A comparison of 20a and 20b with the tree in figure 10 that represents them shows that the verbs *poslal* (sent) and *polučil* (received) do not denote different actions but are different denotations for the same action, which we can agree to denote by the expression *poslal / polučil.* Similar remarks apply to pairs like *dat' / vzjat'* (give / take), *odalživat' / zanimat'* (lend / borrow), *prodavat' / pokupat'* (sell / buy), *obučat / učit'sja* (teach / learn), etc.

In order to model the differences between the members of each pair of verbs the concepts of theme and rheme must be introduced into the SM. The theme is what is spoken about in the sentence and the rheme is what is said about the theme. If 20a and 20b are compared it can be seen that the differences between them come down to the choice of theme and rheme. In 20a the theme is *Ivan* and *Petr* is put into the rheme, but in 20b it is the other way round, *Petr* being the theme and *Ivan* the rheme. Similar relationships hold between the members of the other pairs of verbs, as in:

(21) a) *Brat odolžil den'gi sestre* (brother–lent–money–to sister)

b) *Sestra zanjala den'gi u brata* (sister–borrowed–money–from–brother)

In 21a *brat* is the theme and *sestra* is part of the rheme, but in 21b it is *sestra* that is the theme and *brat* that is in the rheme.

To capture the correlations between theme and rheme in the SM trees the node corresponding to the theme will be circled. Thus the tree in figure 10 can be converted into two trees: figure 11 corresponding to 20a, figure 12 to 20b.

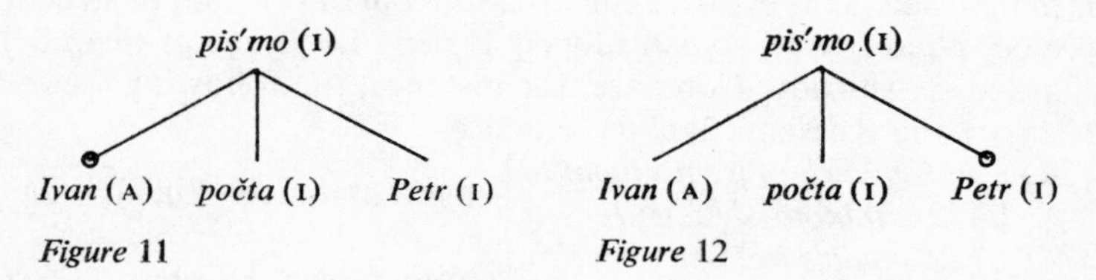


*Figure* 11

*Figure* 12

Four types of SM trees can be distinguished depending on which node corresponds to the theme: a) a tree with the objective as theme; b) a tree with the ablative as theme; c) a tree with the prolative as theme; d) a tree with the locative as theme. These distinctions enable us to deal with the nominative, ergative and stative constructions that occur in natural languages as various empirical manifestations of these types.

Let us consider first of all the nominative and ergative constructions. The nominative construction must be regarded as manifesting the tree in figure 13, which can be given the following interpretation:

(22) An active object (agent) A acts upon an inactive object (patient) I.

The ergative construction manifests the tree in figure 14, which has the interpretation:

(23) An inactive object (patient) I is subjected to the action of an active object (agent) A.

I A I A

*Figure* 13  *Figure* 14

The difference between the nominative and ergative constructions lies in the choice of theme and rheme, with respect to which they are inversely related: the agent is the theme and the patient part of the rheme in the nominative construction, but the patient is the theme and the agent part of the rheme in the ergative construction. The agent and the patient are expressed by surface cases. In the nominative construction the agent is expressed by the nominative case, the patient by some oblique case and in the ergative construction the agent is expressed by the ergative case and the patient by the nominative case.

The nominative and ergative constructions can co-exist in the same language. When this is the case the structure in figure 13 is manifested in the nominative construction and the structure in figure 14 is manifested in the ergative construction, but only if the constructions are considered to be stylistically equivalent, i.e. if one of them is not marked stylistically. Compare, for instance, the following Georgian (24a, c) and Russian (24b, d) sentences.

(24) a) *Monadire-m irem-i mohkla* } (by hunter–deer–killed)
b) *Oxotnikom olen' ubit* }
c) *Monadire irem-sa mohklav* } (hunter–deer–kills)
d) *Oxotnik olenja ubivaet* }

24a contains an ergative construction: the patient *irem-i* is in the nominative case and the agent *monadire-m* is in the ergative case. 24c and 24d contain nominative constructions, the agents *monadire* and *oxotnik* being in the nominative case and the patients *irem-sa* and *olenja* being in an oblique case (*irem-sa* is the dative, *olenja* the accusative).

The ergative construction in 24a and the nominative construction in 24c are stylistically equivalent, the former being used in sentences describing an event in the past, the latter in sentences describing an event in the present. 24c contains a nominative construction, the agent *monadire* being in the nominative case and the patient *irem-sa* being in the dative case.

Although the Russian sentence 24b that translates 24a manifests the structure in figure 13, it cannot be said to contain an ergative construction. The difficulty is that 24b and d are not stylistically equivalent, since 24d is the normal construction in Russian and 24b is stylistically marked. Because of this, 24b is said to contain not an ergative construction but a passive one. There are languages, however, in which it is the ergative construction that is stylistically neutral and the absolutive construction that is marked. We shall not go into any more detail on the relationship between the ergative and the nominative constructions, since it was only necessary to demonstrate that it was possible, in principle, to interpret the structures in figures 13 and 14 as these constructions.[1]

Consider now the tree in figure 15. On the lexical level this tree can be given the interpretations shown in figures 16–18, which correspond to examples 25–27 respectively:

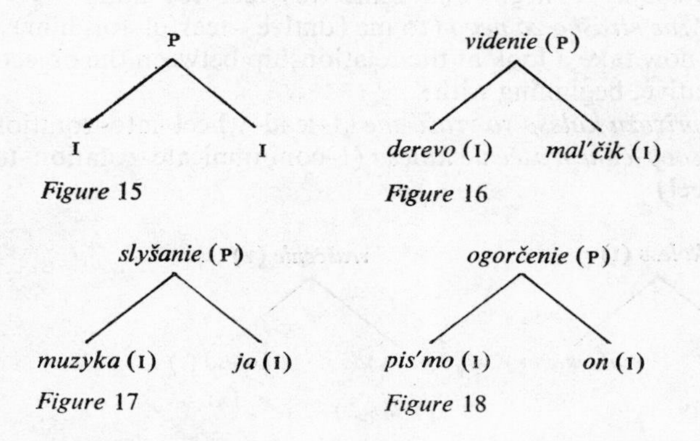


*Figure* 15

*Figure* 16

*Figure* 17

*Figure* 18

(25) *U mal'čika videnie ot dereva* (at–boy–vision (visual image)–from–tree)
= *Mal'čik vidit derevo* (boy–sees–tree)

(26) *U menja slyšanie ot muzyki* (at–me–hearing (aural image)–from–music)
= *Ja slyšu muzyku* (I–hear–music)

[1] On the relationship between the nominative and ergative constructions, see J. Kuryłowicz, Ergativnost' i stadial'nost' v jazyke. *Esquisses Linguistiques*, pp. 95–103. Wroclaw-Kraków: Polska Akademia Nauk.

(27) *U nego ogorčenie ot pis'ma* (at–him–distress–from–letter)
  = *Ego ogorčaet pis'mo* (him–distresses–letter)

25 to 27 are examples of stative constructions, which describe mental processes, i.e. processes of perception and sensation. The participant that perceives or senses is an inactive object that undergoes a mental process and the process itself has its source in a participant that is also an inactive object. It is characteristic of mental processes that they begin and end in inactive objects.

There are languages like Georgian that have a special stative conjugation. Although Russian does not possess a special stative conjugation, many stative verbs occur in constructions with the nominative case and also in constructions with the dative case, the latter being an analogue of the stative constructions. The contrast between the nominative and the dative is illustrated by:

(28) i a) *Mal'čik vidit derevo* (boy (nominative)–sees–tree)
  b) *Mal'čiku vidno derevo* (to boy (dative)–visible–tree)
 ii a) *Ja slyšu muzyku* (I (nominative)–hear–music)
  b) *Mne slyšna muzyka* (to me (dative)–audible–music)
  c) *Mne slyšitsja muzyka* (to me (dative)–hears itself–music)
 iii a) *Ja bojus' za nego* (I (nominative)–fear–for–him)
  b) *Mne strašno za nego* (to me (dative)–fearful–for–him)

Let us now take a look at the relationship between the objective and the locative, beginning with:

(29) a) *Ja privožu koleso vo vraščenie* (I–lead–wheel–into–rotation)
 b) *Ja soobščaju vraščenie kolesu* (I–communicate–rotation–to wheel)

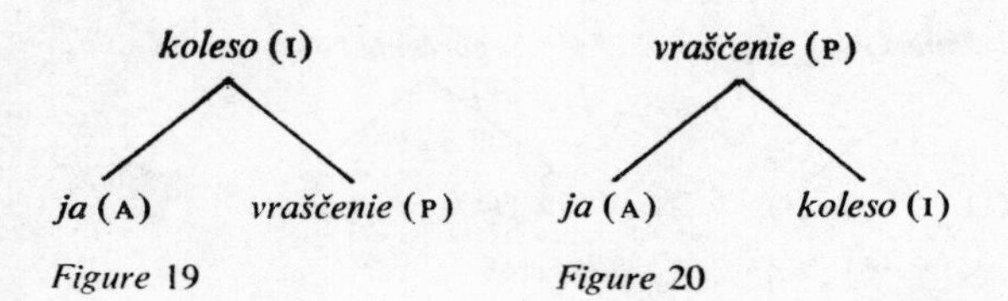


*Figure* 19    *Figure* 20

These synonymous sentences correspond to different trees, 29a being associated with the tree in figure 19, 29b with the tree in figure 20. A comparison of the structure in figure 19 with that in figure 20 shows that they differ in that *koleso* and *vraščenie* change cases. In figure 19 *koleso* is the objective and *vraščenie* the locative, but in figure 20 it is *vraščenie* that is the objective and *koleso* that is the locative. This situation may be called the renaming of terms, since cases, as defined above, are indeed special names of terms.

This renaming of terms is exemplified by the structures in

figures 21 and 22, the former being associated with 30 and the latter with 31:

(30) *Ivan privel Petra v otčajanie* (Ivan–led–Peter–into–despair)
(31) *Ivan vselil v Petra otčajanie* (Ivan–settled–into–Peter–despair)

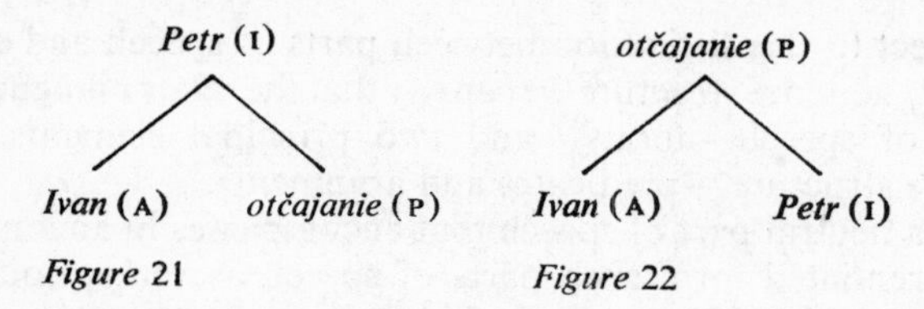


*Figure* 21

*Figure* 22

The renaming of terms can be looked upon as a special operation that transforms synonymous expressions one into the other. To ensure that the renaming operation finds an interpretation in natural language it is essential that one of the terms involved denotes a process. Hitherto the SMs have been represented in the form of trees, but it is now time to proceed to the linear representation of SMs as formulae of the genotype language. These formulae, to be called SM-formulae, are sentences constructed out of two sorts of semions, terms and predicative relators.

In SM-formulae, terms—$T, T^1, T^2, \ldots$—are the names of objects in the broad sense of the word, i.e. not only things but properties and relations. Terms denote things (i.e. material objects), e.g. *stol* (table), *derevo* (tree), *sobaka* (dog), *životnoe* (animal), *čelovek* (person), etc; properties, e.g. *belizna* (whiteness), *krasota* (beauty), *progulka* (walk), *son* (sleep), etc.; relations, e.g. *ubijstvo* (murder), *čtenie* (reading), *polučenie* (receipt/receiving), etc. Properties and relations differ in that properties are ascribed to one object whereas relations are ascribed to two or more objects: e.g. *belizna bumagi* (whiteness–of paper), *krasota ženščin* (beauty–of women), *ego progulka* (his–walk), *moj son* (my–dream); but *ubijstvo proxožego xuliganom* (murder–of passer-by–by hooligan), *čtenie knigi škol'nikom* (reading–of book–by schoolboy), *polučenie sestroj pis'ma ot brata* (receipt–by sister–of letter–from–brother), etc. Predicative relators are the names of non-lexicalised two-, three- and four-place relations specified by cases that are assigned to the relators in the form of subscripts. Each subscript is the image of an SM tree.

Lexicalised predicates are obtained by the application of relators to terms, the latter in the SM-formulae being essentially amorphous lexical elements that are given shape as predicates by the application of the relators. It must be emphasised that the interpretation of terms in the SM-formulae as amorphous lexical elements is essentially different from the interpretation of terms as nouns or noun phrases in the most primitive genotype language.

The set of SM-formulae will be called the case relator language and the rules for generating the SM-formulae will be called the algebra of case relators.[1]

With respect to the distinction between parts of speech and elements of clause / sentence structure we can say that the relator language has one part of speech—terms—and two principal elements of clause / sentence structure—predicates and arguments.

A term is a neutral part of speech that encompasses in an amorphous, undifferentiated form such parts of speech as verbs, nouns, adjectives and adverbs. Terms were said above to be the names of objects in the broadest sense, i.e. the names of things, properties and relations, and nouns were used to exemplify the interpretation of terms. This, however, is no reason to identify terms with nouns. Terms are a neutral part of speech but since we are obliged to use parts of speech when interpreting the terms in Russian, nouns are the most convenient.

The term as a neutral part of speech is not just a construct from which analogues of parts of speech can be derived but a concept that has direct empirical correlates in the analytic languages and in some incorporating languages. For example, there is a neutral part of speech, amorphous lexical elements, in Chinese. Interestingly enough, there are languages in which various parts of speech are distinguished but in which there is only one set of affixes that indicate whether a part of speech is functioning as a predicate, these affixes being added to all parts of speech.

In this respect Yurak Samoyed is interesting, having nouns, adjectives and verbs that all conjugate for person. To be exact, it is not these parts of speech that are conjugated but a compound predicate consisting of a formal predicate and one or other part of speech. Thus the structure of the predicate in Yurak Samoyed can be represented by the formula

(32) RX

in which R is a formal predicate, with personal endings, and X is a variable that can be replaced by any part of speech, as illustrated by the following Yurak Samoyed example from Meščaninov:[2]

[1] My book *Principles of Structural Linguistics* (Mouton, 1971) describes another sort of relator language and relator algebra—a caseless relator language and a caseless relator algebra. The symbol T in the case relator language corresponds to Q in the caseless one. We talk about an algebra of relators and not of semions because in both languages it is relators that are the content semions. The semion denoted by T or Q is, from a formal point of view, empty.

[2] I. I. Meščaninov, *Glagol*, p. 38. Moscow-Leningrad, 1949.

(33) *xasava-m* (I–(am)–man) *ngarka-m* (I–(am)–big)
*xasava-n* (you–(are)–man) *ngarka-n* (you–(are)–big)
*xasava* (he–(is)–man) *ngarka* (he–(is)–big)
*nu-m* (I–stand)
*nu-n* (you–stand)
*nu* (he stands)

It is clear from 33 that it is not a part of speech, noun, adjective or verb, that conjugates but a clause element—the predicate.

Abstracting away from the empirical data and considering the relationship between clause elements and parts of speech theoretically, i.e. with respect to the consequences of the definition of language as a means of communication, we find ourselves obliged to rely on what I shall call the principle of teleological projection. This principle can be formulated thus: *all that is essential in a natural language as a semiotic system serving as a vehicle for verbal communication are those elements without which verbal communication can not take place; therefore, any natural language can be projected on to its potential semiotic system, which is specified by those properties that are necessary for verbal communication.*

If we follow this principle, and by means of a thought-experiment strip away from a natural language everything that is irrelevant to verbal communication, then it will turn out that the minimum, by definition, for any language that is to continue as a vehicle of communication is one part of speech—terms—and two clause elements—predicates and arguments. Indeed, each sentence is by definition the name of a situation, and in accordance with the SM a situation consists of participants and relations between the participants. But it is precisely predicates that are the names of the relations and arguments that are the names of the participants themselves.

Returning to predicate relators, we can introduce the following rules for the transformation of SM trees into case indices:

(34) a) Depending on the number of symbols that must be in the case index, choose a tree with two, three or four nodes,
b) Having chosen an appropriate tree, copy down the case symbols from right to left in the following order: i) the top node; ii) the rightmost node; iii) the second node from the right; iv) the third node from the right.
c) In each index permute the symbols as allowed.

The application of 34a and b to the trees in figures 9, 11 and 13 yields the indices

(35) $R_{lo}$, $R_{aplo}$, $R_{ao}$

Their application to the structures in figures 3, 5 and 7 yields

(36) $R_{apo}$, $R_{ao}$, $R_{lo}$

and their application to the tree in figure 2 yields

(37) $R_{alo}$

Applying 34c to $R_{lo}$, $R_{ao}$ we obtain two new two-place relators with the symbols in the case indices in the reverse order. Applying the rule to $R_{apo}$ and $R_{alo}$ we obtain ten new three-place relators and applying it to $R_{aplo}$ we obtain twenty-three new four-place relators.

The order of symbols in the indices of the relators indicates the case in which each argument stands. For example, the index of the relator $R_{ao}$ shows that the first argument is in the ablative and the second in the objective. On the other hand it is the first argument of the relator $R_{oa}$ that is in the objective and the second argument that is in the ablative. With the relator $R_{aplo}$ the first argument is in the ablative, the second in the prolative, the third in the locative and the fourth in the objective.

Each relator belongs to a specific episemion. $R_{ao}$, $R_{po}$ and $R_{lo}$ and the relators derived from them belong to the episemion $\Delta\alpha\Delta\alpha\beta$. $R_{alo}$, $R_{apo}$ and $R_{plo}$ and the relators derived from them belong to the episemion $\Delta\alpha\Delta\alpha\Delta\alpha\beta$. $R_{aplo}$ and the relators derived from it belong to the episemion $\Delta\alpha\Delta\alpha\Delta\alpha\Delta\alpha\beta$.

I shall now give an example of how the relators operate. The relator $R_{aplo}$ yields the following tree:

(38)
$$\cfrac{\cfrac{\cfrac{\cfrac{\Delta\alpha\alpha\Delta\alpha\Delta\alpha\beta R_{aplo} \qquad \alpha T^1}{\Delta\alpha\Delta\alpha\Delta\alpha\beta(R_{aplo}T^1) \qquad \alpha T^2}}{\Delta\alpha\Delta\alpha\beta((R_{aplo}T^1)T^2) \qquad \alpha T^3}}{\Delta\alpha\beta(((R_{aplo}T^1)T^2)T^3) \qquad \alpha T^4}}{\beta((((R_{aplo}T^1)T^2)T^3)T^4)}$$

The index with $R_{aplo}$ shows that $T^1$ is in the ablative, $T^2$ in the prolative, $T^3$ in the locative and $T^4$ in the objective. Since the index attached to each relator shows which argument stands in which case, the case indices attached to arguments are superfluous. However, where necessary (in complex derivations of one structure from another, which will be discussed later) case indices can be attached to arguments as well. In this instance this would yield $T_a{}^1$, $T_p{}^2$, $T_l{}^3$, $T_o{}^4$.

The semion whose construction is shown in 38 can be written out separately. With the convention about the omission of brackets adopted in the preceding section, the constructed formula will take the form:

(39) $R_{aplo}\ T^1T^2T^3T^4$

In any semion belonging to the episemion $\beta$, i.e. in any sentence, the last argument must be interpreted as the theme of the sentence, the remainder of the semion being interpreted as the rheme. The reason for this is that it is the last argument of a predicate that is directly transformed into a sentence. The repeated operation of a predicate on the preceding arguments produces not a sentence but new complex predicates with fewer places until a complex one-place predicate is formed which applies to the last argument to yield a sentence.

Examples of lexical interpretations of the formulae are given below. Terms are replaced by lexemes, which will be represented as nouns in their dictionary form.

(40) $R_{aplo}$ a) *Moskva Leningrad Tallin poezd* (train)
b) *Idet iz Moskvy čerez Leningrad v Tallin poezd* (goes from–Moscow–through–Leningrad–to–Tallin–train)
c) *Poezd idet iz Moskvy v Tallin čerez Leningrad* (train–goes–from–Moscow–to–Tallin–through–Leningrad)

(41) $R_{aplo}$ a) *Ivan počta Petr pis'mo* (Ivan–post–Peter–letter)
b) *Poslano Ivanom po počte Petru pis'mo* (sent–by Ivan–by–post–to Peter–letter)
c) *Pis'mo poslano Ivanom Petru po počte* (letter–sent–by Ivan–to Peter–by–post)

(42) $R_{aplo}$ a) *Ivan nož Petr rana* (Ivan–knife–Peter–wound)
b) *Nanesena Ivanom nožom Petru rana* (dealt–by Ivan–with knife–to Peter–wound)
c) *Rana nanesena Petru Ivanom s pomošč'ju noža* (wound–dealt–to Peter–by Ivan–with–help–of knife)

(43) $R_{aplo}$ a) *Mal'čik noga dviženie mjač* (boy–foot–movement–ball)
b) *Priveden mal'čikom nogoj v dviženie mjač* (led–by boy–with foot–into–movement–ball)
c) *Mjač priveden v dviženie nogoj mal'čika* (ball–led–into–movement–by foot–of boy)

The substituting of lexemes for terms gives 40a, 41a, 42a and 43a as the interpretations of 39. In each of 40–43, sentences b) and c) represent the closer and closer approximation of a) to natural language. By the convention introduced earlier the theme in 40 is *poezd*, in 41 *pis'mo*, in 42 *rana*, and in 43 *mjač*.

The notion of semantic weight now has to be introduced. By this term is meant the closeness of an argument to the last place of the predicate, and the argument that is in the last place, which is precisely the one that is interpreted as the theme, will be said to have the greatest semantic weight. The semantic weight of the first argument will be held to be equal to 1, that of the second argument to 2, that of the *n*th argument to *n*. If the *n*th argument is the last it is called the theme and the rest of the sentence is called the rheme.

The division into theme and rheme is organised hierarchically. Thus, the *n*th argument of the predicate is the theme of the first level and the rest of the sentence is the rheme of the first level. In the rheme of the first level the argument $(n-1)$ of the predicate is the theme of the second level and the rest of the rheme of the first level is the rheme of the second level, and so on.

It might be asked whether four- and three-place relators can be reduced to two-place relators, that is, whether sentences with four- and three-place relators can be specified by means of sentences with two-place relators. The answer is that they can, if it is assumed that SM arguments are not just terms but can also be sentences. When the latter is the case simple sentences with four- or three-place relators can be specified via complex sentences with two-place relators.

Let $\gamma$ denote '$\alpha$ or $\beta$'. With this symbol the formula $\Delta\gamma\Delta\gamma\beta$ can be constructed and assigned to the two-place relators $R_{ao}$, $R_{po}$, $R_{lo}$. The formula indicates that the first and second argument of the two-place relators can be either $\alpha$ or $\beta$, as illustrated by the following tree:

(44)

$$\dfrac{\dfrac{\Delta\alpha\Delta\alpha\beta R_{ao} \quad \alpha T^1}{\Delta\gamma\beta(R_{ao}T^1)} \qquad \dfrac{\dfrac{\Delta\gamma\Delta\gamma\beta R_{lo} \quad \alpha T^1}{\Delta\gamma\beta R_{lo}T^1} \quad \alpha T^2}{\beta((R_{lo}T^1)T^2)}}{\beta((R_{ao}T^1)\,((R_{lo}T^1)T^2))}$$

Without considering possible interpretations of 44 let us see how many-place relators can be reduced to two-place relators. Consider $R_{aplo}$. In 39 the sentence with this four-place relator $R_{aplo}$ can be represented as an equivalent sentence constructed by means of three two-place relators $R_{ao}$, $R_{po}$, and $R_{lo}$, as in:

(45) $R_{ao}T^1(R_{po}T^2(R_{lo}T^3T^4))$

which can have the following interpretations:

(46) a) $R_{ao}$ *Moskva* ($R_{po}$ *Leningrad* ($R_{lo}$ *Leningrad poezd*)) (cf. 40)
b) $R_{ao}$ *Ivan* ($R_{po}$ *počta* ($R_{lo}$ *Petr pis'mo*)) (cf. 41)
c) $R_{ao}$ *Ivan* ($R_{po}$ *nož* ($R_{lo}$ *Petr rana*)) (cf. 42)
d) $R_{ao}$ *mal'čik* ($R_{po}$ *noga* ($R_{lo}$ *dviženie mjač*)) (cf. 43)

46a corresponds to 40a, 46b to 41a, 46c to 42a, and 46d to 43a. No more examples will be given just now of how a sentence with one many-place relator can be represented as a sentence with several two-place relators but in the next chapter rules will be postulated for the derivation of sentences with many-place relators from sentences with two-place relators.

To conclude this chapter I wish to describe the operation of fusion. As was shown above, two types of predicate have to be distinguished in the case relator language—simple ones and compound ones. A simple predicate is a relator, a pure relational element, that is specified by cases. A compound predicate is a semion that consists of a relator and a term. Consider, for example:

(47) a) $R_{lo}T^1T^2$

b) $R_{lo}$ *vraščenie koleso*

47b is a possible interpretation of 47a. The simple two-place predicate $R_{lo}$ has two arguments, $T^1$ and $T^2$. The simple predicate $R_{lo}$ together with its first argument forms a compound one-place predicate $R_{lo}T^1$. In this compound predicate the marker of predicativeness, $R_{lo}$, and the unspecified lexical element $T^1$ are kept apart.

A sentence with the compound predicate 47 models such Russian sentences as:

(48) a) *Koleso* (*est'*) *vo vraščenii* (wheel–(is)–in–rotation)

b) *Mal'čik* (*est'*) *na progulke* (boy–(is)–on–walk)

c) *Otec* (*est'*) *za rabotoj* (father–(is)–at–work)

In these sentences the two-place copulas (*est'*)*–vo* ((is)–in), (*est'*)*–na* ((is)–on) and (*est'*)*–za* ((is)–at) correspond to $R_{lo}$.

$R_{lo}T^1$ can be replaced by $P_o$, which stands for a simple one-place predicate that has been formed by fusion, like the fusion of $R_{lo}$ and $T^1$. The case index of $P_o$ indicates that the second argument of the two-place predicate $R_{lo}$ serves as the argument of this one-place predicate. The fusion of $R_{lo}$ and $T^1$ yields sentence 49 from 47:

(49) $P_oT$

49 can be given the following interpretation in Russian:

(50) a) *Koleso vraščaetsja* (wheel–rotates)

b) *Mal'čik guljaet* (boy–walks)

c) *Otec rabotaet* (father–works)

Fusion, which will be formally defined in the next chapter, is going to be widely used in the formal semantic system.[1]

[1] The situation model described in this section is related to the localistic theories of case proposed by Hjelmslev, Anderson and Kilby. Cf L. Hjelmslev, La catégorie des cas, *Acta Jutlandica* 7,1 (I–XII, 1–184), 9,2 (I–VII, 1–78), 1935–37; J. M. Anderson, *The Grammar of Case*, CUP 1971; D. A. Kilby, *Deep and Superficial Cases in Russian*, PhD thesis, University of Edinburgh 1972.

## 3. Semantic Theory

1. Definition of the Semantic Theory

In section 1.2 a semantic theory of natural language was said to have two aims: a) to specify the primitive sub-language of the genotype language that is taken as a direct representation of thought; b) to specify the rules that map the primitive sub-language into the expression sub-language of the genotype language, the expression sub-language being considered as the linguistic embodiment of thought. With these aims in mind I shall attempt to construct such a theory. For convenience, I shall talk from now on about 'semantic theory' instead of 'semantic theory of natural language'.

The semantic theory will be constructed on the basis of the relator genotype language. As the primitive sub-language of the genotype language I will take the relator sub-language of the genotype language in which only two-place relators are allowed. The sentences generated in the primitive sub-language of the relator genotype language will be called the axioms of the semantic theory. All the axioms of the semantic theory belong to the episemion $\beta$, i.e. are sentences.

The semantic theory is a formal system in which are postulated:
1. Sentences of the primitive sub-language of the relator genotype language, which are called the semantic axioms.
2. A finite set of rules for semantic derivation.

The semantic axioms and the formulae derivable from them are expressions of the form $\vdash \mathfrak{S}X$, where X is a sentence, $\mathfrak{S}$ is a semantic field (a semantic field is a set of sentences that can be split up into classes of synonymous sentences), and $\vdash$ is the assertion sign. The expression $\vdash \mathfrak{S}X$ is read 'It is asserted that X belongs to a semantic field'. By convention the symbols $\vdash$ and $\mathfrak{S}$ can be omitted from the semantic axioms and the formulae derivable from them.

The rules of semantic derivation are formulae of the form $X \rightarrow Y$, where $\rightarrow$ indicates that the semion X can be replaced by the semion Y. From now on, for simplicity, the phrase 'semantic rules' will be used instead of 'rules of semantic derivation'. In all we can have *n* semantic rules.

A sentence V will be said to be directly derived from a sentence U if V is obtained from U by the application of a semantic rule. To denote direct semantic derivability the sign $\models$ will be used. The expression $U \models V$ means that the sentence V is directly derived from the sentence U.

If there are *n* semantic rules, there are *n* types of direct semantic derivability.

If there is a sequence of sentences $U^0, U^1, \ldots, U^n$, in which each successive sentence is directly derived from the preceding one, $U^n$ is derived from $U^0$ and the sequence $U^0, U^1, \ldots, U^n$ is called the semantic derivation of $U^n$ from $U^0$. Semantic derivability will be denoted by $\vdash$ and the expression $U^0 \vdash U^n$ is to be read 'sentence $U^n$ is derived from $U^0$'.

The use of $\vdash$ to denote derivability is compatible with its use as the assertion sign (as in the above expression $\vdash \Subset X$), since assertion can be regarded as a particular instance of derivability, to be precise, when $n=0$. From this point of view the expression $\vdash X$ has two equivalent interpretations: 'It is asserted that X' or 'X is derived from X'.

The following assertions specify the properties of semantic derivability:

1. $U \vdash U$ for any sentence
2. $U \vdash V$ and $V \vdash Z \rightarrow U \vdash Z$
3. $U \models V \rightarrow U \vdash V$

1) asserts that semantic derivability is reflexive, 2) that semantic derivability is transitive, and 3) that direct semantic derivability is a particular instance of semantic derivability.

Applying the semantic rules to an axiom and the sentences derived from it, we obtain from the axiom a set of semantic derivations.

The linguistic sense of semantic derivations is as follows. It was shown in section 1.1 that the sentences of the primitive sub-language of the genotype language are to be identified with the meanings of sentences, i.e. with situations, for which are to be found linguistic embodiments, linguistic forms which are the sentences of the expression sub-language of the genotype language. Semantic derivations are processes that specify which linguistic forms of sentences correspond to which linguistic meanings of sentences. Each semantic derivation can therefore be regarded as a process that establishes a correspondence between the meaning and linguistic form of a sentence or, which amounts to the same thing, between a situation and the name of a situation. A set of semantic derivations is obtained from one semantic axiom since one and the same meaning can be embodied in a set of linguistic forms, or, to put it another way, one situation can have a set of names.

The following additional remark must be made. As a consequence of assertion 1) about the reflexive property of semantic derivability each axiom can be derived from itself, and thus the primitive sub-language of the relator genotype language also has to be regarded as derivable from itself. The linguistic sense of this consequence is that as a meaning standard the axioms have a dual nature: on the one hand they are identified with the meanings of sentences and on the other hand they can be regarded in themselves as the linguistic forms of those meanings with which they are identified. From the reflexive property of semantic derivability it also follows that the primitive sub-language of the relator genotype language has a dual nature: on one hand it constitutes a set of meaning standards and, on the other hand, since this sub-language can be derived from itself, it must be regarded as its own linguistic form.

The notion of semantic derivability leads to the notion of semantic equivalence. The sentences U and V will be said to be semantically equivalent if V is derivable from U. This will be expressed by the formula $U \vdash V \rightarrow U = V$. Semantic derivability is not symmetric, since the substitution of semions is one-directional, but semantic equivalence is symmetric.

By the semantic equivalence of sentences U and V should be understood that, since V is derivable from U, each of them can replace the other, but the possible use of one instead of the other must not be confused with the derivability of the one from the other. The former refers to the substitution of one sentence for another in the process of communication whereas the latter refers to the substitution of one sentence for another during the application of 'semantic rules'. In the former case the substitution is reversible but in the latter it is one-directional, as is shown by the following example. On the assumption that passive constructions, say *Kniga čitaetsja mal'čikom* (book–is read–by boy), are derived from active ones, in this case *Mal'čik čitaet knigu* (boy–reads–book), only a one-directional substitution of the former for the latter is possible in a semantic derivation, whereas in the process of communication the sentences are mutually substitutable and it is in this sense that they are semantically equivalent.

## 2. Combinators

In semantic rules a fundamental part is played by abstract operators that, following Curry, we shall call combinators. Since combinators are used in the transformation of semions into other semions equivalent in meaning they must be introduced into the genotype language.[1] The present section contains only a formal description of how the combinators operate but the interpretations of linguistic functions obtained by means of the combinators will be examined in the sections devoted to semantic rules and semantic derivations.

Let us begin with that combinator that is called an identificator, denoted by **I**. Let X be a semion. The result of applying **I** to X is identical with X, which is expressed by the equation

(1) **I**X=X

The application of **I** to X can be interpreted as the identity transformation, i.e. the transformation that leaves X unchanged.

Another combinator, called the permutator, is denoted by **C**. If F is a two-place function, **C**F is the converse function, connected with F by the equation

(2) **C**FXY=FYX

The operator **W** is called the duplicator. If F is a two-place function, **W**F is a one-place function, associated with the function F by the equation

(3) **W**FX=FXX

The operator **B** is called the compositor. Let F be a one-place function and let the argument of F be another one-place function whose argument is X. This can be represented by the formula

(4) F(G)X

This sort of expression is sometimes inaccurately called a function from a function but it is more appropriate to call it a 'function from the value of a function'. **B** gives us, instead of two functions F and G, a single complex function **B**FG that is directly dependent on X. The function **B**FG is connected with the functions F and G by the equation

(5) **B**FGX=F(GX)

The complex function **B**FG is obtained thus: first of all **B** is applied to F, yielding the function **B**F, whose argument is the function G. Then **B**F is applied to G, yielding the function **B**FG, whose argument is X. Finally, the application of **B**FG to X yields the complex **B**FGX, which is equivalent to the complex F(GX). It should be noted that in the first complex there are four initial components—**B**, F, G, X—while in the second there are only two—F and (GX). If the brackets are restored in the first complex in accordance with the convention of leftwards grouping, the complex has the form:

(6) (((**B**F)G)X)

or, if the outermost brackets are left out: ((**B**F)G)X.

The combinator **K** is the fictitious argument operator. If G is a

[1] The combinators and the use that is made of them are closely based on Curry's work in combinatory logic. Cf. H. B. Curry & R. Feys, *Combinatory Logic*, vol. 1. Amsterdam, 1958.

no-place function, **K**G is a one-place function connected with G by the equation

(7) **K**GX = G

There are two combinators denoted by Greek letters, $\phi$ and $\psi$. Let us consider $\phi$ first. Let F be a two-place function and let its first argument be the value of a one-place function G whose argument is X and let its second argument be the value of a one-place function whose argument is also X. This can be represented by the formula

(8) F(GX)(HX)

With the combinator $\phi$ we obtain, instead of three functions and H, a single complex function $\phi$FGH directly dependent on X. The function $\phi$**B**FG is connected with the functions F, G and H by the equation

(9) $\phi$FGHX = F(GX)(HX)

The relationship between $\phi$ and two-place functions is the same as that between **B** and one-place functions.

Let us now consider the combinator $\psi$. Let F be a two-place function with its first argument the value of a one-place function D whose argument is X and with its second argument the value of the same one-place function D whose argument is Y. This can be represented by the formula

(10) F(DX)(DY)

With the combinator $\psi$ we obtain instead of the two functions D a single complex function $\psi$FD, directly dependent on X and Y. The function $\psi$FD is connected with the functions F and D by the equation

(11) $\psi$FDXY = F(DX)(DY)

There is a combinator $\mathbf{C}_*$. If F is a one-place function whose argument is X, $\mathbf{C}_*$F is a function connected with the function F by the equation

(12) $\mathbf{C}_*$XF = FX

$\mathbf{C}_*$ is connected with the combinators **C** and **I** by the equation

(13) $\mathbf{C}_*$XY = **CI**XY

This equation is derived as follows:

(14) $\mathbf{C}_*$XY = YX = **I**(YX) = **I**(**I**XY) = **I**YX = **CI**XY

Eight combinators have been described: **I, C, W, B, K,** $\phi$, $\psi$, $\mathbf{C}_*$. (The first seven belong to the class of regular combinators, i.e. combinators that operate on arguments of the function F.) These combinators will play a fundamental part in the postulation of semantic rules. I now wish to discuss two important concepts connected with the effect of the combinators, namely the power of a combinator and combinators of limited effect.

The power of each regular combinator is specified thus:

(15) $\mathbf{X}^1 \equiv \mathbf{X}$

$\mathbf{X}^{n+1} \equiv \mathbf{B}\mathbf{X}\mathbf{X}^n$

($\equiv$ means 'equal by definition'). If **X** is a regular combinator the effect of $\mathbf{X}^n$ consists of the operation of **X** repeated $n$ times. For $n=2$ we obtain the following equations:

$$\mathbf{B}^2\mathrm{FXYZ}=\mathbf{B}(\mathbf{B}\mathrm{F})\mathrm{XYZ}=\mathbf{B}\mathrm{F}(\mathrm{XY})\mathrm{Z}=\mathrm{F}((\mathrm{XY})\mathrm{Z})=\mathrm{F}(\mathrm{XYZ})$$
$$\mathbf{C}^2\mathrm{FXY}=\mathbf{C}(\mathbf{C}\mathrm{F})\mathrm{XY}=\mathbf{C}\mathrm{FYX}=\mathrm{FXY}$$
$$\mathbf{W}^2\mathrm{FX}=\mathbf{W}(\mathbf{W}\mathrm{F})\mathrm{X}=\mathbf{W}\mathrm{FXX}=\mathrm{FXXX}$$
$$\mathbf{K}^2\mathrm{FXY}=\mathbf{K}(\mathbf{K}\mathrm{F})\mathrm{XY}=\mathbf{K}\mathrm{FY}=\mathrm{F}$$

The power is particularly important for **B** and $\boldsymbol{\phi}$. The following assertion holds with respect to these combinators:[1]

(16) For any objects U, X, Y, $\mathrm{Z}^1, \ldots, \mathrm{Z}^n$

$$\mathbf{B}^n\mathrm{UXZ}^1 \ldots \mathrm{Z}^n=\mathrm{U}(\mathrm{XZ}^1 \ldots \mathrm{Z}^n),$$
$$\boldsymbol{\phi}^n\mathrm{UXYZ}^1 \ldots \mathrm{Z}^n=\mathrm{U}(\mathrm{XZ}^1 \ldots \mathrm{Z}^n)(\mathrm{YZ}^1 \ldots \mathrm{Z}^n)$$

It must be remembered that, as laid down in the discussion on how different objects were to be distinguished, the superscript indices in the symbols $\mathrm{Z}^1 \ldots \mathrm{Z}^n$ indicate that these are different objects, whereas the superscript indices attached to the combinators are power indices.

To the class of combinators of limited effect belongs any regular combinator $\mathbf{X}_k$, the subscript index showing that the operation of the combinator is limited to $k-1$ steps and begins with step $k$. From this we obtain the following equations:

(17) $\mathbf{C}_k\mathrm{F}_n\mathrm{X}^1 \ldots \mathrm{X}^k\mathrm{X}^{k+1} \ldots \mathrm{X}^n=\mathrm{F}_n\mathrm{X}^1 \ldots \mathrm{X}^{k+1}\mathrm{X}^k \ldots \mathrm{X}^n$

(18) $\mathbf{W}_k\mathrm{F}_n\mathrm{X}^1 \ldots \mathrm{X}^k\mathrm{X}^{k+1} \ldots \mathrm{X}^n=\mathrm{F}_n\mathrm{X}^1 \ldots \mathrm{X}^k\mathrm{X}^k\mathrm{X}^{k+1} \ldots \mathrm{X}^n$

(19) $\mathbf{K}_k\mathrm{F}_n\mathrm{X}^1 \ldots \mathrm{X}^k\mathrm{X}^{k+1}\mathrm{X}^{k+2} \ldots \mathrm{X}^n=\mathrm{F}_n\mathrm{X}^1 \ldots \mathrm{X}^k\mathrm{X}^{k+2} \ldots \mathrm{X}^n$

(20) $\mathbf{B}_k\mathrm{F}_n\mathrm{X}^1 \ldots \mathrm{X}^k\mathrm{X}^{k+1}\mathrm{X}^{k+2} \ldots \mathrm{X}^n=\mathrm{F}_n\mathrm{X}^1 \ldots \mathrm{X}^k(\mathrm{X}^{k+1}\mathrm{X}^{k+2}) \ldots \mathrm{X}^n$

In the semantic transformations an important part will be played by what are called special permutators, denoted by $\mathbf{C}_{[n]}$ and $\mathbf{C}^{[m]}$. The permutator $\mathbf{C}_{[n]}$ is defined by the equation

(21) $\mathbf{C}_{[n]}\mathrm{FX}^1\mathrm{X}^2 \ldots \mathrm{X}^{n+1}=\mathrm{FX}^{n+1}\mathrm{X}^1\mathrm{X}^2 \ldots \mathrm{X}^n$

and its effect is equal to the product of the operations of the permutators $\mathbf{C}_n, \ldots \mathbf{C}_2, \mathbf{C}_1$. This can be represented by the formula

(22) $\mathbf{C}_{[n]}\equiv\mathbf{C}_n \ldots \mathbf{C}_2\mathbf{C}_1$

By the product of the operations of the permutators is meant that $\mathbf{C}_n$ is applied first, then $\mathbf{C}_{n-1}$, and so on until finally $\mathbf{C}_2$ and $\mathbf{C}_1$ are applied. In the light of these remarks 21 can be rewritten as

(23) $(\mathbf{C}_n \ldots \mathbf{C}_2\mathbf{C}_1)\mathrm{FX}^1\mathrm{X}^2 \ldots \mathrm{X}^{n+1}=\mathrm{FX}^{n+1}\mathrm{X}^1\mathrm{X}^2 \ldots \mathrm{X}^n$

The permutator $\mathbf{C}^{[m]}$ is defined by the equation

(24) $\mathbf{C}^{[m]}\mathrm{FX}^{m+1}\mathrm{X}^1 \ldots \mathrm{X}=\mathrm{FX}^1 \ldots \mathrm{X}^m\mathrm{X}^{m+1}$

The effect of this permutator is equal to the product of the operations of the permutators $\mathbf{C}_1, \mathbf{C}_2, \ldots, \mathbf{C}_m$, which can be represented in the formula

(25) $\mathbf{C}^{[m]}=\mathbf{C}_1\mathbf{C}_2 \ldots \mathbf{C}_m$

$\mathbf{C}_{[n]}$ and $\mathbf{C}^{[m]}$ are the inverses of each other.

[1] For the proof of this assertion cf. Curry & Feys, *op. cit.*, p. 165.

The list of possible combinators has not been exhausted but the most important ones for the semantic theory are those listed above.

The question arises as to which episemions can be assigned to these combinators. Since combinators are specified with respect to functions that are regarded as variables to be replaced by concrete functions of the genotype language, it is not concrete episemions that can be assigned to combinators but abstract episemion formulae containing variables to be replaced by concrete episemions. For convenience the abstract episemion formulae will be called abstract episemions. This means that the question posed at the beginning of this paragraph has to be rephrased thus: which abstract episemions can be assigned to the combinators?

The following method will be used for determining the assignment of abstract episemions to combinators. First we take the formula in the right-hand part of the definition of a combinator and assign this formula the arbitrary abstract episemion z. The formula together with the abstract episemion is treated as the root of a tree for the construction of semions, and a tree is built up by the decomposition of the formula into its elementary components. As the tree is constructed each component is assigned an abstract episemion in accordance with rule b) for the construction of semions. This rule says that if a formula X with an abstract episemion q is decomposed into an operator A and an operand B then, the operand B having been assigned the abstract episemion p, it must be concluded that the operator A should be assigned the abstract episemion $\Delta$pq.

After obtaining a tree for the formula in the right-hand part of the definition of the combinator we construct the corresponding tree for the formula in the left-hand part of the definition, making use of the information obtained for the first tree. This brings us to a specification of the appropriate abstract episemion for the combinator.

By way of illustration, suppose we wish to specify the abstract episemion that should be assigned to the combinator **B**. We begin as follows. Let the abstract episemion z be assigned to the expression F(GX). In accordance with rule b) for the construction of semions it can be supposed that GX has the abstract episemion v and F the abstract episemion $\Delta$vz. This is shown in the tree

$$(26)\quad \frac{\Delta vzF \qquad v(GX)}{zF(GX)}$$

If the expression (GX) has the episemion v, the above-mentioned rule for the construction of episemions allows us to suppose that X has the episemion u and G the episemion $\Delta$uv. This yields the tree

(27)
$$\frac{\Delta vzF \qquad \dfrac{\Delta uvG \qquad uX}{v(GX)}}{zF(GX)}$$

We shall now construct the tree for the formula **B**FGX. If the formula F(GX) has been assigned the abstract episemion z, the formula **B**FGX must also be assigned z. We know from the tree 27 that semion X is assigned the abstract episemion u and that the first stage in the construction of the new tree will be

(28)
$$\frac{\Delta\Delta uv\Delta uz\mathbf{B}FG \qquad uX}{z\mathbf{B}FGX}$$

We know from tree 27 that the semion G is assigned the abstract episemion $\Delta$uv and that the second stage in the construction of the new tree is

(29)
$$\frac{\dfrac{\Delta\Delta uvuz\mathbf{B}F \qquad \Delta uvG}{\Delta uz\mathbf{B}FG} \qquad uX}{z\mathbf{B}FGX}$$

We know from tree 26 that the semion F is assigned the abstract episemion $\Delta$yz and that the final stage in the construction of the tree is

(30)
$$\frac{\dfrac{\dfrac{\Delta\Delta vz\Delta\Delta uv\Delta uz\mathbf{B} \qquad \Delta vzF}{\Delta\Delta uv\Delta uz\mathbf{B}F} \qquad \Delta uvG}{\Delta uz\mathbf{B}FG} \qquad uX}{z\mathbf{B}FGX}$$

It is obvious from the tree 30 that the combinator **B** must be assigned the abstract episemion

(31) $\Delta\Delta vz\Delta\Delta uv\Delta uz$

Let us consider the combinator **W**. Let the expression FXX be assigned the abstract episemion z. According to rule b) for the construction of episemions, if it is supposed that the expression X has the abstract episemion v, then the expression FX must have the abstract episemion $\Delta$vz. It follows that F must have the abstract episemion $\Delta$v$\Delta$vz. This yields the tree

(32)
$$\frac{\dfrac{\Delta v\Delta vzF \qquad vX}{\Delta vzFX} \qquad vX}{zFXX}$$

Going on from this tree it is easy to specify the abstract episemion that must be assigned to the combinator **W**. It is $\Delta\Delta v\Delta vz\Delta vz$. The operation of the combinator **W** is shown in the tree below.

$$\text{(33)}\quad \cfrac{\cfrac{\Delta\Delta \mathrm{v}\Delta \mathrm{vz}\Delta \mathrm{vz}\mathbf{W} \qquad \Delta \mathrm{v}\Delta \mathrm{vzF}}{\Delta \mathrm{vz}\mathbf{W}\mathrm{F}} \qquad \mathrm{vX}}{\mathrm{z}\mathbf{W}\mathrm{FX}}$$

Consider now the combinator $\mathbf{C}_*$. Let the expression YX have the tree

$$\text{(34)}\quad \cfrac{\Delta \mathrm{vzY} \qquad \mathrm{vX}}{\mathrm{zYX}}$$

From this tree it is clear that $\mathbf{C}_*$ has to be assigned the abstract episemion $\Delta\Delta \mathrm{vz}\Delta \mathrm{vz}$.

The operation of the combinator $\mathbf{C}_*$ is shown in the following tree:

$$\text{(35)}\quad \cfrac{\cfrac{\Delta \mathrm{v}\Delta\Delta \mathrm{vzz}\mathbf{C}_* \qquad \mathrm{vX}}{\Delta\Delta \mathrm{vzz}\mathbf{C}_*\mathrm{X}} \qquad \Delta \mathrm{vzY}}{\mathrm{z}\mathbf{C}_*\mathrm{XY}}$$

The combinator **I** must have the abstract episemion $\Delta$zz. This is obvious if we suppose that the expression **I**X is assigned the abstract episemion z.

From these examples of the assignment of abstract episemions to combinators the reader should be able to assign abstract episemions to the other combinators.

## 3. Semantic Axioms

In this section I shall consider the various semantic axioms and rules, which will be interpreted with Russian examples. The list of axioms and rules, of course, is not complete, since we shall concentrate only on those axioms that define the situation model as described on pp. 38–55. In any case, no list of axioms and rules should be considered closed, because a formal system should be tested against empirical data and the results of such experimentation can lead to the list being altered and enlarged.

Let us proceed to the axioms and their interpretation. The following semions will be used in the postulation of the axioms:

1. Two-place relators with case indices;
2. Coordinators $\mathrm{Cr}_1$, $\mathrm{Cr}_2$, . . ., $\mathrm{Cr}_n$, in which the subscript index shows the number of places associated with the coordinator;
3. A negator (operator of negation) N;
4. Elementary terms T, $\mathrm{T}^1$, $\mathrm{T}^2$, . . ., T′, T″, . . .

The indices with the terms show whether two or more terms are identical or not, identical terms having the same indices.

The arguments of the relators can be terms or sentences but only sentences can be the arguments of coordinators. The negator is a one-place predicate with a sentence as its argument. If a sentence is an argument it is referred to as embedded, and a sentence that has another sentence embedded in it is called the main sentence. The two-place predicate-relators belong to one or other of the following episemions: $\Delta\alpha\Delta\alpha\beta$, $\Delta\beta\Delta\beta\beta$, $\Delta\alpha\Delta\beta\beta$, $\Delta\beta\Delta\alpha\beta$. The first episemion denotes the category of predicates both of whose arguments are terms. The second denotes the category of predicates both of whose arguments are embedded sentences and the third denotes the category of predicates whose first argument is a term and whose second argument is a sentence. The predicates denoted by the fourth episemion, however, have as their first argument an embedded sentence and as their second a term.

The unchanging element in the above four episemions is the last symbol, $\beta$, i.e. the value of the function. The arguments have in turn either the value $\alpha$ or the value $\beta$. If the alternating arguments are denoted by the metasymbol $\gamma$ the group of four episemions can be represented by the formula $\Delta\gamma\Delta\gamma\beta$ ($\gamma=\alpha, \beta$).

The relators have case indices denoting the roles associated with the arguments. No matter whether the arguments are terms or sentences they can have the roles objective and ablative, objective and prolative, objective and locative. Since any case from these pairs can correspond either to the first or the second argument, six pairs of case symbols can occur in the case indices: *oa*, *ao*, *op*, *po*, *ol*, *lo*. The constant symbol in each case index is *o*, which can occur with either *a* or *p* or *l*. If the varying case symbols are denoted by the metasymbol *z*, the possible combinations of case symbols can be reduced to two classes, *oz* and *zo* ($z=a, p, l$).

With the metasymbols $\gamma$ and $z$ the relators used in the axioms can be represented as two classes: $\Delta\gamma\Delta\gamma\beta R_{oz}$, $\Delta\gamma\Delta\gamma\beta R_{zo}$.

Below is given a complete list of semion-relators. The metasymbols $\gamma$ and $z$ have been replaced by the appropriate constants.

| | | |
|---|---|---|
| 1. $\Delta\alpha\Delta\alpha\beta R_{oa}$ | 9. $\Delta\alpha\Delta\alpha\beta R_{op}$ | 17. $\Delta\alpha\Delta\alpha\beta R_{ol}$ |
| 2. $\Delta\alpha\Delta\alpha\beta R_{ao}$ | 10. $\Delta\alpha\Delta\alpha\beta R_{po}$ | 18. $\Delta\alpha\Delta\alpha\beta R_{lo}$ |
| 3. $\Delta\beta\Delta\beta\beta R_{oa}$ | 11. $\Delta\beta\Delta\beta\beta R_{op}$ | 19. $\Delta\beta\Delta\beta\beta R_{ol}$ |
| 4. $\Delta\beta\Delta\beta\beta R_{ao}$ | 12. $\Delta\beta\Delta\beta\beta R_{po}$ | 20. $\Delta\beta\Delta\beta\beta R_{lo}$ |
| 5. $\Delta\alpha\Delta\beta\beta R_{oa}$ | 13. $\Delta\alpha\Delta\beta\beta R_{op}$ | 21. $\Delta\alpha\Delta\beta\beta R_{ol}$ |
| 6. $\Delta\alpha\Delta\beta\beta R_{ao}$ | 14. $\Delta\alpha\Delta\beta\beta R_{po}$ | 22. $\Delta\alpha\Delta\beta\beta R_{lo}$ |
| 7. $\Delta\beta\Delta\alpha\beta R_{oa}$ | 15. $\Delta\beta\Delta\alpha\beta R_{op}$ | 23. $\Delta\beta\Delta\alpha\beta R_{ol}$ |
| 8. $\Delta\beta\Delta\alpha\beta R_{ao}$ | 16. $\Delta\beta\Delta\alpha\beta R_{po}$ | 24. $\Delta\beta\Delta\alpha\beta R_{lo}$ |

In addition to the relators there are the coordinators and the negator. The coordinators, together with the episemions assigned to them, are represented by the formulae below:

$$\Delta\beta\Delta\beta\beta Cr_2$$
$$\Delta\beta\Delta\beta\Delta\beta\beta Cr_2$$
$$\ldots\ldots\ldots\ldots$$
$$\Delta\beta^1\Delta\beta^2\ldots\Delta\beta^n\beta Cr_n$$

The negator N belongs to the episemion $\Delta\beta\beta$.

An embedded sentence can be denoted by the metasymbol S. We shall call an 'axiom schema' any sentence formula in which one argument or both arguments of the predicate are denoted by S.

Let us consider the construction of sentences containing one or two embedded sentences. The construction process will be illustrated by tree diagrams. We shall begin with sentences that have an embedded sentence as their first argument. The construction of the sentence begins with the construction of the first argument, i.e. the embedded sentence, after which a two-place relator is applied to the embedded sentence. The one-place predicate that is obtained is applied to the second argument. As an example let us take the construction of the sentence $R_{oa}(R_{lo}T^1T^2)T^3$. Its interpretations will be discussed later, and for the moment it is enough to indicate that one interpretation is *Mat' zastavljaet mal'čika, čtoby mal'čik guljal* (mother–forces–boy–in order that–boy–walk: literally **Mat' kauziruet*, (*čtoby*) *mal'čik byl na progulke*, mother–causes–boy–(in order that)–boy–be–on–walk). The predicate $R_{oa}$ corresponds to the copula *kauziruet*, and $T^3$ corresponds to *mat'*. The predicate $R_{lo}$ corresponds to the locational copula *byl na*, $T^1$ to *progulka*, and $T^2$ to *mal'čik*. The tree diagram corresponding to $R_{oa}(R_{lo}T^1T^2)T^3$ is:

(1)
$$\dfrac{\Delta\beta\Delta\alpha\beta R_{oa} \qquad \dfrac{\dfrac{\Delta\alpha\Delta\alpha\beta R_{lo} \qquad \alpha T^1}{\Delta\alpha\beta(R_{lo}T^1)} \qquad \alpha T^2}{\beta((R_{lo}T^1)T^2)}}{\dfrac{\Delta\alpha\beta(R_{oa}((R_{lo}T^1)T^2)) \qquad \alpha T^3}{\beta((R_{oa}((R_{lo}T^1)T^2))T^3)}}$$

Applying the rule for the omission of brackets, we obtain the formula $R_{oa}(R_{lo}T^1T^2)T^3$.

Let us now examine the construction of a sentence that has an embedded sentence as the second argument. Here too the construction begins with the sentence that functions as an argument. Once this embedded sentence has been constructed it has a one-place predicate applied to it which is obtained from the application of a two-place relator to a term. One example is the formula $R_{lo}T^1(R_{ao}T^2T^3)$, one of whose interpretations is *Ja čuvstvuju aromat rozy* (I–smell–perfume–of rose: literally *(*To, čto*) *aromat idet ot* *rozy, lokalizuetsja vo mne*, (it–that)–perfume–goes–from–rose–locates itself–in–me). The predicate $R_{lo}$ is interpreted as the expression *lokalizuetsja v* (locates itself–in), $T^1$ as *ja* (I: to be exact *mne*, me). The predicate $R_{ao}$ is interpreted as *idet ot* (goes–from), $T^2$ as *roza* and $T^3$ as *aromat*. The tree diagram associated with the above formula is:

(2)
$$\frac{\dfrac{\Delta\alpha\Delta\beta\beta R_{lo} \qquad \alpha T^1}{\Delta\beta\beta(R_{lo}T^1)} \qquad \dfrac{\dfrac{\Delta\alpha\Delta\alpha\beta R_{ao} \qquad \alpha T^2}{\Delta\alpha\beta(R_{ao}T^2)} \qquad \alpha T^3}{\beta((R_{ao}T^2)T^3)}}{\beta((R_{lo}T^1)((R_{oa}T^2)T^3))}$$

Removing the brackets we obtain $R_{lo}T^1(R_{ao}T^2T^3)$.

In sentences where both the arguments of the predicate are sentences the first argument is constructed first. To the first argument is applied a two-place relator and the resulting one-place predicate is applied to the second argument. I will take as an example the sentence $R_{lo}(R_{lo}T^1T^2)(R_{lo}T^2T^3)$, which has as one interpretation *Kogda my prišli, on spal* (when–we–arrived–he–was sleeping: literally **On byl vo sne* (*sostojanii sna*), *kogda my byli v pribytii*, he–was–in–sleep–(state–of sleep)–when–we–were–in–arrival). The first predicate $R_{lo}$ is interpreted as the conjunction *kogda* (when), the second and third predicates as *byli v* (were–in). $T^1$ is interpreted as *son* (sleep), $T^2$ as *on* (he), $T^3$ as *pribytie* (arrival), and $T^4$ as *my* (we). (The relator $R_{lo}$ is interpreted differently in each of its occurrences, the interpretation depending on the interpretation of its arguments). The corresponding tree diagram is shown below:

(3)
$$\frac{\dfrac{\Delta\beta\Delta\beta\beta R_{lo} \qquad \dfrac{\dfrac{\Delta\alpha\Delta\alpha\beta R_{lo} \qquad \alpha T^1}{\Delta\alpha\beta(R_{lo}T^1)} \qquad \alpha T^2}{\beta((R_{lo}T^1)T^2)}}{\Delta\beta\beta(R_{lo}((R_{lo}T^1)T^2)} \qquad \dfrac{\dfrac{\Delta\alpha\Delta\alpha\beta R_{lo} \qquad \alpha T^3}{\Delta\alpha\beta(R_{lo}T^3)} \qquad \alpha T^4}{\beta((R_{lo}T^3)T^4)}}{\beta((R_{lo}(R_{lo}T^1)T^2)((R_{lo}T^3)T^4))}$$

Without brackets, the resulting formula is $R_{lo}(R_{lo}T^1T^2)(R_{lo}T^3T^4)$.

It goes without saying that the tree diagrams showing the construction of predicate structures with many embedded sentences are even more complex.

Since the number of axioms and axiom schemas depends on the number of predicates, we have six axioms and eighteen axiom schemas with relator predicates, which can be represented as three groups in accordance with the array of case symbols: *o* and *a*, *o* and *p*, *o* and *l*. Semions 1–8 go in the first group of axioms, 9–16 in the second group and 17–24 in the third group. The number of axioms and axiom schemas within each group, eight, is determined by the possible combinations of arguments, i.e. of terms and embedded sentences. In all, therefore, there are five groups of axioms and axiom schemas, the first three containing both axioms and axiom schemas, the fourth and fifth containing only axiom schemas. A full list of axioms and axiom schemas is given below, followed by a discussion of their interpretation.

| | | | |
|---|---|---|---|
| 1.1. $R_{ao}T^1T^2$ | 2.1. $R_{po}T^1T^2$ | 3.1. $R_{lo}T^1T^2$ | 4. $CrS^1 \ldots S^n$ |
| 1.2. $R_{oa}T^1T^2$ | 2.2. $R_{op}T^1T^2$ | 3.2. $R_{ol}T^1T^2$ | 5. NS |
| 1.3. $R_{ao}S^1S^2$ | 2.3. $R_{po}S^1S^2$ | 3.3. $R_{lo}S^1S^2$ | |
| 1.4. $R_{oa}S^1S^2$ | 2.4. $R_{op}S^1S^2$ | 3.4. $R_{ol}S^1S^2$ | |
| 1.5. $R_{ao}ST$ | 2.5. $R_{po}ST$ | 3.5. $R_{lo}ST$ | |
| 1.6. $R_{oa}TS$ | 2.6. $R_{op}TS$ | 3.6. $R_{ol}TS$ | |
| 1.7. $R_{ao}TS$ | 2.7. $R_{po}TS$ | 3.7. $R_{lo}TS$ | |
| 1.8. $R_{oa}ST$ | 2.8. $R_{op}ST$ | 3.8. $R_{ol}ST$ | |

The axioms and axiom schemas in the first three groups differ only with respect to the case indices attached to the relators. The axioms within each group differ with respect to the arguments, which are either both terms or both embedded sentences or a combination of term and embedded sentence. It is this that determines that each of the first three groups contains eight axioms and axiom schemas.

A change in the order of symbols in the case indices with the arguments being held constant is interpreted as a change in the theme-rheme structure of the sentence. For example, if the sentences *Pis'mo idet ot Petra* (letter–goes–from–Peter) and *Pis'mo poslano Petrom* (letter–is sent–by Peter) are put in correspondence with $R_{ao}T^1T^2$ then *Petr poslal pis'mo* (Peter–sent–letter) can be put in correspondence with the axiom $R_{oa}T^1T^2$. In the first example the theme of the sentence is the term in the objective case, i.e. *pis'mo*, but in the second sentence the theme is the term in the ablative case, i.e. *Petr*.

To take another example, if the sentence *Ovošči v sumke* (vegetables–(are) in–bag) is put in correspondence with the axiom $R_{lo}T^1T^2$, then the axiom with the symbols in the case index in the reverse order —$R_{ol}T^1T^2$—will correspond to the sentence *Sumka soderžit ovošči* (bag–contains–vegetables). In the first sentence the theme is the term in the objective case, i.e. *ovošči*, and the rheme is *v sumke* but in the second sentence the theme is the term in the locative case, i.e. *sumka*, and the rheme is *soderžit ovošči*.

Axioms that differ only in the order of the symbols in the case indices will be called converse axioms. There is no derivational relation between converse axioms, both axioms in each pair being of equal status.

I will now provide interpretations for individual axioms from each group, beginning with the axioms from the first group, which have to do with ablative-objective and objective-ablative relations. $R_{ao}T^1T^2$ is a sentence with a predicate that has only terms as its arguments. $T^1$ is interpreted as the starting point or the source from which $T^2$ moves or arises. This axiom corresponds to such Russian sentences as *Poezd idet iz Moskvy* (train–goes–from–Moscow), *Pis'mo idet ot Petra* (letter–goes–from–Peter), *Aromat isxodit ot rozy* (perfume–emanates–from–rose), *Vlijanie isxodit ot pisatelja* (influence–emanates–from–writer), *Slyšitsja pesnja* (is heard–song: literally **slyšanie* (*sluxovoj obraz*) *isxodit ot pesni*, hearing (aural image)–emanates–from–song).

The converse axiom $R_{oa}T^1T^2$ is interpreted by the sentences **Moskva otpravljaet poezd* (Moscow–sends out–train), *Roza istočaet aromat* (rose–gives off–perfume), *Pisatel' okazyvaet vlijanie* (writer–exercises–influence), **Pesnja vyzyvaet slyšanie* (*sluxovoj obraz*) (song–calls forth–hearing (aural image)). As before, the difference between the axioms lies in the choice of theme and rheme.

$R_{oa}S^1S^2$ is the schema for axioms whose predicates have embedded sentences as arguments. $S^2$ is a situation that is the source of the situation $S^1$, and the relationship between $S^2$ and $S^1$ expressed by the predicate $R_{oa}$ can be interpreted as the changing of the situation $S^2$ into the situation $S^1$.

In Russian a partial interpretation of $R_{oa}S^1S^2$ is afforded by sentences like *Ivan edet iz Leningrada v Moskvu* (Ivan–is travelling/travels–from–Leningrad–to–Moscow). If $S^1$ is replaced by $R_{lo}T^1T^2$ and $S^2$ by $R_{lo}T^3T^2$ then the axiom $R_{oa}(R_{lo}T^1T^2)(R_{lo}T^3T^2)$ can be interpreted as, e.g., **Ivan v Leningrade, posle čego Ivan v Moskve* (Ivan–(is) in–Leningrad–after–which–Ivan–(is) in–Moscow). The initial situation $S^2$ changes into the situation $S^1$.

The predicate $R_{oa}$, which conveys the idea of a change of situation, can be expressed by words like *preobrazuetsja*, *prevraščaetsja* (is transformed/converted). Thus, the axiom could be interpreted as *Dobryj čelovek prevraščaetsja v zlogo* (good–person–turns–into–evil (one): literally, **Čelovek v dobre prevraščaetsja v čeloveka vo zle*, person–in–good–turns–into–person–in–evil).

The relation between $S^2$ and $S^1$ expressed by the predicate $R_{oa}$ can also be interpreted as one of causation. For instance, *Podul veter, i derev'ja zakačalis'* (began blowing–wind–and–trees–began to sway), in which *podul veter* corresponds to $S^2$ and *i derev'ja zakačalis'* to $R_{oa}S^1$. Another example is *Vygljanulo solnce, poètomu rastajal sneg* (looked out–sun–therefore–melted–snow), in which *vygljanulo solnce* corresponds to $S^2$ and *poètomu rastajal sneg* to $R_{oa}S^1$. In these examples the predicate $R_{oa}$ is interpreted as auxiliary words that express causal/consequential relations, such as *poètomu* (therefore), *v sledstvie čego* (as a result/consequence of which), *i* (and), *v rezul'tate* (as a result), and so on.

$R_{ao}S^1S^2$ is the schema for axioms that are the converses of the preceding one, the difference lying in the choice of theme and rheme. Thus, $R_{ao}S^1S^2$ corresponds to sentences in which the theme is the situation that arises out of another situation, one Russian example being *Ivan priezžaet v Moskvu iz Leningrada* (Ivan–comes–to–Moscow–from–Leningrad: literally **Ivan v Moskve posle togo, kak Ivan* (*byl*) *v Leningrade*, Ivan–in–Moscow–after–that–as–Ivan–(was) –in–Leningrad).

The relations between $S^2$ and $S^1$ expressed by the predicate $R_{ao}$ can be interpreted as relations of consequence and reason. In this case $S^2$, the theme, corresponds to the situation that is the consequence of something, and $S^1$, which is part of the rheme, is the situation that gives rise to something. For example, *Derev'ja zakačalis', tak kak podul veter* (trees–began to sway–as (=*tak kak*)–began to blow–wind). Here $S^2$, *derev'ja zakačalis'*, corresponds to the theme and $R_{ao}S^1$, *tak kak podul veter*, corresponds to the rheme. In the converse axiom *Podul veter* is the theme and *i* (*poètomu*) *derev'ja zakačalis'* the rheme.

Similar remarks apply to the second example, in which $R_{ao}S^1S^2$ is interpreted as *Rastajal sneg potomu, čto vygljanulo solnce* (melted–snow–because (=*potomu, čto*)–looked out–sun). The theme here is $S^2$, *rastajal sneg*, and the rheme is $R_{ao}S^1$, *potomu čto vygljanulo solnce*. In the converse axiom, $R_{oa}S^1S^2$ the theme was *vygljanulo solnce*—$S^2$—and the rheme was *poètomu rastajal sneg*—$R_{oa}S^1$.

The predicate $R_{ao}$ corresponds to conjunctions expressing relations of consequence, like *potomu čto* (because), *tak kak* (as), etc. The relations expressed by these conjunctions or by conjunctions like *poètomu* (therefore), *v sledstvie čego* (as a result of which) are converse. *Potomu čto* indicates that the rheme is the cause and the theme the consequence, whereas *poètomu* indicates that the rheme is the consequence and the theme the cause.

$R_{oa}ST$ is the schema for axioms in which the first argument is an embedded sentence. The relation between the term and the embedded sentence, expressed by the relator $R_{oa}$, can be interpreted as the relation between a source that gives rise to a situation and the situation itself. This axiom, just like $R_{oa}S^1S^2$, can be put in correspondence with sentences like *Ivan edet iz Leningrada v Moskvu* (Ivan–travels–from–Leningrad–to–Moscow). If S is replaced by $R_{lo}T^1T^2$ and interpreted as *Ivan v Moskve* (Ivan–(is) in–Moscow), then the axiom

$R_{oa}(R_{lo}T^1T^2)T^3$ can be interpreted as **Leningrad—èto to, otkuda Ivan v Moskve* (Leningrad–that is the place (=*èto to*)–from which–Ivan–(is) in–Moscow). Here $T^3$—*Leningrad*—is the starting point of the movement that leads to the situation *Ivan v Moskve*. The axiom $R_{oa}(R_{lo}T^1T^2)T^3$ can be regarded as a degeneration of the axiom $R_{oa}(R_{lo}T^1T^2)(R_{lo}T^3T^2)$. In the degenerate structure instead of the second embedded sentence there is one of the terms—in this case $T^3$.

The predicate $R_{oa}$ can also be interpreted as causative copulas like *kauzirovat'* (cause), *zastavljat'* (force). If S is replaced by $R_{lo}T^1T^2$, the complex situation $R_{oa}(R_{lo}T^1T^2)T^3$ can correspond to causative constructions like *Mat' zastavljaet mal'čika guljat'* (mother–forces–boy–to walk: literally, **Mat' zastavljaet, čtoby mal'čik byl na progulke*, mother–forces–that–boy–be–on–walk). Sentences like *Ja obrabatyvaju detal'* (I–am machining–component) and *Ja dvigaju mebel'* (I–am moving–furniture) also correspond to the axiom $R_{oa}(R_{lo}T^1T^2)T^3$ (literally **Ja kauziruju, čtoby detal' byla v obrabotke*, I–cause–that–component–be–in–machining; and **Ja kauziruju, čtoby mebel' byla v dviženii*, I–cause–that–furniture–be–in–movement).

This axiom also corresponds to sentences with causal expressions like *On p'et s toski* (he–drinks–from–melancholy: literally **Toska zastavljaet, čtoby on byl v zapoe*, melancholy–forces–that–he–be–in–drinking).

The axiom $R_{oa}(R_{lo}T^1T^2)T^3$, which was given a causative interpretation, must also be considered a degeneration of the axioms represented by the schema $R_{oa}S^1S^2$. The fact is that in reality causation is a relation that holds between two situations, one of which causes or brings about the other. If we say then that some person brings about a situation the subject that does the causing must be understood to be the degeneration of a situation, the degeneration consisting of the omission of the predicate assigned to the subject.

This means that the sentence *Mat' zastavljaet mal'čika guljat'* should be considered a degeneration of the sentence *Ot materi idut slova, vsledstvie čego mal'čik na progulke* (from–mother–go–words–as result–of which–boy–(is) on–walk). The corresponding axiom is $R_{oa}(R_{lo}T^1T^2)(R_{oa}T^3T^4)$. *Ja obrabatyvaju detal'* is a degeneration of *Ja pol'zujus' stankom, vsledstvie čego detal' v obrabotke* (I–am using–machine tool–as result–of which–component–(is) in–machining). The axiom corresponding to this sentence is $R_{oa}(R_{lo}T^1T^2)(R_{po}T^3T^4)$. Here the degeneration of the second embedded sentence, which involves the omission of its predicate, is accompanied by the renaming of a term, the term in the objective case being relabelled as a term in the ablative.

$R_{ao}TS$ is the schema for axioms that are the converse of the above, the difference again lying in the choice of theme and rheme. In the sentences we have just been discussing the theme is the source of the movement or action but in the sentences we are about to look at the theme is the situation that is brought into existence, i.e. the embedded sentence.

If S is replaced by $R_{lo}T^1T^2$ and interpreted as *Ivan v Moskve* (Ivan–(is) in–Moscow), the axiom $R_{ao}T^1(R_{lo}T^2T^3)$ can be interpreted as **Ivan v Moskve iz Leningrada* (Ivan–(is) in–Moscow–from–Leningrad). If the predicate $R_{ao}$ is interpreted as a causative copula and the first argument as an animate noun, $R_{ao}T^1(R_{lo}T^2T^3)$ can be put in correspondence with sentences like *Mnoju obrabatyvaetsja detal'* (by me–is machined–component), *Mnoju čitaetsja kniga* (by me–is read–book), *Mnoju dvigaetsja mebel'* (by me–is moved–furniture). More literal versions are *(*To, čto*) *detal' v obrabotke, kauziruetsja mnoju* ((It–that)–component–(is) in–machining–is caused–by me), *(*To, čto*) *kniga v čtenii, kauziruetsja mnoju* ((It–that)–book–(is) in–reading–is caused–by me), etc.

$R_{ao}T^1(R_{lo}T^2T^3)$ can also be regarded as a degeneration of the axioms represented by the schema $R_{ao}S^1S^2$.

The second group of axioms have to do with prolative-objective and objective-prolative relations. $R_{po}T^1T^2$ is a sentence with a two-place predicate both of whose arguments are terms. $T^1$, corresponding to the prolative, denotes a point across which there is a movement or an instrument by means of which an action is carried out. $T^2$, corresponding to the objective, is interpreted either as a moving object that cuts across a point p or as an object that uses an instrument p.

This axiom is interpreted as sentences like *Poezd edet čerez Leningrad* (train–goes–through–Leningrad), *Oxotnik edet na olene* (**posredstvom olenja*) (hunter–travels–on–reindeer–(by means–of reindeer)), *Počta dostavljaetsja samoletom* (mail–is delivered–by plane), and also as sentences like *Ja pol'zujus' nožom* (I–use–knife), *On oruduet lopatoj* (he–handles–spade).

With the terms being interpreted in an analogous fashion the converse axiom $R_{op}T^1T^2$ corresponds to sentences in which the theme and rheme have been changed: e.g. **Leningrad propuskaet poezd* (Leningrad–lets pass–train), **Olen'—sredstvo peredviženija dlja oxotnika* (reindeer–(is)–means–of movement–for–hunter), *Samolet dostavljaet počtu* (plane–delivers–mail).

As the arguments of predicates with ablative-objective relations, both these axioms model three-place sentences expressing an instrumental meaning, e.g. *Oxotnik zakalyvaet olenja nožom* (hunter–stabs–reindeer–with knife), *Otec rubit derevo toporom* (father–fells–tree–with axe). Both these sentences correspond to the axiom $R_{oa}(R_{lo}T^1T^2)$

($R_{po}T^3T^4$), more literal versions being *(*To, čto*) *oxotnik pol'zuetsja nožom, kauziruet smert' u olenja* ((it–that)–hunter–uses–knife–causes–death–at–reindeer), *(*To, čto*) *otec pol'zuetsja toporom, kauziruet rubku nad derevom* ((it–that)–father–uses–axe–causes–felling–above–tree).

$R_{po}S^1S^2$ is the schema for axioms with two embedded sentences. The predicate $R_{po}$ expresses circumstantial-instrumental relations between the situations $S^2$ and $S^1$, i.e. the situation $S^1$ is the means by which the situation $S^2$ is obtained. If this schema is replaced by $R_{po}(R_{lo}T^1T^2)(R_{lo}T^3T^2)$ it can be put in correspondence with sentences like **Poezd v Talline čerez Leningrad* (train–(is) in–Tallin–through–Leningrad: literally *Poezd v Talline osuščestvljaetsja čerez to, čto poezd byl v Leningrade*, train–(is) in–Tallin–comes about–through–it–that–train–was–in–Leningrad).

If the schema $R_{po}S^1S^2$ is given a more abstract interpretation it can be put in correspondence with sentences like *Soglašenie bylo dostignuto posredstvom vedenija peregovorov* (*togo, čto velis' peregovory*) (agreement–was–reached–by means–of the holding–of talks (of it–that–talks–were held)). $S^2$ here corresponds to the main clause *soglašenie bylo dostignuto*, and $R_{po}S^1$ corresponds to the preposition and the subordinate clause *posredstvom togo, čto velis' peregovory*. The predicate $R_{po}$ can be interpreted as subordinating conjunctions like *posredstvom togo*, *blagodarja tomu, čto* (thanks to the fact that), etc.

The converse schema $R_{op}S^1S^2$ also models instrumental relations but with the constituents that were the theme becoming the rheme, and vice-versa; e.g. (*to, čto velis' peregovory*) *poslužilo sredstvom dostiženija soglašenija* (*togo, čto soglašenie bylo dostignuto*) ((it–that–were held–talks)–was–means–of attainment–of agreement (of it–that–agreement–was–attained)).

The axiom schemas $R_{po}TS$ and $R_{op}ST$ can be considered as degenerations of the above axioms in which both arguments are embedded sentences. If the first is interpreted as *(*To, čto*) *poezd v Talline, osuščestvljaetsja čerez Leningrad* ((it, that)–train–(is) in–Tallin–comes about–through–Leningrad), or *(*To, čto*) *olen' ubit, osuščestvleno posredstvom noža* ((it–that)–reindeer–killed–brought about–by means–of knife), then the second is interpreted as **Leningrad — to, čerez čto poezd v Talline* (Leningrad–(is) that–through–which–train–in–Tallin) or **Nož orudie togo, čto olen' ubit* (knife–(is) instrument–of it–that–reindeer–killed). In exactly the same way, if $R_{po}TS$ is interpreted as *(*To, čto*) *pis'mo dostavleno, osuščestvleno samoletom* ((it–that)–letter–delivered–brought about–by plane), then the converse schema $R_{op}ST$ must be interpreted as **Samolet — sredstvo togo, čto pis'mo dostavleno* (plane–(is) means–of it–that–letter–delivered).

The third group of axioms involve objective-locative and locative-objective relations. $R_{lo}T^1T^2$ is a sentence in which the arguments of the predicate are terms connected by an objective-locative relation, i.e. the argument $T^2$ is located in/at the argument $T^1$. The predicate $R_{lo}$ corresponds to copulas such as *byt'* (be), *naxodit'sja* (lit. 'find oneself', i.e. 'be'). The term in the locative case, $T^1$, is interpreted as an inanimate noun (either concrete or abstract) or as an animate noun. The term in the objective case is interpreted as a concrete noun, either animate or inanimate. Examples are *Ovošči* (*naxodjatsja*) *v sumke* (vegetables–(are)–in–bag), *Karandaš na stole* (pencil–(is) on–table), *U menja knigi* (at–me–books), *Ivan v toske* (Ivan–(is) in–melancholy). The axiom also corresponds to sentences with one-place predicates denoting an action, e.g. *Mal'čik guljaet* (boy–walks) and *Čelovek rabotaet* (person–works). Literal interpretations are *Mal'čik na progulke* (**v guljanii*) (boy–(is) on–walk–(in–walking)), **Čelovek v rabote* (person–(is) in–work). These interpretations presuppose that a full verb can be reduced to a combination of a copula and an abstract deverbal noun: *guljaet←naxoditsja na progulke; vraščaetsja* (rotates)←*naxoditsja vo vraščenii* (is–in–rotation); *dvigaetsja* (moves) ←*naxoditsja v dviženii* (is–in–movement).

$R_{lo}T^1T^2$ also corresponds to sentences with predicate nominals like *Brat—inžener* (brother–(is) engineer), *Ivan—storož* (Ivan–(is) watchman). Here the arguments are in a relation of abstract location, witness interpretations such as *Brat naxoditsja v klasse inženerov* (Brother–is–in–class–of engineers), **Ivan—v klasse storožej* (Ivan–(is) in–class–of watchmen).

$R_{ol}T^1T^2$ is a sentence with a predicate that is the converse of the predicate in the above sentences. In the latter the objective is the theme but in this sentence the locative is the theme, e.g. *Korobka soderžit karandaš* (basket–contains–pencil), *Sumka soderžit ovošči* (bag–contains–vegetables), *Ja imeju knigi* (I–have–books). Pairs of verbs like *naxodit'sja* (be)–*soderžat'* (contain), *byt'* (be)–*imet'* (have) belong to the class of converse predicates.

$R_{lo}S^1S^2$ is a schema with two embedded sentences. The meaning expressed by this axiom schema is that the situation $S^2$ is located in the situation $S^1$. Here $R_{lo}$ can correspond to subordinating conjunctions like *gde* (where), *kogda* (when). Thus, if $R_{lo}S^1S^2$ is replaced by $R_{lo}(R_{lo}T^1T^2)(R_{lo}T^3T^4)$, the axiom can be interpreted as *Avtomobil' ostanovilsja tam, gde sobralis' ljudi* (car–has stopped–there–where–have gathered–people: literally **Avtomobil' na ostanovke tam, gde ljudi v sbore*, car–(is) on–stop–there–where–people–in–gathering). If $S^1$ is replaced by $R_{lo}T^1T^2$ and $S^2$ by $R_{ol}ST^3$ the axiom $R_{lo}(R_{lo}T^1T^2)$ $(R_{ol}ST^3)$ can be interpreted as *My uslyšali muzyku, kogda kolonna* *byla na ploščadi* (we–heard–music–when–parade–was–in–square: literally **My lokalizovali v sebe* (*to, čto*) *ot muzyki slyšanie* (*sluxovoj obraz*), *kogda kolonna byla na ploščadi*, We–localised–in–ourselves–(it–that)–from–music–hearing–(aural–image)–when–parade–was–in–square).

If $S^1$ is replaced by $R_{ol}T^1T^2$ and $S^2$ by $R_{lo}T^3T^2$, the axiom $R_{lo}(R_{ol}T^1T^2)(R_{lo}(T^3T^2)$ can be interpreted as *Esli u nas budut bilety, my pojdem v teatr* (if–at–us–will be–tickets–we–shall go–to–theatre: literally **Esli my lokalizuem* (*v sebe*) *bilety, to my budem* (*lokalizirovany*) *v teatre*, if–we–locate–(in–selves)–tickets–then–we–shall–be–(localised)–in–theatre).

$R_{ol}S^1S^2$ is the schema for axioms whose predicates are the converse of the ones in the preceding axioms, the difference concerning the choice of theme and rheme. In the above sentences the theme was the situation that was located somewhere but in the following examples the theme is the situation in which the other situation is located.

Thus the axiom $R_{ol}(R_{lo}T^1T^2)(R_{lo}T^3T^4)$ can be interpreted as *Sobralis' ljudi tam, gde ostanovilsja avtomobil'* (have gathered–people–there–where–has stopped–car), and $R_{ol}(R_{ol}ST^1)(R_{lo}T^1T^2)$ can be interpreted as *Kolonna priblizilas', i my uslyšali muzyku* (parade–had approached–and–we–heard–music). $R_{ol}(R_{lo}T^1T^2)(R_{ol}T^3T^2)$ corresponds to sentences like *Esli my v teatre, sledovatel'no my imeem bilety* (if–we–(are) in–theatre–consequently–we–have–tickets).

$R_{lo}TS$ is the schema for axioms with predicates whose arguments are a term and a sentence. If S is replaced by $R_{lo}T^1T^2$ the resulting sentence $R_{lo}T(R_{lo}T^1T^2)$ can be interpreted as *Deti sobralis' na poljane* (children–gathered–in–clearing: literally, **To, čto deti v sbore, imelo mesto na poljane*, it–that–children–in–gathering–took–place–in–clearing). Here T is interpreted as the concrete noun *poljana* (clearing), but if it is interpreted as abstract nouns like *vozmožnost'* (possibility), *neobxodimost'* (necessity), *objazatel'nost'* (obligatoriness), *verojatnost'* (probability), etc., then $R_{lo}TS$ can be regarded as a complex situation in which a simple situation S is located in a modality, i.e. possibility, necessity, and so on. The above axiom $R_{lo}T(R_{lo}T^1T^2)$ can then be interpreted as *Vozmožno, karandaš na stole* (possible–pencil–(is)–on–table), *Dolžno byt', kniga v obrabotke* (must–be–book–(is) in–preparation: literally *(*To, čto*) *karandaš na stole, lokaliziruetsja v vozmožnosti*, it–that–pencil–on–table–is located–in–possibility).

$R_{lo}TS$ has other interpretations too. If the second argument is replaced by $R_{ao}T^1T^2$ and given the interpretation *Aromat idet ot rozy* (perfume–goes–from–rose), *Slyšanie* (*sluxovoj obraz*) *idet ot pesni* (hearing–(aural–image)–goes–from–song), and if the term is interpreted as an animate noun, then the whole axiom can be in correspondence with sentences like *Mne čuvstvuetsja roza* (to me–feels–rose: to be exact, *aromat rozy*, to me–feels–rose–(perfume–of rose)), *Mne slyšitsja pesnja* (to me–hears itself–song). Literal interpretations would be *(*To, čto*) *aromat idet ot rozy, lokalizuetsja vo mne / vosprinimaetsja mnoju* ((it–that)–perfume–goes–from–rose–locates itself–in–me / is perceived–by me), *(*To, čto*) *sluxovoj obraz idet ot pesni, lokalizuetsja vo mne / vosprinimaetsja mnoju* ((it–that)–aural–image–goes–from–song–locates itself–in–me / is perceived–by me).

If S in the converse schema $R_{ol}ST$ is replaced by, e.g., $R_{lo}T^1T^2$, the schema can be interpreted as *Poljana—eto to, gde sobralis' deti* (clearing–(is) it–where–gathered–children). If S is replaced by $R_{oa}T^1T^2$ the axiom $R_{ol}(R_{oa}T^1T^2)T^3$ can be put in correspondence with sentences like *Ja čuvstvuju rozu* (I–feel (smell)–rose), *Ja slyšu muzyku* (I–hear–music): (literally **Ja lokalizuju v sebe to, čto ot rozy idet aromat*, I–locate–in–self–it–that–from–rose–goes–perfume; **Ja lokalizuju v sebe to, čto ot muzyki idet sluxovoj obraz*, I–locate–in–self–it–that–from–music–goes–aural–image).

Now that we have looked at the axiom schemas $R_{ao}TS$ and $R_{oa}ST$ from the first group and $R_{lo}TS$ and $R_{ol}ST$ from the third group, it is worthwhile comparing sentences that have identical surface structures. Such sentences might be, on the one hand, those with verbs denoting actions, e.g. *Ja obrabatyvaju detal'* (I–am machining–component) and *Ja čitaju knigu* (I–am reading–book), and on the other hand those with verbs of perception (i.e. stative verbs), e.g. *Ja vižu dom* (I–see–house) and *Ja slyšu muzyku* (I–hear–music). Both types of sentence correspond to axioms that have a term as one of their arguments and an embedded sentence as the other argument. The difference lies in the distribution of the objective-locative / locative-objective relations (the order is immaterial) and of the objective-ablative / ablative-objective relations between the predicate of the main clause and the predicate of the embedded clause.

In the former examples, i.e. in sentences with verbs denoting actions, the predicate of the main clause is $R_{oa}$ or $R_{ao}$, which means that the term corresponding to the animate noun, i.e. *ja* (I), is regarded as the source of the action, whose object is the embedded clause. The embedded clause itself corresponds to a situation with a locative and an objective, i.e. its predicate is $R_{lo}$ or $R_{ol}$. Consequently, the axioms corresponding to situations involving an action have any of the following four forms: $R_{oa}(R_{ol}T^1T^2)T^3$, $R_{oa}(R_{lo}T^1T^2)T^3$, $R_{ao}T^1(R_{ol}T^2T^3)$, $R_{ao}T^1(R_{lo}T^2T^3)$. The first two axioms correspond to sentences with verbs denoting actions, the verb being in the active voice, e.g. *Ja obrabatyvaju detal'* (I–am machining–component), *Ja čitaju knigu* (I–read–book). The second pair of axioms correspond to sentences in which the verb is in the passive voice, e.g. *Detal' obrabatyvaetsja mnoju* (component–is machined–by me) and *Kniga čitaetsja mnoju* (book–is read–by me).

$R_{oa}(R_{ol}T^1T^2)T^3$ can be interpreted as **Ja kauziruju* (*to, čto*) *obrabotka rasprostranjaetsja na detal'* (I–cause–(it–that)–machining–extend–to–component), **Ja kauziruju to, čto čtenie kasaetsja knigi* (I–cause–it–that–reading–comes in contact with–book).

$R_{oa}(R_{lo}T^1T^2)T^3$ can be given the interpretation **Ja kauziruju* (*to, čto*) *detal' v obrabotke* (I–cause–(it–that)–component–(is) in–machining), **Ja kauziruju to, čto kniga v čtenii* (I–cause–it–that–book –(is) in–reading).

$R_{ao}T^1(R_{ol}T^2T^3)$ can be given the interpretation **To, čto obrabotka rasprostranjaetsja na detal', isxodit ot menja/kauziruetsja mnoju* (it–that–machining–extends–to–component–emanates–from–me/is caused–by me), **To, čto čtenie kasaetsja knigi, isxodit ot menja/kauziruetsja mnoju* (it–that–reading–comes in contact with–book–emanates–from–me/is caused–by me).

$R_{ao}T^1(R_{lo}T^2T^3)$ can be interpreted as *(*To, čto*) *detal' v obrabotke, isxodit ot menja/kauziruetsja mnoju* ((it–that)–component–in–machining–emanates–from–me/is caused–by me), *(*To, čto*) *kniga v čtenii, isxodit ot menja/kauziruetsja mnoju* ((it–that)–book–(is)–in–reading–emanates–from–me/is caused–by me).

With verbs of perception the predicate in the main clause is $R_{lo}$ or $R_{ol}$, which means that the embedded sentence, in the role of objective, is located in/at the term, which is interpreted as an animate noun. The embedded sentence corresponds to a situation with an ablative and an objective, i.e. its predicate is $R_{oa}$ or $R_{ao}$. The axioms corresponding to situations involving perception are: $R_{ol}(R_{oa}T^1T^2)T^3$, $R_{ol}(R_{ao}T^1T^2)T^3$, $R_{lo}T^1(R_{oa}T^2T^3)$, $R_{lo}T^1(R_{ao}T^2T^3)$. The first two sentences correspond to sentences containing stative verbs in the active voice, e.g. *Ja vižu dom* (I–see–house), and the second two sentences correspond to sentences containing stative verbs in the passive voice, e.g. *Mne viden dom* (to me–visible–house).

Interpretations of all four axioms are given below:

$R_{ol}(R_{oa}T^1T^2)T^3$: **Ja lokalizuju v sebe* (*to, čto*) *dom kauziruet videnie* (*zritel'nyj obraz*) (I–locate–in–self–(it–that)–house–causes–vision (visual image)).

$R_{ol}(R_{ao}T^1T^2)T^3$: **Ja lokalizuju v sebe* (*to, čto*) *videnie* (*zritel'nyj obraz*) *isxodit ot doma* (I–locate–in–self–(it–that)–vision (visual image)–emanates–from–house).

$R_{lo}T^1(R_{oa}T^2T^3)$: *(*To, čto*) *dom kauziruet videnie, lokalizuetsja vo mne* ((It–that)–house–causes–vision–locates itself–in–me).

$R_{lo}T^1(R_{ao}T^2T^3)$: **To, čto videnie isxodit ot doma, lokalizuetsja vo mne* (it–that–vision–emanates–from–house–locates itself–in–me).

The fourth group of axioms contains one axiom schema $Cr_nS^1 \ldots S^n$, where Cr is an *n*-place predicate-coordinator. The coordinator structure models compound sentences, the number of places in the predicate Cr corresponding to the number of conjoined clauses. If two clauses are conjoined, the subscript index attached to Cr can be left out, leaving, for example, $CrS^1S^2$, which can be interpreted as *L'et dožd', i šumit more* (pours–rain–and–roars–sea). If more than two clauses are conjoined the subscript index is left in, e.g. in the three-place predicate $Cr_3S^1S^2S^3$, which can be interpreted as *L'et dožd', šumit more, gudit veter* (pours–rain–roars–sea–howls–wind).

The fifth group also contains just one axiom schema, NS. The operator of negation, N, is the only one-place operator in the axiom system, its one argument being a sentence. The above axiom can be interpreted as sentences like *Neverno, čto on ošibaetsja* (untrue–that–he–is making mistake). Negative sentences like *On ne ošibaetsja* (he–not–is making mistake) are obtained by applying the derivational rules to NS.

We will now introduce the notion of reduced axioms and schemas of reduced axioms. A reduced axiom is a sentence with one reduced, i.e. omitted, argument, and by convention only relator axioms can be reduced. Reduced axioms and the schemas of reduced axioms can take one of the eight forms listed below:

1. $R_{(o)z}T$ 5. $R_{(z)o}T$
2. $R_{o(z)}T$ 6. $R_{z(o)}T$
3. $R_{(o)z}S$ 7. $R_{(z)o}S$
4. $R_{o(z)}S$ 8. $R_{z(o)}S$

The bracketed case index shows which argument is omitted.

The reduced axioms can be interpreted as follows. If a complete, i.e. unreduced, axiom is interpreted as *Poezd idet iz Moskvy* (train–goes–from–Moscow) or *Aromat isxodit ot rozy* (perfume–goes–from–rose), then of the corresponding reduced axioms one, $R_{o(a)}T^2$, will be interpreted as *Poezd idet* (train–goes) or *Čuvstvuju aromat* ((I) feel/smell–perfume): literally **Aromat isxodit*, perfume–emanates), and the second, $R_{a(o)}T^1$, will be interpreted as *idet iz Moskvy* (goes–from–Moscow), *isxodit ot rozy* (emanates–from–rose). The reduced axioms can also be interpreted as sentences with indefinite pronouns, such as *Čto-to idet iz Moskvy* (something–goes–from–Moscow) or *Čto-to isxodit ot rozy* (something–goes–from–rose).

The converse reduced axioms, $R_{(o)a}T^2$ and $R_{o(a)}T^1$, corresponding to the complete axiom $R_{oa}T^1T^2$, are interpreted as *Moskva otpravljaet čto-to* (Moscow–sends off–something), *Roza istočaet čto-to* (rose–

gives off–something) and *Čto-to otpravljaet poezd/Poezd otpravljaetsja* (something–sends off–train/train–is sent off), *Čto-to istočaet aromat/Aromat istočaetsja* (something–gives off–perfume/perfume–is given off).

Let us consider two reductions of the axiom schema $1.4R_{oa}S^1S^2$, taking as an example the axiom $R_{oa}(R_{lo}T^1T^2)(R_{lo}T^3T^2)$, which is interpreted as *Poezd idet iz Leningrada v Moskvu* (train–goes–from–Leningrad–to–Moscow: literally *Snačala poezd v Leningrade, potom poezd v Moskve*, at first–train–in–Leningrad–then–train–in–Moscow).

If the first argument is reduced we obtain the sentence $R_{(o)a}(R_{lo}T^3T^2)$, which has to be understood as the transition of an initial situation $S_a$ (the subscript letter is a case index) to a situation that is not denoted by anything, i.e. the transition of the situation $S_a$ to something or other. This transition can be taken as the termination of $S_a$. In such a case the relator $R_{(o)a}$ can be regarded as a termination operator applying to situations, i.e. as an operator that has an aspectual feature labelled terminative. The sentence $R_{(o)a}(R_{lo}T^3T^2)$ can, with respect to the above example, be interpreted as *Poezd perestal byt' v Leningrade* (train–ceased–to be–in–Leningrad).

It should be borne in mind that a sentence with a terminative is equivalent in meaning to a sentence with an operator of negation, $R_{(o)a}(R_{lo}T^1T^2) \equiv N(R_{lo}T^1T^2)$, which is interpreted as *Poezd perestal byt' v Leningrade* (train–ceased–to be–in–Leningrad) = *Poezd ne v Leningrade* (train–not–in–Leningrad).

A second reduction of the axiom schema 1.4 is $R_{o(a)}(R_{lo}T^1T^2)$, which should be understood as the coming into of existence of a situation $S_o$ out of some undetermined situation, i.e. from a practical point of view simply as the coming into existence of a situation $S_o$. The relator here should be regarded as an operator with an aspectual feature that can be labelled inceptive. The sentence $R_{o(a)}(R_{lo}T^1T^2)$ can be interpreted as *Poezd pribyvaet v Moskvu* (train–arrives–in–Moscow: literally **Poezd načinaet byt' v Moskve*, train–begins–to be–in–Moscow).

The most varied sentences with inceptive predicates correspond to the axioms represented by the reduced axiom schema $R_{o(a)}S$. For example, *On stal inženerom* (he–became–engineer) presupposes an initial state in which *On ne byl inžener* (he–not–was–engineer), and *Devuška poblednela* (girl–became pale) presupposes a state in which *Devuška ne byla blednoj* (girl–not–was–pale).

$R_{(o)a}$ and $R_{o(a)}$ can be operators on terms (cf. the reduced axioms 1.1 and 1.2) or on sentences (cf. the reduced schema 1.4), but it is only in the latter case that we can speak of the interpretation of these relators as operators with the aspectual features terminative and inceptive. To distinguish relators with aspectual features from those without the following notational conventions are introduced:

$R_{(o)a}SS \equiv TmS$

$R_{o(a)}S \equiv IcS$

where Tm is the terminative and Ic the inceptive.

Since in the axioms represented by the schema 1.4 the relator $R_{oa}$ denotes the replacement of one situation by another, i.e. the termination of one and the beginning of another, it can also be interpreted as a causative predicate, and the terminative Tm and the inceptive Ic can be regarded as two different cases of the degeneration of the causative predicate.

We shall now concentrate on the interpretation of the other reduced axioms and axiom schemas.

## 4. Semantic Rules

The semantic rules are applied both to axioms and to structures obtained from the axioms by a previous application of the semantic rules. An intermediate structure is an object that is not an axiom but is having a semantic rule applied to it.

A distinction will be drawn between general and special semantic rules. The general rules involve the application of combinators and will be denoted by the symbol of the appropriate combinator in brackets. The special rules are specified by the properties of the relators and the coordinator, and will be denoted by the symbol of the appropriate relator or coordinator. If a relator is applied in more than one rule a number is placed to the right of the symbol for that relator.

### 1. *General rules*

(I) $X \rightarrow \mathbf{I}X$

(C) $FXY \rightarrow \mathbf{C}FYX$

($\mathbf{C}_k$) $FX^1 \ldots X^k X^{k+1} \ldots X^n \rightarrow \mathbf{C}_k FX^1 \ldots X^{k+1} X^k \ldots X^n$

($\mathbf{C}_{[n]}$) $FX^1X^2 \ldots X^n X^{n+1} \rightarrow \mathbf{C}_{[n]} FX^2 \ldots X^n X^{n+1} X^1$

($\mathbf{C}^{[m]}$) $FX^1 \ldots X^m X^{m+1} \rightarrow \mathbf{C}^{[m]} FX^{m+1} X^1 \ldots X^m$

($\mathbf{C}_*$) $XY \rightarrow \mathbf{C}_* YX$

(W) $FXX \rightarrow \mathbf{W}FX$

($\mathbf{W}_k$) $FX^1 \ldots X^k X^k \ldots X^n \rightarrow \mathbf{W}_k FX^1 \ldots X^k \ldots X^n$

(B) $F(GX) \rightarrow \mathbf{B}FGX$

($\mathbf{B}^n$) $F(GX^1 \ldots X^n) \rightarrow \mathbf{B}^n FGX^1 \ldots X^n$

($\mathbf{B}_k$) $FX^1 \ldots X^{k-1}(X^k X^{k+1}) \ldots X^n \rightarrow \mathbf{B}_k X^1 \ldots X^{k-1} X^k X^{k+1} \ldots X^n$

(K) $X \rightarrow \mathbf{K}XY$

($\mathbf{K}_k$) $FX^1 \ldots X^{k-1} Y^1 \ldots Y^n \rightarrow \mathbf{K}_k FX^1 \ldots X^{k-1} X^k Y^1 \ldots Y^n$

($\phi$) $F(GX)(HX) \rightarrow \phi FGHX$

($\psi$) $F(GX)(GY) \rightarrow \psi FGXY$

2. *Special rules*

(R$_T$) $S \rightarrow R_T S$
(R$_{A1}$) $R_{lo}(P^1T^1)(P^2T^1) \rightarrow P^2(R_A(P^1T^1)T^1)$
(R$_{A2}$) $Cr(P^1T^1)(P^2T^1) \rightarrow P^2(R_A(P^1T^1)T^1)$
(Cr) $CrS^1S^2 \rightarrow CrS^2S^1$
(Tm) $R_{(o)a}(R_{lo}T_l{}^1T_o{}^2) \rightarrow Tm(R_{lo}T_l{}^1T_o{}^2)$
(Ic) $R_{o(a)}(R_{lo}T^1T^2) \rightarrow Ic(R_{lo}T^1T^2)$

The general semantic rules do not stand in need of explanation as the properties of the combinators were discussed earlier (p. 58), but the special rules do need to be explained. In these rules the elementary terms T, $T^1$ . . . are to be regarded as representing terms of any complexity and the elementary predicates are to be taken as representing predicates of any complexity.

(R$_T$) is the rule for the nominalisation of an embedded sentence. The relator $R_T$, which will be called the nominaliser, is a semion belonging to the episemion $\Delta\beta\alpha$. Its operation is shown in 1:

(1) $$\frac{\Delta\beta\alpha R_T \qquad \beta S}{\alpha(R_T S)}$$

The rule (R$_T$) also models the transformation in 2:

(2) a) **On skazal, on pridet*→ *On skazal, čto on pridet*
b) He said he would come→He said that he would come

(b is a translation of a.)

(R$_{A1}$) is the rule that relativises an embedded sentence. The relator $R_A$, which will be called the relativiser, is a semion belonging to the episemion $\Delta\beta\Delta\alpha\alpha$. Its function is to convert the first embedded sentence into an operator attached to one of the terms of the second embedded sentence. The rule of relativisation can be applied on condition that both embedded sentences contain identical terms. The effect of the relativiser is shown in 3:

(3) $$\frac{\dfrac{\Delta\beta\Delta\alpha\alpha R_A \qquad \beta S}{\Delta\alpha\alpha(R_A S)} \qquad \alpha T}{\alpha((R_A S)T)}$$

Rule (R$_{A1}$) models the transformation of a complex sentence with an adverbial clause into a complex sentence with a relative clause, e.g.

(4) *Kogda čelovek myslit, on živet* (when–person–thinks–he–lives)
*Čelovek, kotoryj myslit, živet* (person–who–thinks–lives)

In the interpretation of the genotype sentences related by the rule (R$_{A1}$) one of the identical terms in the initial sentence is interpreted as a personal pronoun. In the derived sentence, the term in the embedded sentence that is the operator for the identical term in the matrix sentence, is interpreted as a relative pronoun like *kotoryj* (who/which/that).

($R_{A2}$) differs from ($R_{A1}$) in its left-hand part. While in ($R_{A1}$) the operator with the embedded sentences is $R_{lo}$, in ($R_{A2}$) the operator is the two-place coordinator $\Delta\beta\Delta\beta\beta$Cr. ($R_{A2}$) models the transformation of compound sentences into complex sentences with a relative clause, e.g.

(5) *Ja vstretil prijatelja, i on pokazal mne gorod* (I–met–friend–and–he–showed–me–town)
*Ja vstretil prijatelja, kotoryj pokazal mne gorod* (I–met–friend–who showed–me–town)

As for ($R_{A1}$), the rule ($R_{A2}$) can be applied only if there are identical terms in both embedded sentences. In the interpretation of genotype sentences related by ($R_{A2}$) one of the identical terms is pronominalised, this process being analogous to the pronominalisation that occurs in the interpretation of sentences related by ($R_{A1}$).

The rule (Cr) shows that the coordinator can permute elements. The sentences that are its arguments change places without the meaning of the whole sentence being changed, e.g.

(6) *Šumit les, idet dožd'* (roars–wood–goes–rain)→*Idet dožd', šumit les*

The last two special rules introduce aspectual operators. The rule (Tm) denotes the ending of the action described by the embedded sentence, and the operator of the ending of an action is called the terminative. The rule (Ic) denotes the beginning of the action described by the embedded sentence, and the operator of the beginning of an action is called the inceptive. Both rules for the introduction of aspectual operators are connected with the specific nature of the reduced axioms discussed in the preceding section (pp. 64–80).

In addition to the general and special semantic rules there are supplementary rules called rules of fusion. These are divided into two sorts:

1. *Rules of fusion* (fu1) by which relator predicates and predicates consisting of sequences of combinators and relators combined with terms are transformed into what I will call synthetic predicates. This transformation of relator predicates into synthetic predicates models the natural language process whereby compound predicates consisting of a dummy verb and a full noun or adjective are transformed into single, full verbs, e.g.

(7) a) *izdaet zvuk* (gives out–sound)→*zvučit* (sounds)
b) *naxoditsja na progulke* (is–on–walk)→*guljaet* (walks)
c) *javljaetsja učitelem* (is–teacher)→*učitel'stvuet* (teaches)
d) *zanimaetsja čteniem* (is occupied–with reading)→*čitaet* (reads)
e) *delaet rabotu* (does–work)→*rabotaet* (works)

f) *imeet želanie* (has–wish)→*želaet* (wishes)
g) *vyzyvaet razdraženie* (calls forth–annoyance)→*razdražaet* (annoys)
h) *okazyvaet vlijanie* (exercises–influence)→*vlijaet* (influences)
i) *byl pečal'nyj* (was–sad)→*pečalilsja* (grieved)
j) *delaet belym* (makes–white)→*belit* (whitens)

2. *Rules of fusion* (fu2) by which complex predicates consisting of sequences of combinators and relators are transformed either into a coordinator or into relators with a greater number of symbols in the case indices than any one of the relators in the sequence.

With the rules (fu2), as with the rules (fu1), the symbols in the case indices are transferred to the synthetic predicates and derived relators with the appropriate arguments. If two identical symbols are obtained one of them can be relabelled with the case symbols of the embedded sentence that contains the corresponding term in the initial axiom.

The following list contains the postulated rules (fu1) and (fu2):

(fu1.1) $R_{lo}T_{l} \rightarrow P_{o}$
(fu1.2) $R_{po}T_{p} \rightarrow P_{o}'$
(fu1.3) $R_{oa}T_{o} \rightarrow P_{a}$
(fu1.4) $R_{lo}T_{o} \rightarrow P_{oo}$
(fu1.5) $R_{ao}T_{a} \rightarrow P_{a}'$
(fu1.6) $\mathbf{B}R_{lo}R_{lo}T_{l} \rightarrow P_{oo}'$
(fu1.7) $\mathbf{B}R_{ol}(R_{oa}T_{o}) \rightarrow P_{al}$
(fu1.8) $\mathbf{B}R_{oa}(R_{lo}T_{l}) \rightarrow P_{oa}$
(fu1.9) $\mathbf{B}(\mathbf{C}R_{lo})R_{oa}T_{o} \rightarrow P_{al}$
(fu1.10) $\mathbf{B}(\phi R_{lo})R_{lo}T_{l} \rightarrow P_{(o)}''$
(fu1.11) $\mathbf{C}(\mathbf{B}(\mathbf{C}R_{ao})(R_{lo}T_{l})) \rightarrow P_{ao}$
(fu1.12) $\mathbf{C}(\mathbf{B}(\mathbf{C}R_{lo})(R_{oa}T_{o})) \rightarrow P_{la}$
(fu1.13) $\mathbf{C}(\mathbf{B}(\mathbf{C}(\mathbf{B}R_{oa}(R_{lo}T^{1})))(R_{po}T_{p}{}^{2})) \rightarrow P_{oa}$
(fu1.14) $\mathbf{C}_2(\mathbf{B}(\mathbf{B}(\mathbf{C}(\mathbf{B}R_{oa}(R_{lo}T))))R_{po}) \rightarrow P_{poa}$
(fu1.15) $\mathbf{B}^2(\mathbf{B}R_{oa}R_{ol})R_{lo} \rightarrow P_{ola}$
(fu2.1) $\mathbf{B}(\mathbf{B}R_{oa})R_{lo} \rightarrow R_{loa}$
(fu2.2) $\mathbf{B}^2R_{oa}R_{lo} \rightarrow R_{loa}$
(fu2.3) $\mathbf{B}(\mathbf{C}(\mathbf{B}(R_{oa})R_{lo}))R_{lo} \rightarrow R_{lao}$
(fu2.4) $\mathbf{C}(\mathbf{B}(\mathbf{B}(\mathbf{C}(\mathbf{B}R_{oa}(R_{lo}T_{1}))))R_{po}) \rightarrow R_{poa}$
(fu2.5) $\mathbf{C}^{[3]}(\mathbf{B}^3(\mathbf{C}R_{po})(\mathbf{B}(\mathbf{C}(\mathbf{B}(\phi R_{po})R_{oa}))R_{lo})) \rightarrow R_{plao}$
(fu2.6) $\phi R_{lo} \rightarrow \mathbf{C}_2$

## 5. Derivation of the Analogues of Simple Sentences with Full Predicates

It was shown earlier that, in sentences with relator predicates, only the terms correspond to full words in natural languages, the relators being interpreted as various sorts of copulas and auxiliary words—conjunctions and prepositions. In the interpretation of relators copular words were used like *kauzirovat'* (cause), *lokalizovat'* (locate), *imet'* (have), *byt'* (be), *naxodit'sja na* (lit. 'find oneself–on', i.e. 'be–on'), *soderžat'* (contain), *okazyvat'* (exercise (influence, etc.)). Full predicates of natural language were reduced to a combination of copular elements and abstract nouns, e.g. *vraščaetsja* (rotates)—*naxodit'sja vo vraščenii* (be–in–rotation); *vraščaet* (rotate: transitive) —*kauziruet* (*nečto*) *vo vraščenii* (cause–something–in–rotation); *zvučit* (sounds)—*izdaet zvuk* (gives out–sound); and so on. Formal analogues for the full predicates are not postulated in the semantic theory but are derived from relator sentences that function as axioms. We shall shortly provide derivations of the genotype analogues of simple sentences of Russian containing full predicates—one-, two-, three- and four-place.

Each derivation will consist of numbered lines, the first line containing some axiom. The number of lines will be called the length of the derivation. If in some derivation a sentence $S_i$ is obtained from a sentence $S_{i-1}$ by the application of a semantic rule X, the semantic rule X will be said to be applied on step *i* of the derivation. Each application of a semantic rule is a step in a derivation. The first line is obtained on the null step in the derivation, the second on the first step, and line *i* on the step $i-1$.

To the right of the first line in each derivation will be the symbol A, standing for 'axiom'. To the right of the subsequent lines will be the symbols for the semantic rules by which each line is derived from the preceding one.

The analogues of one-place full predicates are obtained by applying the operation of fusion, which substitutes a simple predicate for a complex one. Simple predicates will be called synthetic.

As examples we shall set out the derivation of analogues of sentences with active—(1) and (2)—and stative—(3)—one-place predicates.

| | | |
|---|---|---|
| (1) a) | *On rabotaet* | (he–works) |
| b) | *On guljaet* | (he–walks) |
| (2) a) | *On kopaet* | (he–digs) |
| b) | *On pilit* | (he–saws) |
| (3) a) | *Paxnet roza* | (smells–rose) |
| b) | *Slyšitsja pesnja* | (is heard–song) |

The analogue of 1a, b is derived from the axiom 3.1 (cf. the previous section, p. 68):

(4) $R_{lo}T_lT_o$

The axiom is interpreted as:

(5) a) *On (est') na rabote* (he–(is)–at–work)
b) *On (est') na progulke* (he–(is)–on–walk)

The analogue of 1 is obtained in one step and the length of the derivation is equal to two:

(6) 1. $((R_{lo}T_l^1)T_o^2)$ (A)
2. $P_oT_o$ (fu1.1)

Fusion converts the relator predicate $R_{lo}T_1$ into the simple predicate $P_o$ and the case index on this synthetic predicate is copied from the second argument $T_o^2$. In the initial axiom brackets have been put in to make it obvious which symbols constitute the complex predicate $R_{lo}T_l^1$ that is converted into the synthetic predicate $P_o$.

The analogues of 2a and b are derived from the axiom 2.1 (cf. p. 68):

(7) $R_{po}T_p^1T_o^2$

This axiom is interpreted as:

(8) a) *On oruduet piloj* (he–uses–saw)
b) *On oruduet lopatoj* (he–uses–spade)

The analogue of 8 is obtained in one step too:

(9) 1. $((R_{po}T_p^1)T_o^2)$ (A)
2. $P_oT_o$ (fu1.2)

Fusion and the replacement of $R_{po}T_p$ by $P_o$ models the process by which primitive predicates like *oruduet lopatoj* and *oruduet piloj* are compressed into derived synthetic predicates like *kopaet* (digs) and *pilit* (saws).

The analogues of 3a and b with the stative verbs *paxnet* (smells) and *slyšitsja* (is heard) are derived from the axiom 1.2 (cf. p. 68):

(10) $R_{oa}T_o^1T_a^2$

This axiom is interpreted as:

(11) a) *Roza izdaet zapax* (rose–gives out–smell)
b) *Pesnja kauziruet slyšanie* (*sluxovoj obraz*) (song–causes–hearing (aural image))

The analogue of 3 is also obtained in one step:

(12) 1. $(R_{oa}T_o^1)T_a^2$ (A)
2. $P_aT_a$ (fu1.3)

Here the simple predicate is assigned the case index of the ablative, copied from the second argument $T_a$. The replacement of $R_{oa}T_o$ by $P_a$ models the transformation of compound predicates like *izdaet zapax* (gives out–smell) and *kauziruet slyšanie* (causes–hearing) into simple verbal predicates like *paxnet* (smells) and *slyšitsja* (is heard).

A compound predicate is one that consists of a copula and a noun either in the nominative or in an oblique case, e.g. *byl učitel'* (was–teacher: nominative case), *byl učitelem* (was–teacher: instrumental case), *okazyvaet vlijanie* (exercises–influence), *proizvodit vpečatlenie* (produces–impression), *privodit v otčajanie* (leads–to–despair), *dovodit do isteriki* (leads–to–hysterics).

The analogues of sentences with two-place predicates are obtained from axioms with embedded sentences. Consider the derivation of the analogues of sentences with active verbs—13, 14—and stative verbs—15:

(13) a) *On obrabatyvaet detal'* (he–machines–component)
b) *On progulyvaet sobaku* (he–walks–dog)
(14) a) *On kopaet zemlju* (he–digs–ground)
b) *On pilit drova* (he–saws–wood)
(15) a) *Ja njuxaju rozu* (I–sniff–rose)
b) *Ja slyšu pesnju* (I–hear–song)

The sentences in 13, like those in 1, have as their analogue a sentence derived from an axiom one of whose arguments is a term in the locative. The sentences in 14, like those in 2, have as their analogue a sentence derived from an axiom containing a term in the prolative and the sentences in 15, like those in 3, have as their analogue a sentence derived from an axiom with a term in the ablative. However, in the analogues of two-place synthetic predicates these arguments are in embedded sentences.

Since the structure of the axioms and the type of semantic rule is the same for 13 and 15, we shall consider first the derivation of analogues of sentences obtained from axioms with a locative and an ablative in the embedded sentence. The analogue of the sentences in 13 is derived from the axiom postulated in schema 1.8. The embedded sentence coincides with the axiom 3.1 (cf. p. 68):

(16) $R_{oa}(R_{lo}T_l^1T_o^2)T_a^3$

This axiom is interpreted as:

(17) a) **Ja kauziruju, (čtoby) detal' byla v obrabotke* (I–cause–(that)–component–be–in–machining)
b) **Ona kaziruet, (čtoby) sobaka byla na progulke* (she–causes–(that)–dog–be–on–walk)

The analogue of the sentences in 13 is obtained in two steps:

(18) 1. $R_{oa}(R_{lo}T_l^1T_o^2)T_a^3$ (A)
2. $\mathbf{B}R_{oa}(R_{lo}T_l^1)T_o^2T_o^3$ (**B**)
3. $P_{oa}T_o^2T_a^3$ (fu1.8)

In the second line of the derivation the predicate $R_{oa}$, *kauziruet*, and the complex predicate $R_{lo}T_l^1$, *naxodit'sja v obrabotke* (be–in–machining) and *naxodit'sja na progulke* (be–on–walk), are drawn together into the compositor **B**. The new complex predicate $\mathbf{B}R_{oa}(R_{lo}T_l^1)$ can be interpreted as *kauziruet byt' v obrabotke, kauziruet byt' na progulke* (cf. 17). In the third line of the derivation this complex predicate is subjected to fusion, which replaces it with the simple predicate $P_{oa}$

corresponding to a full two-place predicate like *obrabatyvae* (machines), *progulyvaet* (walks).

Passive constructions with verbs denoting actions like

(19) *Detal' obrabatyvaetsja im* (component–is machined–by him)

are derived from the axiom postulated in schema 1.7:

(20) $R_{ao}T_a(R_{lo}T_lT_o)$

The axiom 20, the converse of 16, is given the interpretation:

(21) *(*To, čto*) *detal' v obrabotke, kauziruetsja im* ((it–that)–component–in–machining–is caused–by him)

The derivation takes four steps and its length is five:

(22) 1. $R_{ao}T_a^1(R_{lo}T_l^2T_o^3)$ (A)
2. $\mathbf{C}R_{ao}(R_{lo}T_l^2T_o^3)T_a^1$ (C)
3. $\mathbf{B}(\mathbf{C}R_{ao})(R_{lo}T_l^2)T_o^3T_a^1$ (B)
4. $\mathbf{C}(\mathbf{B}(\mathbf{C}R_{ao})(R_{lo}T_l^2))T_a^1T_o^3$ (C)
5. $P_{ao}T_a^1T_o^3$ (fu1.11)

The permutator **C** is applied twice in the derivation. The second and third lines are only of formal significance in that they involve the permutation and movement of terms ($T_o$ is raised from the embedded sentence into the main one). In the fourth line $T_o$ is moved into the position of theme. In the fifth line the complex predicate, which can be interpreted as **Kauziruetsja byt' v obrabotke* (is caused–to be–in–machining), is replaced by the simple predicate corresponding to the verb *obrabatyvaetsja* (is machined). The case indices on $T_a$ and $T_o$ are copied on to the synthetic predicate $P_{ao}$.

The genotype analogue of passive constructions like those in 19 can also be obtained from axiom 16. This is done by extending the derivation in 18 by one step and applying the permutator **C**. The penultimate line of the derivation would then be

$\mathbf{C}(\mathbf{B}R_{oa}(R_{lo}T_l^1))T_a^3T_o^2$.

The fact that it is possible to obtain the genotype analogues of passive constructions in two ways reflects the fact that the correlation between active and passive constructions in natural language can be handled in two ways. They can either be regarded as independent of each other or as being related in that one is derived from the other. These considerations also apply to the analogues of absolute and ergative constructions in languages with ergatives.

The analogue of the sentences with stative verbs in 15 is derived from the axiom postulated in schema 3.8, representing a sentence with one embedding. The embedded sentence is the same as the axiom 1.2:

(23) $R_{ol}(R_{oa}T_o^1T_a^2)T_l^3$

This axiom is interpreted as:

(24) **Ja lokalizuju* (*vosprinimaju*) *to, čto roza izdaet zapax* (I–locate–(perceive)–it–that–rose–gives out–smell)

The derivation is completed in two steps:

(25) 1. $R_{ol}(R_{oa}T_o{}^1T_a{}^2)T_l{}^3$ (A)
2. $\mathbf{B}R_{ol}(R_{oa}T_o{}^1)T_a{}^2T_l{}^3$ (**B**)
3. $P_{al}T_a{}^2T_l{}^3$ (fu1.7)

The semantic rules applied in 25 are the same as those applied in 18. 25 and 18 differ only with respect to the case indices attached to the predicates in the main and embedded sentences, and it is this that determines the differences in the case indices in the final synthetic predicate.

The second last line of 25 contains a complex predicate that can be interpreted as *lokalizuju izdavat' zapax* (I locate–to give out–smell) and *lokalizuju kauzirovat' slyšanie* (I locate–to cause–hearing), (like *zastavljaju byt' na progulke*, I force–to be–on–walk), i.e. as a construction of the accusative with the infinitive type. This complex predicate is then compressed into a simple two-place predicate that is interpreted as *njuxaju* (I sniff) or *slyšu* (I hear).

Converse sentences like *Mne slyšitsja pesnja* (to me–hears–song) have as their analogues genotype sentences derived from the axiom postulated in schema 3.7 and including the axiom 1.2:

(26) $R_{lo}T_l{}^1(R_{oa}T^2T^3)$

The derivation is completed in four steps:

(27) 1. $R_{lo}T_l{}^1(R_{oa}T_o{}^2T_a{}^3)$ (A)
2. $\mathbf{C}R_{lo}(R_{oa}T_o{}^2T_a{}^3)T_l{}^1$ (**C**)
3. $\mathbf{B}(\mathbf{C}R_{lo})(R_{oa}T_o{}^2)T_a{}^3T_l{}^1$ (**B**)
4. $\mathbf{C}(\mathbf{B}(\mathbf{C}R_{lo})(R_{oa}T_o{}^2))T_l{}^1T_a{}^3$ (**C**)
5. $P_{la}T_l{}^1T_a{}^3$ (fu1.12)

Since the structure of 27 is identical with the structure of 22, there is no need to go into the interpretation of each line. The only thing that must be pointed out is that the complex predicate in the fourth line is replaced in the fifth line by the predicate $P_{la}$, which is interpreted as a stative verb like *slyšitsja* (is heard) or *čuvstvujetsja* (is felt). The sentences obtained via the derivations 27 and 22 differ only in the order of the symbols in the case indices, i.e. in the choice of theme and rheme.

The genotype analogue of *Mne slyšitsja pesnja* (to me–hears–song) can be obtained directly from the axiom in 23 if a change is made in the derivation in 25. This change involves applying the permutator **C** after the second line, which gives as the third line: $\mathbf{C}(\mathbf{B}R_{lo}(R_{oa}T_o{}^1)T_l{}^3T_a{}^2$. With this derivation sentences like *Mne slyšitsja pesnja* could be regarded as deriving from the sentences in 15.

The derivation of the sentences 14a, b is very different from the derivations in 18 and 22, mainly because of the different initial axioms. The initial axiom here is that postulated in schema 1.4, representing a sentence with two embedded sentences. The embedded sentences are identical with the axioms 3.1 and 2.1. The entire initial axiom is:

(28) $R_{oa}(R_{lo}T_l{}^1T_o{}^2)(R_{po}T_p{}^3T_o{}^4)$

and is interpreted as:

(29) a) **On pol'zuetsja lopatoj, v rezul'tate čego zemlja v raskopke* (*sostojanii byt' raskopannoj*) (he–uses–spade–as–result–of which–ground–in–excavation–(state–to be–excavated))

b) **On pol'zuetsja piloj, čto kauziruet to, čto drova v raspilke* (he–uses–saw–which–causes–it–that–wood–in–sawing)

The derivation is completed in five steps

(30) 1. $R_{oa}(R_{lo}T_l{}^1T_o{}^2)(R_{po}T_p{}^3T_o{}^4)$ (A)
2. $\mathbf{B}R_{oa}(R_{lo}T_l{}^1)T_o{}^2(R_{po}T_p{}^3T_o{}^4)$ (**B**)
3. $\mathbf{C}(R_{oa}(R_{lo}T_l{}^1))(R_{po}T_p{}^3T_o{}^4)T_o{}^2$ (**C**)
4. $\mathbf{B}(\mathbf{C}(\mathbf{B}R_{oa}(R_{lo}T_l{}^1)))(R_{po}T_p{}^3)T_o{}^4T_o{}^2$ (**B**)
5. $\mathbf{C}(\mathbf{B}(\mathbf{C}(\mathbf{B}R_{oa}(R_{lo}T_l{}^1)))(R_{po}T_p{}^3))T_o{}^2T_o{}^4$ (**C**)
6. $P_{oa}T_oT_a$ (fu1.13)

The second line in 30 shows the formation of a complex predicate like **kauziruet byt' v raspilke* (cause–to be–in–sawing) and the raising of the argument $T_o$ from the embedded sentence into the main one. In the third line the permutator **C** moves $T_o{}^2$ into the position of theme. The fourth line shows the formation of a still more complex predicate for which it is difficult to find a good interpretation, and also the raising of the argument $T_o{}^4$, i.e. *ja* (I). In the fifth line the permutator changes the position of the theme and the rheme, $T_o{}^4$ moving out of the rheme into the position of theme and $T_o{}^2$ moving into the rheme. In the sixth line the complex predicate is replaced by a simple one and the case index attached to $T^4$ is changed to the ablative, as the embedded sentence from which the term was removed is in the ablative.

The observations that were made about the derivation of sentences like 19 and like *Mne slyšitsja pesnja* (to me–hears–song) apply also to the derivation of the passive constructions corresponding to the sentences in 29. That is to say, sentences like 31 can be obtained from the same axiom as those in 29 but in a different number of steps, or they can be obtained from a different axiom. For 29 the axiom is that postulated in schema 1.4, the embedded sentences being identical with the axioms 1.3 and 1.2.

(31) *Drova piljatsja mnoju* (wood–is sawn–by me)

The initial axiom in the derivation is:

(32) $R_{oa}(R_{lo}T_l{}^1T_o{}^2)(R_{op}T_o{}^3T_p{}^4)$

The second argument in 32 is interpreted as:

(33) *Pila ispol'zuetsja mnoju* (saw–is used–by me)

I now wish to consider the derivations of the analogues of sentences with three-place predicates, such as those in 34 and 35:

(34) *Oxotnik zakalyvaet olenja nožom* (hunter–stabs–deer–with knife)

(35) a) *Vrač pomeščaet bol'nogo v gospital'* (doctor–places–patient–in–hospital)

b) *Brat daet den'gi sestre* (brother–gives–money–to sister)

The analogue of 34 is derived from the axiom in 28, which is interpreted as:

(36) *Oxotnik* ($T_o^4$) *pol'zuetsja nožom* ($T_o^3$), *čto javljaetsja pričinoj togo, čto olen'* ($T_o^2$) *mertv* (**v smerti* ($T_l^1$)) (hunter ($T_o^4$)–uses–knife ($T_o^3$)–which–is–reason–for it–that–deer ($T_o^2$)–(is) dead–(in–death ($T_l^1$))

The derivation of the analogue of 34 is the same as that shown in 30 as far as the fourth line, i.e. it is the same as the derivation of the analogues of the sentences in 14, so only the final part of the derivation is given, beginning with the fourth line:

(37)
4. $\mathbf{B}(\mathbf{C}(\mathbf{B}R_{oa}(R_{lo}T_l^1)))(R_{po}T_p^3)T_o^4T_o^2$ (**B**)
5. $\mathbf{B}(\mathbf{B}(\mathbf{C}(\mathbf{B}R_{oa}(R_{lo}T_l^1))))R_{po}T_p^3T_o^4T_o^2$ (**B**)
6. $\mathbf{C}(\mathbf{B}(\mathbf{B}(\mathbf{C}(\mathbf{B}R_{oa}(R_{lo}T_l^1))))R_{po})T_p^3T_o^2T_o^4$ (**C**)
7. $P_{poa}T_p^3T_o^2T_a^4$ (fu2.4)

In the fourth line of the derivation the argument $(R_{po}T_p)$ is interpreted as *pol'zuetsja nožom* (uses–knife). In the fifth line the term $T_p^3$ (*nož*) is raised by the application of the compositor **B** and the resulting complex predicate is three-place. In the sixth line $T_o^4$ is transferred to the position of theme and in the seventh line the complex predicate is replaced by a simple one corresponding to the three-place predicate $R_{poa}$, which can be interpreted as *ubivaet* (kills). It is worthwhile mentioning that three-place predicates that have as one of their arguments a prolative—in the above examples the prolative has an instrumental meaning—can be derived from two-place predicates interpreted as deverbal nouns like *pilit* (saws), or *hammers, knifes.* Thus, sentences like 14 or like

(38) a) The hunter knifed the deer

b) He hammered at the nail

are obtained via the derivation in 30, and sentences like 34 or

(39) a) He killed the deer with a knife

b) He struck at the nail with a hammer

are obtained via the derivation in 37, which is a continuation of 30 from the fourth line.

The analogue of the sentences in 35 with three-place predicates is derived from the axiom postulated in schema 1.8. The embedded sentence is the same as axiom 3.1:

(40) $R_{oa}(R_{lo}T_l^1T_o^2)T_a^3$

From the same axiom are derived the analogues of sentences with two-place predicates expressed by denominal verbs:

(41) a) *Vrač gospitaliziruet bol'nogo* (doctor–hospitalises–ill (man))
b) The police jailed the robber

The axiom in 40 is interpreted as:

(42) a) **Vrač kauziruet* (*to, čto*) *bol'noj v gospitale* (doctor–causes–(it–that)–ill (man)–in–hospital)
b) **Policija kauziruet* (*to, čto*) *grabitel' v tjurme* (police–cause–(it–that)–robber–in–prison)

The derivation of sentences with three-place predicates like *pomeščaet* (places), *kladet* (puts) and *daet* (gives) is a continuation of the derivation in 18, and is given here in full:

(43) 1. $R_{oa}(R_{lo}T_l^1T_o^2)T_a^3$ (A)
2. $\mathbf{B}R_{oa}(R_{lo}T_l^1)T_o^2T_a^3$ (**B**)
3. $\mathbf{B}(\mathbf{B}R_{oa})R_{lo}T_l^1T_o^2T_a^3$ (**B**)
4. $R_{loa}T_l^1T_o^2T_a^3$ (fu2.1)

In the second line of the derivation a complex predicate is obtained that can be interpreted as infinitive constructions like *kauziruet byt' v gospitale* (causes–to be–in–hospital), *kauziruet byt' u sestry* (causes–to be–at–sister). A second application of the compositor **B** in the third line raises $T_l$, i.e. the argument in the locative—*gospital', sestra.* In the fourth line the complex predicate is replaced by the three-place relator predicate $R_{loa}$, which corresponds to full three-place verbs like *pomeščaet, kladet, daet.* The second and third lines could have been reduced to one if $\mathbf{B}^2$ had been applied. This would have given us in the second line an analogue of a three-place predicate of the form:

(43′) $\mathbf{B}^2R_{oa}R_{lo}T_l^1T_o^2T_a^3$

A comparison of the derivations in 18 and 43 shows that three-place predicates with a locative, like three-place predicates with a prolative, are obtained by continuing the derivational process applied to analogues of sentences with two-place predicates.

I will not spend any time on deriving the analogues of the sentences in 44, which are the converse of 35.

(44) a) *Sestra polučaet den'gi ot brata* (sister–receives–money–from–brother)
b) *Brat snabžaet sestru den'gami* (brother–provides–sister–with money)

The same remarks apply here as apply to the pairs of sentences 13 and 19—*Ja obrabatyvaju detal'* (I–machine–component) and *Detal' obrabatyvaetsja mnoju* (component–is machined–by me)—and 15b, *Ja slyšu pesnju* (I–hear–song) and *Mne slyšitsja pesnja* (to me–hears–song) (cf. pp. 86, 87). The converse sentences can either be derived from different axioms or from the same axiom but in a different number of steps.

To conclude this section I wish to discuss the derivation of analogues to sentences with four-place predicates, e.g.:

(45) *Poezd edet iz Moskvy v Tallin čerez Leningrad* (train–goes–from–Moscow–to–Tallin–through–Leningrad)

The analogue of such sentences is derived from the axiom:

(46) $R_{po}T_{p}^{1}(R_{oa}(R_{lo}T_{l}^{2}T_{o}^{3})(R_{lo}T_{l}^{4}T_{o}^{3}))$

The structure of the axiom is as follows. The axiom schema 2.7 includes as an embedded sentence the axiom schema $R_{oa}S^{1}S^{2}$ (1.3). Each of the arguments in this schema is identical with the axiom 3.2. The above complex axiom can be interpreted as:

(47) **To, čto snačala poezd v Moskve, zatem poezd v Talline, osuščestvljalsja čerez Leningrad* (it–that–train–in–Moscow–then–train–in–Tallin–was brought about–through–Leningrad)

The derivation of sentences with four-place predicates is completed in nine steps, the main task of the derivation being to apply the transformations that raise the terms one by one from the embedded sentences into the main sentence. This requires a series of operations that compress predicates and permute arguments. Since this type of derivation is fairly complex we shall set ourselves the simpler goal of deriving the analogue of sentences with three-place predicates. This analogue corresponds to the first embedded sentence (axiom schema 1.3) and is interpreted as:

(48) *Poezd edet iz Moskvy v Tallin* (train–goes–from–Moscow–to–Tallin)

Cf. the derivation in 49, which consists of five steps:

(49)
1. $R_{oa}(R_{lo}T_{l}^{1}T_{o}^{2})(R_{lo}T_{l}^{3}T_{o}^{2})$ (A)
2. $\phi R_{oa}(R_{lo}T_{l}^{1})(R_{lo}T_{l}^{3})T_{o}^{2}$ ($\phi$)
3. $\mathbf{B}(\phi R_{oa})R_{lo}T_{l}^{1}(R_{lo}T_{l}^{3})T_{o}^{2}$ (**B**)
4. $\mathbf{C}(\mathbf{B}(\phi R_{oa})R_{lo})(R_{lo}T_{l}^{3})T_{l}^{1}T_{o}^{2}$ (**C**)
5. $\mathbf{B}(\mathbf{C}(\mathbf{B}(\phi R_{oa})R_{lo}))R_{lo}T_{l}^{3}T_{l}^{1}T_{o}^{2}$ (**B**)
6. $P_{loa}T_{l}^{3}T_{a}^{1}T_{o}^{2}$ (fu2.3)

In the second line of the above derivation the combinator $\phi$, which factorises functions with identical arguments, raises $T_{o}^{2}$ from the embedded sentences into the main one. In the third line the compositor **B** carries out the same operation on $T_{l}^{1}$. After **C** applies in the fourth line to move $T_{l}^{1}$ nearer to $T_{l}^{2}$, the compositor **B** applies again in the fifth line to raise the last argument $T_{l}^{3}$ into the main sentence. In the sixth line the complex predicate that has resulted from these operations is replaced by the simple three-place predicate $P_{lao}$, which is interpreted as *edet* (*otkuda–kuda*), (goes–(from where–to where)). For lines 2–5 no reasonable linguistic interpretation has been found, but the initial and final lines can be interpreted quite naturally.

To obtain a four-place predicate it is necessary to add the

predicate $R_{po}T_p$ to each of the first five lines in 49. This predicate is interpreted as *osuščestvljaetsja čerez Leningrad* (is brought about–through–Leningrad). What this means is that the analogue of sentences with three-place predicates and all the lines in its derivation from the appropriate axiom are transformed into embedded sentences associated with the predicate $R_{po}T_p$. Cf. the derivation:

(50) 1. $R_{po}T_p{}^1(R_{oa}(R_{lo}T_l{}^2T_o{}^3)(R_{lo}T_l{}^4T_o{}^3))$ (A)
2. $R_{po}T_p{}^1(\phi R_{oa}(R_{lo}T_l{}^2)(R_{lo}T_l{}^4)T_o{}^3)$ ($\phi$)
3. $R_{po}T_p{}^1(\mathbf{B}(\phi R_{oa})R_{lo}T_l{}^2(R_{lo}T_l{}^4)T_o{}^3)$ (**B**)
4. $R_{po}T_p{}^1(\mathbf{C}(\mathbf{B}(\phi R_{oa})R_{lo})(R_{lo}T_l{}^4)T_l{}^2T_o{}^3)$ (**C**)
5. $R_{po}T_p{}^1(\mathbf{B}(\mathbf{C}(\mathbf{B}(\phi R_{oa})R_{lo}))R_{lo}T_l{}^4T_l{}^2T_o{}^3)$ (**B**)
6. $\mathbf{C}R_{po}(\mathbf{B}(\mathbf{C}(\mathbf{B}(\phi R_{oa})R_{lo}))R_{lo}T_l{}^4T_l{}^2T_o{}^3)T_p{}^1$ (**C**)
7. $\mathbf{B}^3(\mathbf{C}R_{po}(\mathbf{B}(\mathbf{C}(\mathbf{B}(\phi R_{oa})R_{lo}))R_{lo}))T_l{}^4T_l{}^2T_o{}^3T_p{}^1$ ($\mathbf{B}^3$)
8. $\mathbf{C}^{[3]}(\mathbf{B}^3(\mathbf{C}R_{po}(\mathbf{B}(\mathbf{C}(\mathbf{B}(\phi R_{oa})R_{lo}))R_{lo}))T_p{}^1T_l{}^4T_l{}^2T_o{}^3$ ($\mathbf{C}^{[3]}$)
9. $R_{plao}T_p{}^1T_l{}^2T_a{}^4T_o{}^3$ (fu2.5)

The same explanations apply to the first five lines of the above derivation as applied to the first five lines of that in 49. In the sixth line the permutator **C** applies, causing $T_p$ and the embedded sentence to change places (having already undergone the operations discussed with respect to 49). In the seventh line the compositor $\mathbf{B}^3$ draws together the predicate of the main sentence and the predicate of the embedded sentence, thus freeing all three terms $T_l{}^2$, $T_l{}^4$, and $T_o{}^3$ to be raised into the main sentence. The complex predicate obtained in this line is four-place. In the eighth line the permutator $\mathbf{C}^3$ applies, causing the arguments to change places, whereby $T_o{}^3$ is moved into the position of theme. In the ninth line the predicate undergoes fusion and is replaced by the four-place relator $R_{plao}$. $T_l{}^4$ is relabelled $T_a{}^4$, since this term in the initial axiom is part of the embedded sentence that is in the ablative. The ninth line is the analogue of 45, i.e. a sentence with a four-place predicate.

The derivations that have been discussed in this section show how we obtain the genotype analogues of simple sentences with full predicates. Such sentences, whether they have two-, three- or four-place predicates, are derived from axioms with embedded sentences i.e. from complex sentences. This derivational process has linguistic motivation in that, from the point of view of applicational grammar, many simple sentences of Russian have complex underlying structures and the purpose of the derivation is to show how something that is 'simple' is obtained from something that is 'complex', and in fact to show how complex these 'simple' sentences are.

The degree of complexity of simple sentences with full predicates is specified by the number of lines in the derivation (the length of the derivation) and, correspondingly, by the number of rules that have to be applied to obtain the genotype analogue. Let us suppose that there is a derivation of a sentence containing the analogue of a full predicate and that the length of this derivation is $n$ (i.e. the derivation has $n$ lines). The degree of complexity of the predicate can be measured by the number of operators at the line $n-1$, i.e. at the line just before the complex predicate is replaced by a simple one. For example, the degree of complexity of a four-place predicate like *idet* (goes) is 7 (cf. 50), and the degree of complexity of a three-place predicate like *ubivaet* (kills) is 5 (cf. 37). The degree of complexity of a three-place predicate like *daet* (gives) is 2 (cf. 43), and so on.

6. Derivations of the Analogues of Complex Sentences

By analogues of complex sentences we mean particularly sentences containing non-finite verb forms, i.e. sentences with infinitive phrases, participial and gerundial constructions, and nominalisations like *priezd otca* (arrival–of father), *belizna snega* (whiteness–of snow). We also include sentences with attributive adjectives among the analogues of complex sentences, since such adjectives are treated in applicational grammar as resulting from the compression of relative clauses.

Let us begin with infinitive constructions. The derivational process by which derived structures are obtained from axioms will be represented as before in the form of a column consisting of the lines in the derivation. The first line contains an axiom, the second line the result of applying the first rule, the third line the result of applying the second rule, and so on.

Subjective and objective infinitive constructions are obtained from axioms postulated by means of the same schema but in a different number of steps. The derivation of subjective infinitives is the more complex one. To illustrate the problem I will discuss the derivation of the genotype analogues of two sentences containing the same finite verb form. Since such paired constructions do not exist in Russian, I shall use examples from English.

(1) a) I want him to come
b) I want to come

The analogues of the sentences in 1 are derived from axioms with similar structure, the only difference being the presence or absence of identical terms. The analogue of 1a is derived from the axiom in 2:

(2) $R_{lo}(R_{lo}T_l^1(R_{lo}T_l^2T_o^3))T_o^4$

This axiom, which is postulated in schema 3.8, represents a sentence with two embeddings. The first embedded sentence is the same as the axiom postulated in schema 3.6 and the second is the same as the axiom 3.1. The entire axiom in 2 is interpreted as **To, čto on v pribytii,* *lokalizuetsja v xotenii, i ja lokalizujus' v ètom* (it–that–he–(is) in-coming–is located–in–wanting–and–I–locate myself–in–that). The derivation is completed in four steps:

(3) 1. $R_{lo}(R_{lo}T_l^1)(R_{lo}T_l^2T_o^3))T_o^4$ (A)
2. $R_{lo}(R_{lo}T_l^1(P_oT_o^3))T_o^4$ (ful.1)
3. $\mathbf{B}R_{lo}R_{lo}T_l^1(P_oT_o^3)T_o^4$ (**B**)
4. $P_{oo}(P_oT_o^3)T_o^4$ (ful.6)
5. $\mathbf{B}P_{oo}P_oT_o^3T_o^4$ (**B**)

What the above derivation does is compress the initial axiom with two embedded sentences so that the embedded sentences are got rid of, the analogue of a complex predicate obtained and $T_o^4$ released from the most deeply embedded sentence. In the course of the derivation several relator predicates with their terms and the more complex predicates derived from them are replaced by full (synthetic) predicates. In the derivation of analogues of complex sentences synthetic predicates can be substituted on any step in the derivation, whereas in the derivations presented in the preceding section this substitution could take place only in the last step. There is only one condition placed on the possible sequences of semantic rules: the last line must not contain any relator predicates, only synthetic predicates being allowed.

I will now explain the various steps in 3. In the second line the relator predicate in the most deeply embedded sentence, together with its first argument $T^2$, is replaced by the synthetic predicate $P_o$. In the third line the compositor **B** deletes the first embedded sentence, factorising $R_{lo}$, which is the predicate of the main sentence and the predicate of the first embedded sentence. In the fourth line the complex predicate $\mathbf{B}R_{lo}R_{lo}T_l$ is replaced by a second synthetic predicate to which is transferred the case index from the arguments of the complex predicate. In the fifth line the compositor **B** deletes the second embedded sentence, pulling together the predicates of the main and the embedded sentences and raising the term $T_o^3$. The fifth line is interpreted as 1a, the complex predicate $\mathbf{B}P_{oo}P_o$ corresponding to the combination of finite and non-finite verb forms *want to come*. The arguments $T_o^3$ and $T_o^4$ are interpreted as *him* and *I*. The intermediate lines in the derivation in 3 have no linguistic interpretation.

The derivation of the subjective infinitive construction 1b is one step longer. The initial axiom differs from that in 2 in that the term $T_o^3$ occurs twice, once in the main sentence and once in the second embedded sentence:

(4) $R_{lo}(R_{lo}T_l^1(R_{lo}T_l^2T_o^3))T_o^3$

The derivation is completed in five steps. Up to line five it is identical with 3, since only the numerical index above the occurrences of the terms $T_o$ is affected. Because of this only the last two lines of the derivation are given:

(5) 5. $\mathbf{B}P_{oo}P_oT_o^3T_o^3$ (**B**)
6. $\mathbf{W}(\mathbf{B}P_{oo}P_o)T_o^3$ (**W**)

The fifth line corresponds to an ungrammatical sentence with co-referential subject and object:

(6) He³ wanted him³ to come

In the sixth line the identical terms are fused by an application of the duplicator, which finally yields the analogue of sentence 1b with a subjective infinitive.

The analogue of sentences containing a stative verb such as *see*, *hear*, *smell*, *feel* with an infinitive in its complement has a more complex derivation than the analogue of 1a, i.e. of sentences containing volitional verbs. I wish now to examine the derivation of the analogues to the following sentences:

(7) a) I see him run
b) I hear the birds sing

These analogues are derived from the axiom:

(8) $R_{lo}T_l^1(R_{oa}T_o^2(R_{lo}T_l^3T_o^4))$

The above axiom is postulated in axiom schema 3.7 and represents a sentence with two embedded sentences, the first one being the same as the axiom postulated in schema 1.6 and the second being the same as the axiom 3.1. With respect to 7a the axiom in 8 is interpreted as **To, čto on v bege, kauziruet videnie, i èto lokalizuetsja vo mne* (it–that–he–(is) in–running–causes–vision–and–that–is located–in–me).

The analogue of 7 is derived in five steps:

(9) 1. $R_{lo}T_l^1(R_{oa}T_o^2(R_{lo}T_l^3T_o^4))$ (A)
2. $\mathbf{C}R_{lo}(R_{oa}T_o^2(R_{lo}T_l^3T_o^4))T_l^1$ (**C**)
3. $\mathbf{C}R_{lo}(R_{oa}T_o^2(P_oT_o^4))T_l^1$ (fu1.1)
4. $\mathbf{B}(\mathbf{C}R_{lo})R_{oa}T_o^2(P_oT_o^4)T_l^1$ (**B**)
5. $P_{al}(P_oT_o^4)T_l^1$ (fu1.9)
6. $\mathbf{B}P_{al}P_oT_o^4T_l^1$ (**B**)

In the second line the permutator **C** moves $T_l^1$ from the rheme into the position of theme. In the third line the operation of fusion applies to replace the relator predicate and one of its arguments in the second embedded sentence with the synthetic predicate $P_o$. In the fourth line the compositor **B** pulls together the predicates of the main sentence and the first embedded sentence, raising $T_l^2$ into the main sentence. In the fifth line the complex predicate $\mathbf{B}(\mathbf{C}R_{lo})R_{oa}T_o^2$ undergoes fusion, being replaced by the synthetic predicate $P_{al}$. The case indices of the ablative and the locative are transferred from the arguments of the complex predicate to the synthetic predicate. In the sixth line the compositor **B** deletes the second embedded sentence, the complex predicate $\mathbf{B}P_{al}P_o$ being interpreted as a combination of finite and non-finite verb forms, e.g. *see run*, *hear sing*. The sixth line corresponds to the sentences in 7.

The derivation of sentences containing causative verbs with infinitive complements, e.g. *make*, *force*, is different from the derivations in 3 and 9, as will be seen from the derivation of the analogue to sentences like:

(10) a) *Mat' zastavljaet mal'čika guljat'* (mother–forces–boy–to walk)

b) I made him work

The analogue of 10 is derived from the axiom:

(11) $R_{oa}(R_{lo}T_l^1T_o^2)T_a^3$

This axiom is postulated in schema 1.8. The embedded sentence is the same as the axiom 3.1. 11 is interpreted as *Mat' zastavljaet, čtoby mal'čik byl na progulke* (mother–forces–that–boy–be–on–walk) and *Ja zastavljaju, čtoby on byl na rabote* (I–force–that–he–be–at–work).

The analogue of such infinitive constructions is derived in two steps, the derivation being made simple by the simplicity of the initial axiom, which contains only one embedded sentence as compared with the axioms 2 and 8, which contain two embedded sentences. This two-step derivation is:

(12) 1. $R_{oa}(R_{lo}T_l^1T_o^2)T_a^3$ (A)

2. $\mathbf{B}R_{oa}(R_{lo}T_l^1)T_o^2T_a^3$ (**B**)

3. $P_{oa}T_o^2T_a^3$ (fu1.8)

The derivation above has already been discussed in connection with the derivation of analogues of full predicates, cf. p. 86, derivation 18. What has to be emphasised here is that $P_{oa}$ can be interpreted either as a simple predicate of causation like *progulyvaet* (*sobaku*), (walks–(dog)) or as a combination of a causative 'dummy' verb and a non-finite verb form, e.g. *zastavljaet guljat'* (forces–to walk), or *makes work*.

It was mentioned earlier that sentences with nominalisations are assigned analogues like those of complex sentences. This can be illustrated by the derivation of sentences like those in 13 with deverbal nominals and subjective genitives:

(13) a) *Ja slyšu penie ptic* (I–hear–singing–of birds)

b) *Ja čuvstvuju nastuplenie vesny* (I–feel–approach–of spring)

These sentences, which contain the stative verbs *slyšu* (I hear) and *čuvstvuju* (I feel), are derived from the axiom in 8, just like the sentences in 7, which also have stative verbs. The analogue of 13 is derived in seven steps:

(14) 1. $R_{lo}T_l^1(R_{oa}T_o^2(R_{lo}T_l^3T_o^4))$ (A)

2. $\mathbf{C}R_{lo}(R_{oa}T_o^2(R_{lo}T_l^3T_o^4))T_l^1$ (**C**)

3. $CR_{lo}(R_{oa}T_o{}^2(P_oT_o{}^4)T_l{}^1$ (fu1.1)
4. $\mathbf{B}(CR_{lo})R_{oa}T_o{}^2(P_oT_o{}^4)T_l{}^1$ (**B**)
5. $P_{al}(P_oT_o{}^4)T_l{}^1$ (fu1.9)
6. $P_{al}(R_T(P_oT_o{}^4))T_l{}^1$ ($R_T$)
7. $P_{al}(\mathbf{B}R_TP_oT_o{}^4)T_l{}^1$ (**B**)
8. $P_{al}(\mathbf{C}_*T_o{}^4(\mathbf{B}R_TP_o))T_l{}^1$ ($\mathbf{C}_*$)

This derivation is identical with that in 9 up to the fifth line but in the interest of clarity the derivation has been set out in full. The fact that the initial axioms for the sentences in 7 and 13 are identical, and also the first five lines of the two derivations, shows indisputably how closely related are Russian and English sentences with stative verbs. Sentences like 7b, *I hear the birds sing*, and 13a, *Ja slyšu penie ptic*, are undoubtedly synonymous, since 7b is translated into Russian by 13a as its closest equivalent, and vice-versa.

But a comparison of 9 and 14 reveals immediately that the derivation of the analogues to Russian sentences with nominalised predicates is more complex. Since 14 is partly the same as 9, we shall concentrate only on the last three steps.

In the sixth line the nominalising operator $\Delta\beta\alpha R_T$ transforms the embedded sentence $P_oT_o$—*Pojut ptici* (are singing–birds)—into a noun phrase, $R_T(P_oT_o)$, which can be interpreted as a subordinate clause introduced by *čto* (that), *kak* (how), etc. The sixth line is interpreted as a complex sentence:

(15) a) *Ja slyšu, čto pojut ptici* (I–hear–that–are singing–birds)
b) *Ja čuvstvuju, kak približaetsja vesna* (I–feel–how–is approaching–spring)

In the seventh line the operator **B** draws together the nominaliser $R_T$ and the predicate $P_o$. The resulting complex one-place function $\mathbf{B}R_TP_o$ can be interpreted as participles: *pojuščie* (singing), *približajuščajasja* (approaching). The attributive nature of the function $\mathbf{B}R_TP_o$ is shown in the tree diagram:

(16)
$$\cfrac{\cfrac{\Delta\Delta\Delta\beta\alpha\Delta\Delta\alpha\beta\Delta\alpha\alpha\mathbf{B} \qquad \Delta\beta\alpha R_T}{\Delta\Delta\alpha\beta\Delta\alpha\alpha(\mathbf{B}R_T) \qquad \Delta\alpha\beta P_o}}{\Delta\alpha\alpha((\mathbf{B}R_T)P_o)}$$

Here the arguments of the compositor **B** are the nominaliser $R_T$ and the one-place predicate $\Delta\alpha\beta P_o$. The function denotes a complex semion belonging to the category of modifiers of nouns, i.e. $\Delta\alpha\alpha$. The seventh line of the derivation in 14 is interpreted as:

(17) a) *Ja slyšu pojuščix ptic* (I–hear–singing–birds)
b) *Ja čuvstvuju približajuščujusja vesnu* (I–feel–approaching–spring)

In the eighth line the combinator $\mathbf{C}_*$ transforms $T_o$ into a predicate and $\mathbf{B}R_TP_o$ into an argument. The eighth line is interpreted as 13.

It is obvious that 7b, 13, 15 and 17 are synonymous. As was shown in the analysis of the derivation in 14, their analogues are derived from the same axiom but in a different number of steps. The derivational history of the genotype analogues of this small class of synonymous sentences is shown in figure 23.

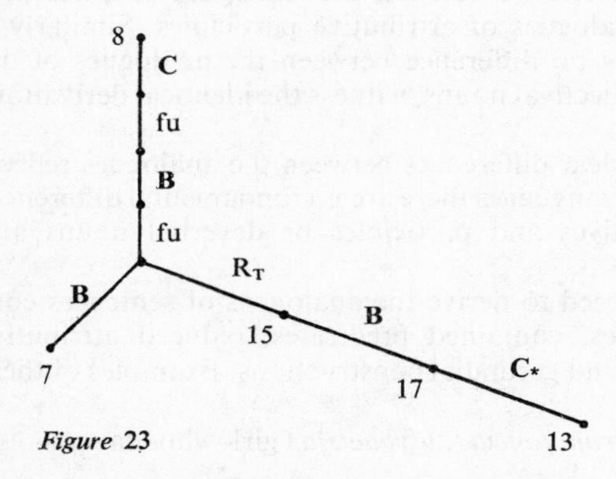


*Figure* 23

The nodes of the tree in figure 23 correspond to sentences of the genotype language, and the lines joining the nodes correspond to steps in the semantic derivation. The branches at the foot of the diagram correspond to the semantic derivations obtained from the axiom 8. The lines are labelled with the names of the semantic rules that are applied. When a sentence of the genotype language can be interpreted as a phenotype sentence, the corresponding node is labelled with the number of the appropriate Russian or English example among those previously discussed in this section.

Let us now consider how the genotype analogues of attributive adjectives and the nouns formed from them can be derived, for instance the adjective in 18a and the corresponding noun in 18b:

(18) a) *Ja ljubujus' krasivym ozerom* (I–admire–beautiful–lake)

b) *Ja ljubujus' krasotoj ozera* (I–admire–beauty–of lake)

The analogues of both these sentences are derived from the same axiom as are the sentences in 7, 15, 17 and 13, i.e. from the axiom in 8. Here 8 is interpreted as *To, čto ozero v krasote, kauziruet ljubovanie, čto lokalizuetsja vo mne* (it–that–lake–(is) in–beauty–causes–admiration–which–is located–in–me). This interpretation differs from that on p. 96 with respect to the predicate $R_{lo}T_l^3$, which was interpreted there as a sequence consisting of a copula and a deverbal noun, but which is here interpreted as a sequence consisting of a copula and a deadjectival noun.

The derivation of the analogue to 18b is completely identical with the derivation of the analogue to 13, cf. 14. In the seventh line, which was earlier associated with sentences containing participles in attributive position, we obtain the analogue of 18a. That the analogues of 18a and 17 have identical derivations indicates that in applicational analyses there is no difference between the analogues of attributive adjectives and the analogues of attributive participles. Similarly it turns out that there is no difference between the analogues of deverbal nouns and deadjectival nouns, witness the identical derivations assigned to 13 and 18b.

The lack of any clear differences between the analogues reflects the fact that in natural languages there are no fundamental differences between either adjectives and participles or deverbal nouns and deadjectival nouns.

We can now proceed to derive the analogues of sentences containing relative clauses, conjoined predicates, reduced attributive clauses, or participial and gerundial constructions. Examples of these are:

(19) a) *Devočka, kotoraja tancuet, ulybaetsja* (girl–who–dances–smiles)
b) *Tancujuščaja devočka ulybaetsja* (dancing–girl–smiles)
c) *Devočka ulybaetsja, kogda tancuet* (girl–smiles–when–dances)
d) *Devočka ulybaetsja i tancuet* (girl–smiles–and–dances)
e) *Tancuja, devočka ulybaetsja* ((while) dancing–girl–smiles)

The analogues of these sentences are derived from the axiom:

(20) $R_{lo}(R_{lo}T_l{}^1T_o{}^2)(R_{lo}T_l{}^3T_o{}^2)$

This axiom is postulated in axiom schema 3.3 and represents a sentence with two embedded sentences, both of the latter corresponding to the axiom 3.1.

The axiom in 20 can be interpreted as **Kogda devočka v tance, devočka v ulybke* (when–girl–(is) in–dance–girl–(is) in–smile). The genotype analogue of 19a is derived in three steps:

(21) 1. $R_{lo}(R_{lo}T_l{}^1T_o{}^2)(R_{lo}T_l{}^3T_o{}^2)$ (A)
2. $R_{lo}(R_{lo}T_l{}^1T_o{}^2)(P_oT_o{}^2)$ (fu1.1)
3. $R_{lo}(P_oT_o{}^2)(P_oT_o{}^2)$ (fu1.1)
4. $P_o(R_A(P_oT_o{}^2)T_o{}^2)$ ($R_A$)

In the second and third lines the two-place relator predicates are replaced with one-place synthetic predicates. The third line is interpreted as 22a, or 22b if one of the identical terms is pronominalised.

(22) a) **Kogda devočka tancuet, devočka ulybaetsja* (when–girl–dances–girl–smiles)

b) *Kogda devočka tancuet, ona ulybaetsja* (when–girl–dances–she –smiles)

In the fourth line the embedded sentence is relativised by the relativising operator $\Delta\beta\Delta\alpha\alpha R_A$. This relativised sentence, $R_A(P_oT_o^2)$, becomes an operator on the term $T_o^2$ in the second embedded sentence, this term being identical with the $T_o^2$ in the relativised sentence. The last line of the derivation is interpreted as 19a, i.e. as corresponding to a sentence with a relative clause in it. $T_o$ in the embedded sentence is interpreted as a relative pronoun, in this case *kotoraja* (who).

The genotype analogue of 19b can be obtained by adding two steps to the derivation in 21. The final part of the new derivation, beginning with the fourth line, is:

(23) 4. $P_o(R_A(P_oT_o^2)T_o^2)$ $(R_A)$
5. $P_o(\mathbf{B}R_AP_oT_o^2T_o^2)$ $(\mathbf{B})$
6. $P_o(\mathbf{W}(\mathbf{B}R_AP_oT_o^2))$ $(\mathbf{W})$

In the fifth line the compositor draws together the relativiser $R_A$ and the predicate $P_o$. The resulting complex predicate, $\mathbf{B}R_AP_o$, has as its arguments two identical terms, $T_o^2$, which in the sixth line are fused into one term by an application of the duplicator **W**. The fifth line has no linguistic interpretation but the sixth corresponds to 19b. The derivation in 23 is not the only way in which the genotype analogues of attributive participles can be obtained, since another way was mentioned in connection with the derivation of the analogue to 17: cf. the seventh line in 14. However, no matter the type of derivation, attributive participles are regarded in applicational grammar as derived structures that are obtained via reduced predicates. The exact nature of the derived structure is determined by the initial axiom. The analogue of 19b, $\mathbf{B}R_AP_o$, and the analogue of 17, $\mathbf{B}R_TP_o$, have very similar derived structures.

The analogue of sentences with conjoined verbs (e.g. 19c) is derived from the axiom in 20 by the application of other semantic rules:

(24) 1. $R_{lo}(R_{lo}T_l^1T_o^2)(R_{lo}T_l^3T_o^2)$ (A)
2. $\phi R_{lo}(R_{lo}T_l^1)(R_{lo}T_l^3)T_o^2$ $(\phi)$
3. $\phi R_{lo}(R_{lo}T_o^1)P_oT_o^2$ (fu1.1)
4. $\phi R_{lo}P_{oo}P_oT_o$ (fu1.1)
5. $CrP_{oo}P_oT_o$ (fu2.6)

In the second line the combinator $\phi$ factors out $T_o^2$, which occurs in both the embedded sentences, and draws together the predicate of the main sentence and the predicates of the embedded sentences. In the third line the relator predicate $R_{lo}T_l^3$ is replaced by a synthetic one-place predicate, $P_o$. One possible interpretation of this line is:

(25) **Devocka ulybaetsja, kogda v tance* (girl–smiles–when–in–dance)

In the fourth line the relator predicate $\phi R_{lo}T_o{}^1$ is replaced by a synthetic one-place predicate, $P_o$. The complex three-place predicate $R_{lo}$ is still interpreted as the conjunction *kogda* (when). The fourth line can be given the interpretation *Devočka ulybaetsja, kogda tancuet* (=19c).

In the next step in the derivation the predicate $R_{lo}$ can be replaced by the three-place ordinator-predicate $\Delta\beta\Delta\beta\beta$Cr, which can be interpreted as a conjunction like *i* (and). If the genotype objects are replaced by words of a natural language, e.g. Russian, the fifth line is of the form:

(26) **I* (*tancuet* (*ulybaetsja devočka*)) (and (dances (smiles girl)))

The derivation by which the analogue of the gerundial construction in 19e is obtained is partially similar to the derivation in 22, as can be seen from:

(27) 1. $R_{lo}(R_{lo}T_l{}^1T_o{}^2)(R_{lo}T_l{}^3T_o{}^2)$ (A)
2. $\phi R_{lo}(R_{lo}T_l{}^1)(R_{lo}T_l{}^3)T_o{}^2$ ($\phi$)
3. $\phi R_{lo}(R_{lo}T_l{}^1)P_oT_o{}^2$ (fu1.1)
4. $\mathbf{B}(\phi R_{lo})R_{lo}T_l{}^1P_oT_o{}^2$ (**B**)
5. $P_o{}''P_oT_o{}^2$ (fu1.10)

The above derivation is identical with that in 24 as far as the third line. In the fourth line the compositor **B** draws together the complex predicate $\phi R_{lo}$ and the predicate $R_{lo}$ in the embedded sentence, at the same time raising $T_l{}^1$. The resulting complex predicate $\mathbf{B}(\phi R_{lo})R_{lo}T_l{}^1$ can be interpreted as:

(28) **kogda naxoditsja v tance* (when–is–in–dance)

The substitution of the simple predicate $P_o$ for this complex one models the reduction of 28 to a gerund such as *tancuja* (dancing). $\mathbf{B}(\phi R_{lo})R_{lo}$—*kogda naxoditsja v* (when–is–in)—can be put in correspondence with the suffix of the gerund.

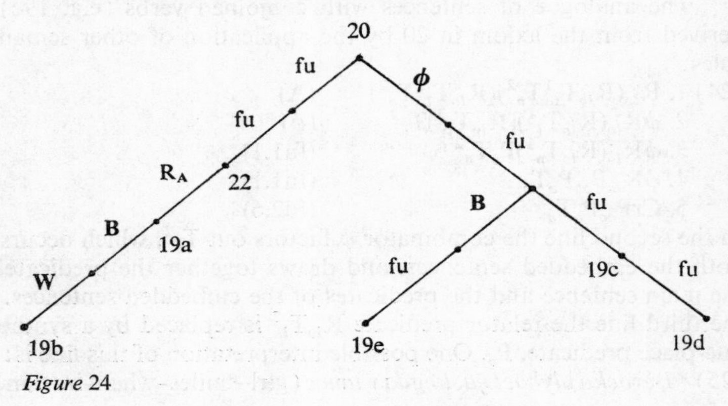


*Figure* 24

Having obtained the genotype analogues of the examples in 19, which form a class of synonymous sentences, we can construct a derivational tree for these analogues. The tree is shown in figure 24. As in the tree in figure 23, the axiom from which the analogues of 19 are derived is placed at the root of the tree. (The sentences in 22 also derive from this axiom.) The labels on the branches are those of the semantic rules that are applied and if after any sequence of steps the analogue of a grammatical sentence is obtained, the number of the sentence is placed next to the corresponding node in the tree.

## 7. Semantic Fields

Another notion can now usefully be introduced, namely that of a semantic field. A semantic field in the genotype language is a set of derivations from a single axiom, and can be represented by a labelled tree called the tree of the semantic field. The root of the tree corresponds to the axiom and each branch corresponds to a semantic derivation. The nodes on each branch correspond to the sentences that are derived, the initial node, i.e. the root, corresponding to the axiom, the intermediate nodes to the intermediate sentences in the semantic derivation, and the final node to the final derived sentence. The lines joining the nodes correspond to the steps in the derivation and are labelled with the symbols for the rules by whose application the sentence corresponding to each node has been obtained. The tree of a semantic field can also display information about its interpretation in a natural language. Assuming that there is an accompanying description of the sentences in the natural language, this is done by taking the numbers of the appropriate examples in that description and assigning them to the nodes that correspond to the genotype sentences whose interpretation is to be indicated. Each branch is called a subfield.

Each semantic field in the genotype language is paralleled by a semantic field in the phenotype language, the latter being a class of synonymous sentences that interpret the genotype semantic field. A subfield of the phenotype semantic field is a set of sentences that interpret a genotype subfield.

The derivational trees in figures 23 and 24 are examples of semantic fields. The first models the derivation of sentences with infinitive complements, as in 7 of the previous section, with subordinate clauses introduced by *čto* (that), as in 15, and with nominalisations, as in 13 and 17. The second field comprises the analogues of sentences with attributive clauses, like 19a; with participial constructions, like 19b; with subordinate adverbial clauses, like 19c and 22; with conjoined predicates, like 19d; and with gerundial constructions, like 19e.

I would like to discuss other semantic fields, some richer than figures 23 and 24, some poorer. The fields will be interpreted as sentences of English, since I wish to take into account certain constructions that do not occur in Russian, for example, sentences with infinitive complements, sentences with infinitives in subject position, sentences with the dummy subject *it* and an extraposed clause, and a few other constructions.

The first of the four fields I want to look at contains sentences with verbs like *expect* and *believe*. As examples I will take the following nine sentences:

(1) Mary expects John will arrive
(2) Mary expects John to arrive
(3) John is expected to arrive by Mary
(4) Mary expects that John will arrive
(5) ?That John will arrive is expected by Mary
(6) Mary expects John's arrival
(7) John's arrival is expected by Mary
(8) *Mary expects it that John will arrive
(9) It is expected by Mary that John will arrive

The analogues of 1–9 are derived from the axiom:

(10) $R_{lo}T_l^1(R_{oa}T_o^2(R_{lo}T_l^3T_o^4))$

This axiom, which was 8 in the previous section, is postulated in axiom schema 3.7 and represents a sentence with two embedded sentences, the first corresponding to the axiom schema 1.6 and the second to the axiom 3.1. 10 can be interpreted as:

(11) **Džon v pribytii, čto kauziruet ožidanie, kotoroe lokalizuetsja v Meri* (John–(is) in–arrival–which causes expectation–which–is located–in–Mary)

The field of verbs of expecting and believing can be broken down into four subfields depending on which semantic rules apply in the derivation of the analogues to these sentences. The first subfield brings together 1–3; the second, 1, 4 and 5; the third, 1, 4, 6 and 7; and the fourth, 1, 4, 8 and 9. The analogue of each sentence in a subfield (apart from the first sentence) is derivationally related to the analogue of the preceding sentence, i.e. is obtained from it by the application of one or more semantic rules. 1, which is a member of all the subfields, is derived from the axiom in 10 by four semantic rules:

(12) 1. $R_{lo}T_l^1(R_{oa}T_o^2(R_{lo}T_l^3T_o^4))$ (A)
2. $\mathbf{C}R_{lo}(R_{oa}T_o^2(R_{lo}T_l^3T_o^4))T_l^1$ (C)
3. $\mathbf{C}R_{lo}(R_{oa}T_o^2(P_oT_o^4))T_l^1$ (fu1.1)
4. $\mathbf{B}(\mathbf{C}R_{lo})R_{oa}T_o^2(P_oT_o^4)T_l^1$ (B)
5. $P_{al}(P_oT_o^4)T_l^1$ (fu1.9)

In the second line the permutator **C** moves $T_l^1$, *Mary*, into the position of theme. In the third line, as a result of fusion, the synthetic predicate $P_oT_o^4$ is substituted for the relator predicate $R_{lo}T_l^3T_o^4$. This corresponds to the transformation **Naxoditsja v pribytii* (is–in–arrival)→ *pribyvaet* (arrives). In the fourth line the compositor **B** pulls together the predicate of the main sentence and the predicate of the embedded sentence, creating a complex predicate that can be interpreted as *est' v ožidanii* (is–in–expectation). In the fifth line fusion applies again to replace this complex predicate with the synthetic predicate *ožidaet* (expects). The fifth line is the analogue of 1, which is a member of all four subfields.

The other sentences in the first subfield, 2 and 3, are obtained by the application of semantic rules to the final line in 12, as illustrated in 13, beginning at line five:

(13) 5. $P_{al}(P_oT_o^4)T_l^1$ (fu1.9)
6. $\mathbf{B}P_{al}P_oT_o^4T_l^1$ (**B**)
7. $\mathbf{C}(\mathbf{B}P_{al}P_o)T_l^1T_o^4$ (**C**)

The sixth line of 13 is obtained by applying the compositor **B**. The complex predicate $\mathbf{B}P_{al}P_o$ is interpreted as *expects to arrive* and the whole sentence corresponds to 2. In the seventh line the permutator **C** moves $T_o^4$, *John*, from the rheme into the position of theme, yielding the analogue of 3, in which $T_l^1$ is interpreted as *by Mary*.

The second subfield, i.e. 1, 4 and 5, is also obtained by extending the derivation in 12. The extended derivation is set out in 14, though only from the fifth line since the steps in 12 and 14 are the same up to that point:

(14) 5. $P_{al}(P_oT_o^4)T_l^1$ (fu1.9)
6. $P_{al}(R_T(R_oT_o^4))T_l^1$ ($R_T$)
7. $\mathbf{C}P_{al}T_l^1(R_T(P_oT_o^4))$ (**C**)

As was said earlier, the fifth line corresponds to 1, which belongs to all the subfields. In the sixth line the operator $\Delta\beta\alpha R_T$, *that*, nominalises the embedded sentence to generate the analogue of 4. In the seventh line the theme and the rheme are permuted to generate the analogue of 5, which has as its theme the nominalised embedded sentence.

The third subfield, consisting of 1, 4, 6 and 7, is, like the other subfields, an extension of 12:

(15) 5. $P_{al}(P_oT_o^4)T_l^1$ (fu1.9)
6. $P_{al}(R_T(P_oT_o^4)T_l^1$ ($R_T$)
7. $P_{al}(\mathbf{B}R_TP_oT_o^4)T_l^1$ (**B**)
8. $P_{al}(\mathbf{C}_*T_o^4(\mathbf{B}R_TP_o))T_l^1$ ($\mathbf{C}_*$)
9. $\mathbf{C}P_{al}T_l^1(\mathbf{C}_*T_o^4(\mathbf{B}R_TP_o))$ (**C**)

Lines five and six correspond to sentences 1 and 4. In the seventh line the compositor **B** combines the nominaliser $R_T$ with the predicate of the embedded sentence $P_o$, the resulting complex $\mathbf{B}R_TP_o$ being interpreted as an attributive participle (cf. p. 98). The seventh line as a whole has no interpretation but on p. 98 the sentence containing $\mathbf{B}R_TP_o$ was interpreted as:

(16) a) *Ja slyšu pojuščix ptic* (I–hear–singing–birds)
b) *Ja čuvstvuju približajuščujusja vesnu* (I–feel–approaching–spring)

(These examples were numbered 17a and 17b in the previous section.)

The combinator $\mathbf{C}_*$ moves $T_o^4$ into the function and transforms $\mathbf{B}R_TP_o$ into an argument, in which role it is interpreted as the deverbal noun *arrival* (cf. pp. 98–9). The eighth line corresponds to 6. In the ninth line the passive equivalent of 6, i.e. 7, is obtained, with the nominalised embedded sentence *John's arrival* as its theme. $T_l^1$ is interpreted as the prepositional phrase *by Mary* and the predicate $\mathbf{C}P_{al}$ is interpreted as the passive construction *is expected.*

The fourth subfield, consisting of 1, 4, 8 and 9, is derived in the same way as the others:

(17) 5. $P_{al}(P_oT_o^4)T_l^1$ (fu1.9)
6. $P_{al}(R_T(P_oT_o^4))T_l^1$ $(R_T)$
7. $\mathbf{K}_1P_{al}(R_T(P_oT_o^4))T_0T_l^1$ $(\mathbf{K}_1)$
8. $\mathbf{C}^{[2]}(\mathbf{K}_1P_{al})T_l^1(R_T(P_oT_o^4))T_0$ $(\mathbf{C}^{[2]})$

Lines five and six correspond to sentences 1 and 4. In the seventh line the combinator $\mathbf{K}_1$ places $T_0$ after the nominalised embedded sentence, $T_0$ being interpreted as the dummy *it*. The whole line can be interpreted as the ungrammatical sentence 8, though it is only the verb in the main clause that causes the ungrammaticality. If instead of *expect* a verb like *hate* or *like* is used the sentence becomes correct:[1]

(18) a) Mary likes it that John will arrive
b) Mary hates it that John will arrive

To obtain the analogue of 9 it is necessary to substitute $T_0$ for the last argument and $T_l^1$, *by Mary*, for the first one (the syntactic link between the preposition-governed noun and the predicate is the weakest). To carry out these operations the permutator $\mathbf{C}^{[2]}$ is applied in the eighth line, which moves $T_0$ into first place in the sentence. This yields the analogue of 9.

All the derivations that have just been discussed are identical up to the fifth or sixth line, after which, if the process does not end there, a different set of semantic rules is applied in each derivation. The genotype semantic field corresponding to the field of verbs of expecting and believing is shown in figure 25. At the root of this tree is the number of the initial axiom, and the lines joining the nodes are labelled

[1] Translator's note: in fact the sentences in 18 are stylistically bad but the construction type in itself is correct, witness sentences such as *Mary likes it that John comes every day to keep her company*.

with the symbols for the operators or operations that are applied in the course of the derivation. Opposite the appropriate nodes are the numbers of the sentences that interpret the corresponding genotype sentences. It is clear from figure 25 that in this particular field the final step in the derivation must be permutation.

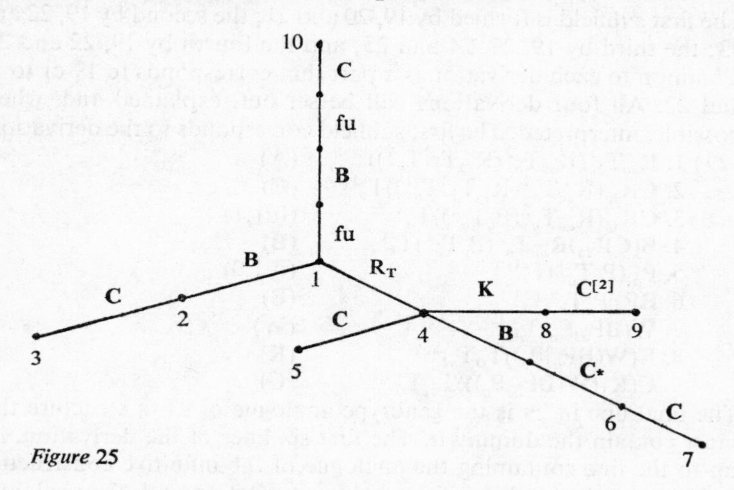


*Figure 25*

The second semantic field whose derivation is to be discussed is that of emotive verbs like *please* and *upset*. Compare the following examples:

(19) Mary is pleased she came
(20) Mary is pleased to come
(21) It pleased Mary to come
(22) Mary is pleased that she came
(23) ?That she came pleased Mary
(24) ?Mary is pleased about her coming
(25) ?Her coming pleased Mary
(26) It pleased Mary that she came.

This field differs from the previous one in that it contains a sentence, 20, with an infinitive whose subject is identical with the subject of the main verb; and a sentence, 21, containing a construction the converse of that in 20; and it also differs in that it contains no sentence like 2 in which the subject of the infinitive is identical with the object of the main verb.

This field consists of four subfields, each with its own derivation, though all the derivations begin with the same axiom:

(27) $R_{lo}T_l^1(R_{oa}T_o^2(P_{lo}T_l^3T_o^1))$

The above axiom is different from that in 10 in that it has the identical terms $T_l^1$ and $T_o^1$. Axiom 27 is interpreted here as:

(28) **Mèri v pribytii, čto kauziruet udovol'stvie, kotoroe lokalizuetsja v Mèri* (Mary–(is) in–arrival–which–causes–pleasure–which–is located–in–Mary)

The first subfield is formed by 19, 20 and 21; the second by 19, 22 and 23; the third by 19, 22, 24 and 25; and the fourth by 19, 22 and 26. Common to each derivation is a part that corresponds to 19 or to 19 and 22. All four derivations will be set out, explained and, where possible, interpreted. The first subfield corresponds to the derivation:

(29)
1. $R_{lo}T_l^1(R_{oa}T_o^2(R_{lo}T_l^3T_o^1))$ (A)
2. $\mathbf{C}R_{lo}(R_{oa}T_o^2(R_{lo}T_l^3T_o^1))T_l^1$ (C)
3. $\mathbf{C}R_{lo}(R_{oa}T_o^2(P_oT_o^2))T_o^2$ (fu1.1)
4. $\mathbf{B}(\mathbf{C}R_{lo})R_{oa}T_o^2(P_oT_o^1)T_l^1$ (**B**)
5. $P_{al}(P_oT_o^1)T_l^1$ (fu1.9)
6. $\mathbf{B}P_{al}P_oT_o^1T_l^1$ (**B**)
7. $\mathbf{W}(\mathbf{B}P_{al}P_o)T_{ol}^1$ (**W**)
8. $\mathbf{K}(\mathbf{W}(\mathbf{B}P_{al}P_o))T_0T_{ol}^1$ (**K**)
9. $\mathbf{C}(\mathbf{K}_1(\mathbf{W}(\mathbf{B}P_{al}P_o)))T_{ol}T_0$ (**C**)

The final line in 29 is the genotype analogue of 21, a structure that must contain the dummy *it*. The first six lines of the derivation, i.e. up to the line containing the analogue of the infinitive construction in 20, have already been discussed in connection with the analogues of complex sentences (cf. the derivation in 5 and the accompanying explanations on p. 96). For this reason I am going to concentrate on individual lines that have to be explained if this field of synonymous sentences is to be understood. Attention will also be drawn to the fact that 29 shares its first six lines with 13 in the *expect/believe* field (p. 105), from which was obtained the analogue of infinitive constructions like that in 2.

The fifth line, which had no interpretation among sentences with verbs of volition like *want*, was assigned interpretation 1 from the sentences containing *expect* or *believe*, and corresponds to 19 among the sentences containing emotive verbs. One of the identical terms is interpreted as *she* and, in contrast with 1, the predicate of the main sentence is interpreted as a passive construction, *is pleased*. The sixth line has no interpretation, but cf. 6 on p. 96—*He*[3] *wanted him*[3] *to come*—which provides at least a hypothetical interpretation from the sentences with verbs of volition. In the seventh line the duplicator **W** fuses the identical terms together, generating the analogue of 20.

In the eighth line the combinator **K** puts $T_0$ in the place immediately following the predicate and in the ninth line the permutator **C** moves the complex argument $T_0$, corresponding to the dummy subject *it*, into final position. The complex predicate can be put in correspondence with the active verb *pleased* and the whole of the ninth line can be put in correspondence with 23.

The second subfield corresponds to the derivation in 30, which, being identical with 29 up to the fifth line, begins with the fifth line:

(30) 5. $P_{al}(P_o T_o^1) T_l^1$ (fu1.9)
6. $P_{al}(R_T(P_o T_o^1)) T_l^1$ $(R_T)$
7. $\mathbf{C} P_{al} T_l^1 (R_T(P_o T_o^1))$ **(C)**

30 is identical with 13 up to line six, which is interpreted as 22, cf. 4 in the field of *expect/believe* verbs. The difference between 4 and 22 lies in the interpretation of $P_{al}$, which in the former corresponds to the active verb *expect*, in the latter to the passive construction *is pleased*. The seventh line corresponds to the converse construction in 23, cf. 5 in the first field. $\mathbf{C}P_{al}$ corresponds to the active verb *pleased* in 23 but to the passive *is expected* in 5.

The third subfield is obtained via the derivation in 31, which is identical with 30 up to the sixth line and with 15 up to the ninth line. Because of this the first four lines are omitted:

(31) 5. $P_{al}(P_o T_o^1) T_l^1$ (fu1.9)
6. $P_{al}(R_T(P_o T_o^1)) T_l^1$ $(R_T)$
7. $P_{al}(\mathbf{B} R_T P_o T_o^1) T_l^1$ **(B)**
8. $P_{al}(\mathbf{C}_* T_o^1 (\mathbf{B} R_T P_o)) T_l^1$ $(\mathbf{C}_*)$
9. $\mathbf{C} P_{al} T_l^1 (\mathbf{C}_* T_o^1 (\mathbf{B} R_T P_o))$ **(C)**

Lines five to nine in the above derivation have already been examined in detail in connection with 15. Line five corresponds to 19, line six to 22, and the seventh line, as in 15, has no interpretation, although it is easily interpreted with respect to other verbs, as in 16 on p. 106. The eighth line corresponds to 24, $T_o^1$ being interpreted as the possessive pronoun *her*. The ninth line is interpreted as 25. The last two lines find a more natural interpretation in sentences containing verbs of expecting and believing than in sentences containing emotive verbs, as is clear from a comparison of 6 and 7 on the one hand, and 24 and 25 on the other. The doubtful status of the latter two is indicated by the question marks against them.

The fourth subfield includes two objects that are identical with objects in the other subfields, namely with 19 and 22. This identity is obvious from 32, in which, as usual, the first four lines are left out.

(32) 5. $P_{al}(P_o T_o^1) T_l^1$ (fu1.9)
6. $P_{al}(R_T(P_o T_o^1)) T_l^1$ $(R_T)$
7. $\mathbf{K}_1 P_{al}(R_T(P_o T_o^1)) T_0 T_l^1$ $(\mathbf{K}_1)$
8. $\mathbf{C}_2(\mathbf{K}_1 P_{al})(R_T(P_o T_o^1)) T_l^1 T_0$ $(\mathbf{C}_2)$

The fifth line corresponds to 19, the sixth to 22. The seventh line can be interpreted as a genotype structure like *Mary is pleased about it that she came.* As was said before, this genotype sentence only makes sense linguistically if the predicate $\mathbf{K}_1\mathrm{P}_{al}$ is interpreted as a verb like *hate* or *like* (cf. 18 on p. 106). In the eighth line the permutator $\mathbf{C}_2$ moves the dummy argument $\mathrm{T}_0$ into final position to yield the analogue of 26. Whereas in the seventh line $\mathbf{K}_1\mathrm{P}_{al}$ corresponds to the passive construction *is pleased*, in the eighth line $\mathbf{C}_2(\mathbf{K}_1\mathrm{P}_{al})$ corresponds to the active verb *pleased.* Cf. the converse relationship between 4 and 9 in the subfield of verbs of expecting and believing. A comparison of all such pairs of related sentences in the subfield of verbs of expecting and subfield of emotive verbs (i.e. 2–3 and 20–21; 4–5 and 22–23; 6–7 and 24–25; 8–9 and 22–26) reveals that in one field the relationship between constructions with and without prepositions is the reverse of the relationship in the other field. Consider, for example, 33, which represents the general type of converse relation in the subfield of verbs of expecting, and 34, which represents the general type in the subfield of emotive verbs.

(33) I expect it→It is expected by me
(34) I am pleased about it→It pleased me

The tree for the semantic field of emotive verbs is shown in figure 26.

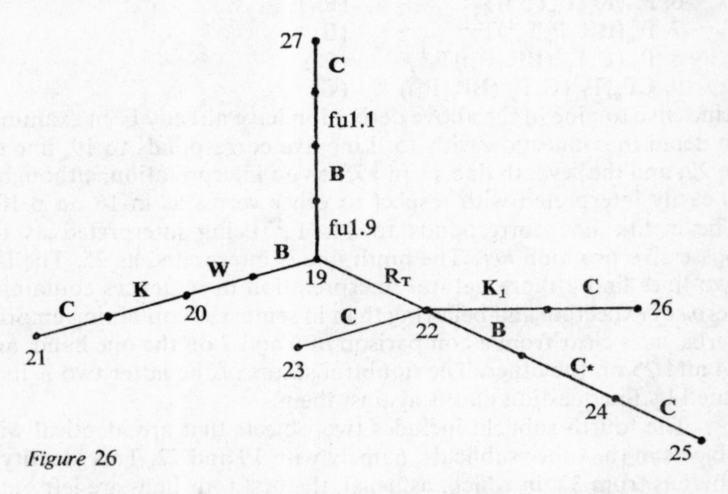


*Figure* 26

The third semantic field that is to be discussed is the small modal one, consisting in all of six sentences:

(35) Perhaps, John will arrive
(36) John may arrive
(37) It is possible for John to arrive
(38) That John will arrive is possible

(39) It is possible that John will arrive
(40) John's arrival is possible
All six sentences are derived from the axiom:
(41) $R_{lo}T_l^1(R_{lo}T_l^1T_o^3)$
This axiom is postulated in axiom schema 3.7. The embedded sentence is the same as axiom 1.3. In the modal field 41 is interpreted as **To, čto Džon v pribytii, lokalizuetsja v vozmožnosti* (it–that–John–(is) in–arrival–is located–in–possibility).

There are three subfields in this field: one that includes 35, 36 and 37; a second that includes 35, 38 and 40; and a third that includes 35, 38 and 40. Each subfield has its own derivation, although the derivations have some lines in common. The derivation corresponding to the first subfield is:

(42) 1. $R_{lo}T_l^1(R_{lo}T_l^2T_o^3)$ (A)
2. $R_{lo}T_l^1(P_oT_o^3)$ (ful.1)
3. $P_o(P_o^1T_o^3)$ (ful.1)
4. $\mathbf{BP}_oP_o^1T_o^3$ (**B**)
5. $\mathbf{K}_1(\mathbf{BP}_oP_o^1)T_0T_o^3$ ($\mathbf{K}_1$)
6. $\mathbf{C}(\mathbf{K}_1(\mathbf{BP}_oP_o^1))T_o^3T_0$ (**C**)

The first line in 42 corresponds to the axiom. In the second line a synthetic predicate is formed inside the embedded sentence, the change from $R_{lo}T_l^2T_o^3$ to $P_oT_o^3$ modelling the derivation of a full one-place predicate from a copular construction, e.g. **est' v pribytii* (is–in–arrival)→*pribyvaet* (arrives). In the third line the operation of fusion is applied again, modelling the transformation of **lokalizuetsja v vozmožnosti* (is located–in–possibility)→*vozmožno* (possibly/perhaps). The fusion takes place in the main sentence and the resulting one-place predicate, $P_o$, has as its argument the embedded sentence $(P_oT_o^3)$. The third line is interpreted as 35. In the fourth line the predicates of the main and the embedded sentences are joined in one unit to form a complex one-place predicate that can be interpreted as *may arrive*. The fourth line as a whole corresponds to 36. 37 is the converse of 36 in that from being the subject *John* becomes the object. This conversion can be performed only by means of the dummy argument, which in line five is inserted into object position and then in line six moved into subject position by the operation of permutation. The complex predicate $\mathbf{C}(\mathbf{K}_1(\mathbf{BP}_oP_o))$ can be interpreted as *is possible* and the whole sixth line corresponds to 37.

The derivation in 43 corresponds to the second subfield. Since all the derivations in the modal field have the first three lines in common, 43 begins at the third line:

(43) 3. $P_o(P_o^1T_o^3)$ (ful.1)
4. $P_o(R_T(P_o^1T_o^3))$ ($R_T$)

5. $P_o(\mathbf{B}R_TP_o{}^1T_o{}^3)$ **(B)**
6. $P_o(\mathbf{C_*}T_o{}^3(\mathbf{B}R_TP_o{}^1))$ **(C$_*$)**

The third line corresponds to 35. In the fourth line the nominalising operator $\Delta\beta\alpha R_T$ transforms the embedded sentence into a noun phrase. If $R_T$ is interpreted as a conjunction like *that* and if the predicate of the main sentence is interpreted as *is possible*, then the fourth line will correspond to 38. The derivation can be extended by applying the compositor **B** to $R_T$ and then to $P_o$. The complex predicate $\mathbf{B}R_TP_o$, as was observed on p.98, can be interpreted as a participle but here the fifth line has no interpretation (cf. 18 on p.106 for an interpretation). In the sixth line the combinator **C** transforms $T_o{}^3$, *John*, into a function and $\mathbf{B}R_TP_o{}^1$ into an argument, the resulting sentence corresponding to 40.

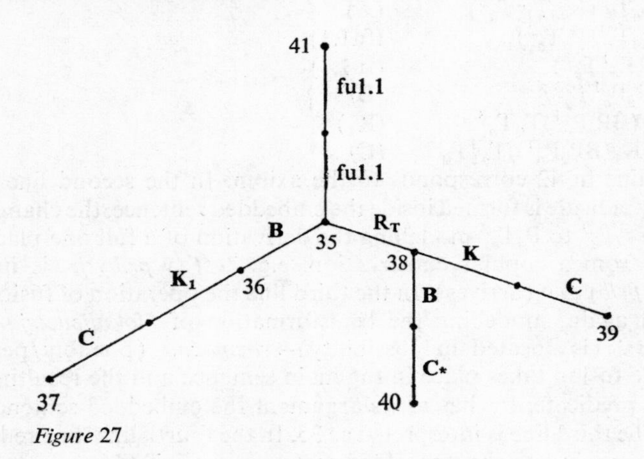


*Figure* 27

The derivation in 44 is that of the third subfield:

(44) 3. $P_o(P_o{}^1P_o{}^3)$ (ful.1)
4. $P_o(R_T(P_o{}^1T_o{}^3))$ ($R_T$)
5. $\mathbf{K}P_oT_0(R_T(P_o{}^1T_o{}^3))$ **(K)**
6. $\mathbf{C}(\mathbf{K}_oP_o)(R_T(P_o{}^1T_o{}^3))T_0$ **(C)**

As the interpretation of the third and fourth lines has already been discussed I will say no more about them here. In the fifth line the dummy argument $T_0$ is moved by the operator **K** into the first position after the predicate $P_o$. This yields an intermediate structure that can be interpreted as the hypothetical sentence

(45) **is possible it that John will arrive*

This intermediate structure is necessary if 39, the converse of 38, is to be derived. In 38 the nominalised embedded sentence, corresponding to $(R_T(P_oT_o^3))$, is the subject but in 40, which is obtained in the sixth line, it is moved into object position. Into subject position goes instead the dummy argument $T_0$, which was the empty object in the fifth line.

The modal field is represented by the tree in figure 27.

The last semantic field we shall look at is the causative one, which consists of only two sentences:

(46) I forced him to come

(47) He was forced to come by me

The analogues of these sentences are derived from the axiom

(48) $R_{oa}(R_{lo}T_lT_o)T_a$

This axiom is postulated in axiom schema 1.8 and the embedded sentence is the same as axiom 3.1. 48 is interpreted as:

(49) **Ja kauziruju (to, čtoby) on byl v pribytii* (I–cause–it–that–he–be–in–arrival)

The derivation of the causative field is:

(50) 1. $R_{oa}(R_{lo}T_lT_o)T_a$ (A)
2. $\mathbf{B}R_{oa}(R_{lo}T_l)T_oT_a$ (**B**)
3. $P_{oa}T_oT_a$ (ful.8)
4. $\mathbf{C}P_{oa}T_aT_o$ (**C**)

The above derivation is identical up to the third line with the derivation in 12 in the section on complex sentences (cf. p.97). The third line is interpreted as 46, $T_a$ corresponding to *I*, $T_o$ to *him*, and the predicate $P_{oa}$ to the infinitival complex *forced to come*. In the fourth line the permutator **C** causes $T_a$ and $T_o$ to change places, thereby generating the analogue of 47, which is the converse of 46. The derivational tree of the causative field is set out in figure 28. If the trees in figures 25, 26, 27 and 28 are compared it will be seen that there is a good deal of variation among the semantic fields with respect to the number and length of the derivations and the type of semantic rules that are applied.

*Figure* 28

# 4. Semantic Theory as the Basis for Grammars of Natural Languages

## 1. On Defining a Grammar of a Natural Language

The purpose of studying any natural language is to write a grammar of it. A natural language can be considered as a set of sentences each of which can be described in terms of a content plane and an expression plane, the former being called the meaning of the sentence, the latter being expression or physical manifestation. (Instead of 'content plane' and 'expression plane' the terms 'signifié' and 'signifiant' can be used.) The term 'sentence' is applied here not just to a sentence as such but to any group of sentences that form a coherent whole. Abstracting away from the expression plane, we can consider the content plane of a sentence to be a unit of meaning, which we shall call a situation. Comparing sentences and situations, we can see that sentences are bilateral units consisting of two components, a signifié and a signifiant, whereas a situation is unilateral in that it has only one component, a signifié. A grammar is a set of rules that map the infinite set of unilateral units—situations—into an infinite set of bilateral units—sentences. To know a language is to be able to put any sentence or equivalent sentences into correspondence with the appropriate situation, and vice-versa. A grammar can thus be thought of as a special operator that maps situations on to sentences and sentences on to situations.

The grammar of a language is a complex logical mechanism stored in the brain of each person that speaks that language, but since it is not open to direct, immediate observation we can do no more than form hypotheses as to its structure. We are obliged, that is, to construct hypothetical formal systems that can serve as cybernetic models of these grammars that exist in objective reality but are hidden from our immediate view. By comparing the cybernetic models with observed linguistic facts we can constantly improve them, bringing them closer and closer to the real grammars.

It follows that the term 'grammar of a natural language' is ambiguous, since it can be understood either as denoting a special kind of logical mechanism stored in speakers' brains and not open to direct inspection or as denoting a cybernetic model that represents a hypothesis about the structure of the logical mechanism. To avoid this ambiguity the term 'objective grammar' will be used to denote the logical mechanism stored in speakers' brains and the term 'construct-grammar' will be used to denote the cybernetic models.

To denote the knowledge of the objective grammar that is available to the speaker of a language I shall borrow Chomsky's term 'linguistic competence'.

Linguistic competence varies from person to person, different people being sensitive to language in different degrees. This sensitivity (or *Sprachgefühl*) is precisely what Chomsky would call a person's level of linguistic intuition or linguistic competence. In addition to variation from person to person it must also be recognised that a single individual can possess different levels of competence at different periods in his life. As Chomsky has proposed, the linguist's grammar should model linguistic competence, but since linguistic competence is a subjective state that varies from person to person it is more reasonable to assume that the purpose of constructing a grammar is to model not linguistic competence but the objective content of this competence that is not affected by the individual's degree of awareness, i.e. what was called above the objective grammar.

This objective grammar has a unique ontological status because, on the one hand, it exists only in human consciousness but, on the other, Man is forced to treat it as an object that exists independently of him. Objective grammars belong to a special world, which can be called the world of semiotic systems or the semiotic world. The essential property of this world is that genetically it is the product of human consciousness but ontologically it is independent of human consciousness. If by the material nature of the world we mean that it belongs to objective reality, then it is not just the physical world that is to be considered material but also the semiotic world.

As objective grammars are not open to direct observation, we shall adopt the practice of scientists and identify the construct-grammar with the objective grammar, not forgetting, of course, that this identification is hypothetical and that we must be constantly perfecting the construct-grammar by testing it against linguistic facts. From now on, therefore, the term 'grammar' will be systematically used in two senses, equivalent both to 'objective grammar' and 'construct-grammar'. (As a synonym of 'grammars of natural languages' I shall use 'phenotype grammars'.)

The term 'genotype language' will similarly be used in two senses, to denote both the semiotic basis of natural languages, which exists in objective reality but is not open to direct inspection, and the artificial, specially constructed language that is a hypothesis about the objective semiotic basis.

The next task is to draw up the formal conditions that, I believe, must govern the construction of any phenotype grammars that are to be adequate. The formal conditions that follow encompass all the essential details of what might be called the theory of constructing phenotype grammars.

*Condition* 1. In the construction of a phenotype grammar three levels of representation have to be distinguished for situations: 1) the content plane; 2) the expression plane; 3) the level on which the content plane and the expression plane meet. The first level, that of the content plane, will be called the semantic level, the second will be called the phonological level and the third, on which content and expression plane meet, will be called the morphological level. Each level must be split into two sub-levels. The sub-levels of the semantic one are the primitive semantic (or deep-semantic) level and the expressive semantic (or surface-semantic) level. The phonological level splits up into the phonological level proper (or deep-phonological level) and the phonetic (or surface-phonological) level. Similarly, the morphological level consists of deep-morphological and surface-morphological levels.

*Condition* 2. By analogy with the different levels of the representation of situations mentioned under condition 1 a phenotype grammar must have three components that operate in sequence: 1) a semantic component, 2) a morphological component and 3) a phonological component.

Operating with unilateral units of meaning called phenotype semions the semantic component constructs the deep-semantic level, which is mapped into the surface-semantic level of representation.

The morphological component projects the surface-semantic level onto the phonological one, in the process creating bilateral units—called sentences—consisting of a signifié and a signifiant. The projection takes place in three stages. In the first stage the surface situation is projected onto the appropriate deep sentence, i.e. onto a sentence consisting of deep wordforms, these being wordforms that have a global representation, with no indication of the division into morphemes. Attached to each deep wordform is an index formed from the symbols denoting the syntactically determined morphological characteristics of that deep wordform. In the second stage these deep wordforms are transformed into surface wordforms, i.e. into wordforms in which the morpheme boundaries are shown. In the third stage the morphemes are transformed into their phonological representation, i.e. into morphs. In the morphological component there are also word-order rules which are applied to the deep wordforms.

The phonological component projects the phonological level of representation onto the phonetic one.

*Condition* 3. The semantic component of a phenotype grammar must be analogous to the semantic theory. This means, firstly, that the deep-semantic level of representation must be constructed as a projection of the primitive sub-language of the relator genotype language and, secondly, that all the rules that map the primitive sub-language of the relator genotype language into the expression sub-language of the relator genotype language must also apply in the phenotype grammar to project the deep-semantic level of representation on to the surface-semantic level.

Instead of 'deep-semantic representation of a situation' I will use the term 'deep situation', and instead of 'surface-semantic representation of a situation' I will use the term 'surface situation'. Deep situations are the axioms of the phenotype grammar and to each axiom of the semantic theory there can correspond an infinite set of deep situations. This means that each axiom of the semantic theory appears as an axiom schema of the phenotype grammar in the course of the latter's construction.

For the construction of deep situations or, which amounts to the same thing, axioms of the phenotype grammar, rules are postulated for the insertion of meaning units, called elementary phenotype semions, into the axioms of the semantic theory. The elementary phenotype semions are unilateral units of meaning that can be called meaning-atoms, and each deep situation is a combination of elementary phenotype semions, i.e. meaning-atoms. The elementary phenotype semions that form a deep situation have indices showing the associated genotype cases and other semantic features such as number and gender.

Two sorts of rule are involved in the transformation of deep situations into surface ones: 1) genotype semantic rules and 2) special phenotype semantic rules. The genotype semantic rules are transferred en bloc from the semantic theory into the semantic component of the phenotype grammar. The special semantic rules replace the indices of genotype cases with the indices of phenotype case relations and perform various other transformations, which will be exemplified in the fragment of Russian grammar in the following section.

Thus the semantic components of phenotype grammars can be regarded as various extensions of the semantic theory. In fact, the semantic component of any phenotype grammar is the semantic theory fleshed out with elementary phenotype semions and supplemented with semantic indices and special phenotype rules.

Since this is the nature of the semantic component of a phenotype grammar, the semantic theory must be taken as the basis for the construction of phenotype grammars.

*Condition* 4. The operator-operand relation, on which the description of the genotype language rests, must be kept as the basis for the description of phenotype languages.

Since it follows from condition 4 that the structure of every complex unit in both the genotype and phenotype languages must be described as the hierarchical combination of simple units carried out by applying operators to operands, a further distinction must be drawn between genotype and phenotype applicational grammars. For instance, we must specify whether we are dealing with a genotype applicational grammar of Russian or a phenotype one.

*Condition* 5. When a deep-semantic representation of a situation is projected onto a phonological representation the meaning of the situation must remain constant. This condition, which ensures that sentences derived from the same deep situation are synonymous, can be called the principle of the preservation of meaning during the derivation of sentences in a phenotype grammar.

*Condition* 6. On the level of the phonological representation of a situation phonological oppositions can not be neutralised.

This condition is needed to ensure that the morphological rules are as simple as possible, the point being that the homonymy of morphs that results from such neutralisations complicates the morphological rules.

These six conditions are general principles governing the construction of applicational grammars of natural languages or applicational phenotype grammars. Certain aspects of the construction process require explanation and I shall first of all examine in detail the morphological and phonological components of applicational phenotype grammars.

The morphological component can usefully be taken first. The semantic component of an applicational phenotype grammar yields surface situations consisting of combinations of surface phenotype semions. What happens next is that the structures of the content plane are mapped into units of the expression plane, i.e. phonological objects, by the generative mechanism of the applicational grammar. As we know, the elementary phonological objects are distinctive features and it is this set of universal distinctive features that is used to code the varied structures of the content plane. If it is asked what role the phoneme plays, the answer is that in a generative grammar it makes more sense to think of a phoneme as simply an abbreviation for a bundle of distinctive features.

On the level of phonological representation the elementary morphological unit is the morph.[1] The morph is a minimal unit that is formed as a result of some elementary semion or bundle of elementary semions being mapped into some phonological object, and can thus be regarded as consisting of a signifié and a signifiant. The signifié is a simple or complex semion, i.e. a simple or complex unit of the content plane and the signifiant is a simple or complex phonological object, i.e. a unit of the expression plane that can not be broken up into smaller units with respect to the correlation with the content plane. A class of morphs with the same signifié but different signifiants is called a morpheme, and the morphs representing the same morpheme are called the allomorphs of that morpheme.

In an applicational phenotype grammar what are called the morphological rules map the content plane on to the expression plane.

The inclusion of morphological rules in the phonological component brings us up against serious difficulties. Consider, for example, the allomorphs /y/, /a/ and /e/ in the plural forms of such Russian words as *stoly* (tables), *goroda* (towns) and *krestjane* (peasants). (The nominative singular forms of these words are *stol*, *gorod* and *krestjanin* respectively.) The distinctions between these allomorphs are not phonologically conditioned and are of a completely different character from the distinction between the allomorphs /got/ and /god/ in the Russian words *god* (year: pronounced *got*) and *gody* (years). The latter pair of allomorphs exists because in Russian voiced consonants are devoiced in word-final position.

Problems also arise with word formation. In German the formation of diminutives involves umlaut, as in *Wort-Wörtchen* and *Hut-Hütchen* but the difference between the allomorphs /vort/ and /vört/, /hut/ and /hüt/ is not phonologically conditioned.

We must distinguish clearly two essentially different types of variation in morphs, that which is not phonologically conditioned and that which is. The first type can be dealt with by the morphology but the second must be handled in the phonology.

The actual mapping of semions, units of the content plane, on to phonological objects, units of the expression plane, belongs not to phonology but to morphology, since it is the latter that encompasses the processes that map the content plane on to the expression plane. Phonology, on the other hand, includes processes that take place in the expression plane itself independently of the content plane. One

[1] The following definitions are preliminary in nature and have been formulated without taking into account the full complexity of the relations between the content and expression planes. I also ignore here certain details concerning the work of the morphological component which will be explained in the next section.

simple example that illustrates the point neatly is that of the plural noun allomorphs in English: /s/, /z/ and /iz/. As is well-known, the difference between these allomorphs is phonologically conditioned: 1) after /š/, /ž/, /z/, /č/ and /ǰ/ the allomorph /iz/ occurs, as in /glasiz/–*glasses*, /saiziz/–*sizes*, /bušiz/–*bushes*, /ružiz/–*rouges*, /arčiz/ –*arches*; 2) /z/ occurs after vowels or voiced consonants, as in /šu:z/–*shoes*, /bedz/–*beds*, /egz/–*eggs*; 3) /s/ occurs after voiceless constants, as in /kats/–*cats*, /buks/–*books*.

That these differences really are phonologically conditioned can be seen from the fact that the same differences are to be found in the allomorphs of the present tense, third person singular morpheme, as in 1) /fišiz/–*fishes*, /ri:čiz/–*reaches*; 2) /si:z/–*sees*, /digz/–*digs*; 3) /piks/–*picks*, /mi:ts/–*meets*; and also in the allomorphs of the possessive morpheme, as in 1) /*jonziz*/–Jones's; 2) /bilz/–*Bill's*; 3) /a:nts/–*aunt's*.

The morphology has to deal with morphs not only within the word but also in the sentence, especially in languages where linear order functions as a signifiant. Compare the two English sentences *Ann sees Irene* and *Irene sees Ann*, in which the signifiés 'subject' and 'object' are distinguished only by the order of the morphemes *Ann* and *Irene*. We can say that with respect to these signifiés it is the order that functions as the signifiant. In the corresponding Russian sentences, however, the signifiant of the 'subject' is /a/ and that of the 'object' is /u/, as in *Anna vidit Irinu* (Ann–sees–Irene) and *Irina vidit Annu* (Irene–sees–Ann). It is facts like these that allow us to talk not only of the morphology of the word but also of the morphology of the sentence.

I now wish to take a closer look at the phonological component of an applicational phenotype grammar. The task of the phonological component is to explain and predict differences between allomorphs by means of a hypothetical abstract phonological system and phonetic processes that map the abstract phonological system into a concrete phonological system.

This way of describing the task of a generative phonology can be justified by the following examples involving differences between allomorphs:

/grup/ and /grub/ in the words *grub* and *grubyj* (both = 'coarse')
/gas/ and /gaz/ in the words *gaz* (gas) and *gazy* (gases)
/noš/ and /nož/ in the words *nož* (knife) and *nožik* (little knife)
/druk/ and /drug/ in the words *drug* (friend) and *druga* (of friend)

It can be concluded from the huge set of similar oppositions that the differences between these allomorphs are caused by the devoicing of voiced consonants in word final position. In order to make a general statement based on this conclusion it can be assumed that in Russian there are two phonological levels: an abstract (or deep) one and a concrete (or surface) one. On the abstract phonological level voiced and voiceless consonants are distinguished in word final position but the difference is obliterated on the concrete level by the devoicing of word final voiced consonants. That is to say, the opposition of voiced and voiceless consonants is neutralised only on the concrete phonological level.

The next example of variation between allomorphs is taken from English. From observations of the many occurrences of these allomorphs it can be hypothesised that in English the consonant clusters /šz/, /žz/, /čz/, /ǰz/, /tz/ and /kz/ are possible on the abstract phonological level. The insertion of a vowel between sibilants and the devoicing of voiced consonants immediately preceded by voiceless ones leads to the occurrence on the concrete phonological level of the phoneme sequences /žiz/, /šiz/, /čiz/, /ǰiz/, /ts/ and /ks/.

This hypothesis enables the allomorph /z/ to be considered as the abstract representative of the corresponding morpheme from which the allomorphs /iz/ and /s/ are obtained on the concrete phonological level via the processes mentioned in the preceding paragraph.

A wider range of facts enables the statement of these processes to be refined. For instance, the various allomorphs of the past tense morpheme—/t/, /d/ and /id/—show that the insertion of vowels occurs not just between sibilants but in general between consonants articulated in the same manner. However, what is of immediate interest here is not the exactness of the generalisations but the very fact that hypotheses about phonological processes like the above can be arrived at by generalising from observed facts.

The generalisation of observed facts makes it necessary to postulate two phonological levels and to formulate appropriate hypotheses about phonological processes. Hypotheses of this sort that do no more than generalise from observed facts will be called summation hypotheses, since they simply sum up our observations.

In a generative phonology summation hypotheses about phonological processes must be supplemented by a fundamentally different type, which can be called postulation hypotheses. Facts are the basis of any hypothetical constructions, whether summation hypotheses or postulation hypotheses, but there is an essential difference between the two types in that the former derive from generalisations, summations of observed facts, whereas the latter deal with imaginary phonological objects and processes that are in principle unobservable at any particular stage of a language.

This can be illustrated by an example from Russian, in which there can be observed an alternation of phonemes that is not brought about by any directly observable phonetic processes: e.g. /k/, /č/ and /c/ in *durak* (fool), *durač'e* (set of fools) and *durackij* (foolish); /g/, /ž/ and /z/ in *drugu* (to friend), *druželskij* (friendly) and *druz'ja* (friends); /e/, /o/ and /∅/ in *pročest'* (to read through), *pročel* ((he) read), *pročla* ((she) read); and many others. If we are giving a synchronic analysis of Russian the alternations can be handled by indicating the morphemes in the environment in which they take place. Indeed this method is widely used in synchronic grammars. However, this method is inconvenient in that it leads in the long run to huge lists of morpheme environments and yields a synchronic description that is a mere statement of empirical facts. To go beyond such statements we need to adopt the hypothesis that the level on which the alternation of phonemes occurs is the result of deep, not directly observable, phonetic processes. In this way the alternation of phonemes can be described by means of a finite set of phonological rules organised into a coherent system. Of course, this is achieved at the cost of imaginary phonemes and imaginary phonetic processes.

As far as Russian is concerned, attempts have been made to explain the alternation of phonemes by assuming that Modern Russian has a deep phonological system containing short and long vowels, to be precise the reduced vowels /ŭ/ and /ĭ/. A set of primitive consonants is postulated in which there are no affricates or soft consonants. Also postulated is a set of phonetic processes by which the observed morphological structures can be derived from hypothetical morphological structures that are represented as combinations of primitive phonemes, combinations of primitive distinctive features. As was said above, phonemes are taken to be abbreviations, labels for bundles of distinctive features. It is this sort of proposal that I call a postulation hypothesis, and it is just such rules and primitive objects that constitute the essence of the phonological component. In this component summation and postulation hypotheses are integrated into a single abstract phonological system that can be used to explain the observed differences between the allomorphs of a morpheme, that is, to explain the observed variation among morphemes, which consists of various types of alternation between phonemes.

The formal apparatus on the content plane is based on the operator-operand relation, every complex structure on that plane being obtained by the successive applications of operators to operands, and this same operator-operand relation is transferred to the expression plane to become the essential property of the phonological component of the applicational generative model. Corresponding to the distinction between operators and operands on the content plane, a distinction will be drawn between operators and operands on the expression plane—to be more exact, on the expression plane of those bilateral units called morphs that are obtained as a result of the content plane being mapped into the expression plane.

Of course, there is no mutual one-one relation between the operators and operands on the one plane and those on the other plane, but this is not of any consequence for the phonological component of the applicational model. What is of consequence is that, with respect to their expression plane, derivational affixes can be regarded as operators whose operands are either primitive roots or stems of varying derivational complexity that have been obtained by the application of one or more operators to primitive roots. This means that any word containing at least one derivational affix has an applicational structure. The number of affixes applied to the root determines a word's degree of derivational complexity, in that a word consisting of a root and *n* affixes will be said to be of the *n*th degree of derivational complexity.

A stem consisting of a root and *n* affixes applied to the root will be called a stem of the *n*th degree of derivational complexity. When determining a word's degree of complexity in this fashion we do not distinguish between different sorts of derivational affixes, such as word-forming and word-changing affixes, since this distinction is not crucial for the phonological component. What is crucial is that the degree of derivational complexity is determined by the number of affixes applied to the root, regardless of what the affixes are.

The above definitions of degree of derivational complexity and stem permit us to assume that the phonological processes are iterative, which in turn means that each set of phonological rules can be applied to words in a given order and any number of times depending on the number of steps in the derivation of the word. The iterative processes apply in cycles. In the first cycle the phonological rules are applied to a root, in the second cycle to a stem of the first degree of derivational complexity, in the third cycle to a stem of the second degree of complexity, and so on until in the last cycle the rules are applied to the whole word.

The cyclical application of the phonological processes is supported by the fact that the system of phonological rules can be considered as historical phonological processes superimposed on a synchronic cross-section of a language. Adopting an analogy with biology one can say that, in a certain respect, generative phonology is to historical phonology as ontogenesis is to phylogenesis. It is well-known in historical phonology that after some phonetic law ceases to operate the process of morphological analogy takes over and stems are levelled out. For example, at one period in the history of Russian, after the fall of the jers (the disappearance of the reduced vowels mentioned earlier), a phonetic law came into operation by which unstressed *e* became *o* before a hard non-sharp consonant. This law led to *med* (honey) becoming *mjod*, *pes* (dog) becoming *pjos*, and *nesem* (we shall carry) becoming *nesjom*, etc. This sound change could not occur in *mede* (prepositional case of *med*) or *pesik* (little dog) or *nesete* (you will carry) because in these words *e* occurred before a soft sharp consonant. However, after this phonetic law stopped operating stems were levelled by morphological analogy and the words *mjede*, *pjosik* and *nesjote*, etc., were formed. These are events from the history of Russian, but morphological analogy cannot be invoked in a synchronic phonological description of Modern Russian since the task of the analyst is to penetrate beneath the surface of the synchronic cross-section and reveal the underlying, purely phonological, processes. However, the difficulty that arises out of these considerations can be resolved if the synchronic phonetic processes are regarded as cyclical phonological processes, and I will now demonstrate how the results of the above historical changes can be described synchronically.

We shall assume that *mede*, *nesjote*, *pjosik* in Modern Russian are derived from the initial abstract forms (*med*<*e*), ((*nes*<*e*)<*te*), (*pjos*<*ik*). < signals the application of an operator to an operand, the symbol to the right of < being the operator, the symbol to the left being the operand. The following phonological rules will be used:

1. c→c′

This rule says that non-sharp hard consonants become sharp soft consonants before high front vowels.

2.1.1. ŭ́→o
2.1.2. ĭ́→e

This rule says that if the reduced vowels *ŭ* and *ĭ* are stressed and are not in word-final position they become *o* and *e* respectively.

2.2.1. ŭ→o
2.2.2. ĭ→e

This rule says that if *ŭ* and *ĭ* are unstressed, and if the following syllable contains *ŭ* or *ĭ*, then they become *o* and *e* respectively.

2.3.1. ŭ→∅
2.3.2. ĭ→∅

This rule says that the reduced vowels are replaced by zero if they are in word-final position or if the following syllable contains a full vowel.

3. e→o: *e* becomes *o* before a non-sharp hard consonant.

4. e→ĕ: Long *e* changes into short *e*
5. o, a, e→i (non-sharp)

This rule says that unstressed *o*, *a*, *e* become *i* after non-sharp soft consonants.

The concrete phonological representations of the above-mentioned words are set out below. The rules have to be applied in the order in which they are given.

Initial word: (*med*<*e*)

| *first cycle* | | *second cycle* | |
|---|---|---|---|
| a) *m'ed* | by rule 1 | a) (*m'od*<*e*) | by rule 3 |
| b) *m'od* | by rule 3 | b) (*m'od*<*ĕ*) | by rule 4 |
| | | c) (*m'od*<*i*) | by rule 5 |

Initial word: ((*nes*<*e*)<*te*)

| *first cycle* | | *second cycle* | |
|---|---|---|---|
| a) *n'es* | by rule 1 | a) (*n'os'*<*e*) | by rule 1 |
| b) *n'os* | by rule 3 | b) (*n'os'*<*o*) | by rule 3 |

*third cycle*

| | |
|---|---|
| a) ((*n'os'*<*o*)<*t'e*) | by rule 1 |
| b) ((*n'is'*<*o*)<*t'i*) | by rule 5 (applied twice) |

Initial word: ((*pĭs*<*ik*)<*ŭ*)

| *first cycle* | | *second cycle* | |
|---|---|---|---|
| a) *p'is* | by rule 1 | a) (*p'os'*<*ik*) | by rule 1 |
| b) *p'es* | by rule 2.1.2 | b) ((*p'os'*<*ik*)<∅) | by rule 2.3.1 |
| c) *p'os* | by rule 3 | | |

These examples of phonological derivations show that the application of the phonological rules does not disturb the applicational structure of the word, i.e. it does not disturb the operator-operand relation holding between the components of the word. In their form the phonological rules are productions, in Post's sense of the term, that transform abstract applicational phonological structures into concrete applicational phonological structures.

There are other problems that must now be taken up. For instance, it might seem strange that in an applicational phenotype grammar there is no level containing a syntactic representation of situations. When the construction of phenotype grammars was discussed nothing was said about syntax because each applicational phenotype grammar is an interpreted formal system, i.e. a formal system in which syntactic structures are postulated along with their interpretation. The construction of syntactico-semantic formal systems is allowed for in mathematical logic and it is to this sort of formal system that applicational phenotype grammars belong.[1] Strictly speaking, indeed, we should speak not about semantic levels of representation of a situation but about syntactico-semantic levels. However, since each formal semantic system must have its syntax the term 'semantic level of representation' will be used for short.

The morphological component of an applicational phenotype grammar includes a group of rules that determine the order of words in the sentence.[2] These rules apply after the semions have been mapped into words. I would like to discuss the schemas for these rules and to see what they can contribute to the comparative study of word-order.

First of all the notion of structural position must be introduced. It can be defined in this way. A phrase can be broken up into components, one of which is its main operator, the others being the operands of the operator. If a phrase X is split up into a main operator A and its operands $B^1, \ldots, B^n$, A and $B^1, \ldots, B^n$ are first degree components of X. The phrase X is a component of itself or a null degree component. The term 'main operator' is explained by the fact that there are also second degree operators. For example, if A is applied to $B^1$ the second degree operator $(AB^1)$ is obtained whose operands are $B^2, \ldots, B^n$ and if this new operator $(AB^1)$ is applied to $B^2$ another second degree operator is obtained whose operands are $B^3, \ldots, B^n$, and so on. If the first degree components of the phrase A are themselves phrases, then they in turn can be split up into a main operator and its operands. These components, first degree components of the first degree components of X, will be called second degree of X. In general, first degree components of the $n$th degree components of a phrase X will be called $(n+1)$ degree components of X. This means that each $n$th degree component of X (where $n \neq 0$) is either the main operator in some component of the $(n-1)$ degree or the $n$th operand of the main operator in the $(n-1)$ degree component. Where $(n-1)=0$ this $(n-1)$ degree component is either the main operator in the $n$th degree component or its $n$th operand.

The relation between the first degree components of a phrase and the phrase itself is one of immediate syntactic subordination. This relation holds between the main operator in a phrase and the phrase itself and also between the operands in the phrase and the phrase itself. From the fact that each $n$th degree component $(n \neq 0)$ of a complex phrase is either the main operator of an $(n-1)$ degree component or the $n$th operand of the latter, it follows that each $n$th

[1] Cf. H. B. Curry, *Foundations of Mathematical Logic*. New York, 1963.

[2] It was remarked earlier that morphology is being taken in the broadest sense and thus includes word-order in sentences.

degree component of X, where $n \neq 0$, is in a relation of immediate syntactic subordination with any $(n-1)$ degree component of X. Each *n*th degree component of X is either identical with X or is connected with it via a chain of relations of immediate syntactic subordination. The structural syntactic position of a component Y in a phrase X can now be said to be the chain of these relations that binds Y or, in the limiting case of Y coinciding with X, a relation of identity with X.

The notion of structural syntactic position having been defined, the concept of a code of structural syntactic positions will be introduced. This code is a set of numerical indices that are in a one-one correspondence with the structural syntactic positions: to each index there corresponds only one position and to each position there corresponds only one index.

The construction of indices will now be specified.

1. The index 0 corresponds to the structural syntactic position of the whole phrase, i.e. to a null degree position.

2. If the index *i* is put in correspondence with the structural syntactic position of component Y in phrase X, then the index 0 will correspond to the position of the main operator immediately subordinate to Y and the indices 1, 2, . . ., *n* will correspond to the positions of the first, second, . . ., *n*th operand of that operator.

The following example will illustrate how indices are correlated with positions.

(1) *Včera brat prines sestre učebnik anglijskogo jazyka* (yesterday–brother–brought–sister–grammar–of English–of language)

This whole sentence is assigned the index 00. The operand of *včera* (yesterday) is the component *brat prines sestre učebnik anglijskogo jazyka*, which must be assigned 01 as its index. The main operator immediately subordinate to the component *brat prines sestre učebnik anglijskogo jazyka* is *prines* (brought), which must have the index 010. The first operand of this operator is *sestre* (to sister), which will have the index 011, the second operand is *učebnik anglijskogo jazyka*, which will have 012 as its index, and the third operand is *brat*, which has the index 013. The main operator immediately subordinate to the component *učebnik anglijskogo jazyka* is *anglijskogo jazyka*. Its index is 0120 and the index of its operand, *učebnik*, is 0121. The main operator of the component *anglijskogo jazyka* is *anglijskogo*, to which is assigned the index 01200, and its operand is *jazyka*, which has the index 01201.

The assigning of indices to components can be represented in the form of a derivation. For example, the derivation in 2 illustrates the assigning of indices to the components of 1:

(2) 1. *Včera brat prines sestre učebnik anglijskogo jazyka*
0

2. *Včera* | *brat prines sestre učebnik anglijskogo jazyka*
00 | 01

| 3. *Včera* | *brat* | *prines* | *sestre* | *učebnik anglijskogo jazyka* | |
|---|---|---|---|---|---|
| 00 | 013 | 010 | 011 | 012 | |
| 4. *Včera* | *brat* | *prines* | *sestre* | *učebnik* | *anglijskogo jazyka* |
| 00 | 013 | 010 | 011 | 0120 | 0121 |

| 5. *Včera* | *brat* | *prines* | *sestre* | *učebnik* | *anglijskogo* | *jazyka* |
|---|---|---|---|---|---|---|
| 00 | 013 | 010 | 011 | 0120 | 01210 | 01211 |

Going by the different number of ciphers in the indices we can distinguish different levels in the division of the sentence into its components. Components of a phrase X with single-cipher indices belong to the null level of division, components with two-cipher indices to the first level, components with three-cipher indices to the second level, and components with $n$-cipher indices to the $(n-1)$ level.

Which structural positions the components of a phrase have does not depend on the linear order of the words, as the components, with their indices, can be arranged in any linear order or even arranged in a plane or in space without the structural positions of the words being in the least affected. This is explained by the fact that the structural positions of the components are invariant relative to the arrangement of the components in a line, in a plane or in space. However, since the words of a phrase are uttered in a definite temporal sequence one after the other, which is reflected in the linear order of words in the written representation of the spoken language, the concepts of abstract and concrete linear syntactic position will have to be brought in.

'Abstract syntactic position' is defined thus. Suppose there are components A and B of a phrase X that are directly subordinate to the same component C. Suppose also that A and B are arranged linearly. This means that either B follows A or A follows B. The positions of A, to the left or right of B, constitute A's abstract linear syntactic positions; and the positions of B, to the left or right of A, constitute B's abstract linear syntactic positions.

The definition of 'concrete syntactic position' is as follows. Suppose a phrase X contains the words A and B arranged in linear order, which means that either B follows A or A follows B. The positions of A, to the left or right of B, constitute A's concrete linear syntactic positions; and the positions of B, to the left or right of A, constitute B's concrete linear syntactic positions.

The definitions of abstract and concrete linear syntactic positions differ, as a comparison will show, in that the former takes into account the different levels of division into components whereas the latter does not, treating the words in the phrase simply as a linear sequence of objects.

Corresponding to the difference between abstract and concrete linear syntactic positions a distinction can also be drawn between two sorts of word-order rules: 1) rules that are based on the distinction between abstract syntactic positions and 2) rules that are based on the distinction between concrete linear syntactic positions. Rules of the first sort fall into two sub-types; those that specify the position of operands relative to their main operator and those that specify the position of the operands of the same main operator relative to each other.

In connexion with the two types of word order the concepts must be introduced of free and fixed order of operands relative to their main operator. If a set of operands can occur to the right or the left of their main operator their order will be said to be free relative to their main operator. If, however, the operands can occupy only one place relative to their main operator—either only to the right or only to the left—then their order will be said to be fixed relative to their main operator.

It is also necessary to distinguish the free and fixed order of operands relative to each other. Two operands of a main operator will be said to be freely ordered with respect to each other if one operand can occur either to the right or the left of the other one, but if one operand can occur either only to the right or only to the left they will be said to be in a fixed order relative to each other.

Let us consider phrases with a fixed order of operands relative to their main operator. The main operator will be called a syntactic prefix if all its operands are positioned to its right, but it will be called a syntactic suffix if all its operands are positioned to its left. If some of its operands occur to its right and others to its left the main operator will be described as a syntactic infix.

The genotype language is one in which the operands are in a fixed order relative to their main operators and to each other and in which the main operator functions as a syntactic prefix. This fixed order is preserved even in the semantic component of an applicational phenotype grammar and it is only the morphological component that maps the fixed order of main operator and its operands into an order appropriate to the language under consideration. Thus the fixed order of operands relative to their main operator and to each other that is adopted in the genotype language serves as a standard for the specification of word order in natural languages.

A word is needed concerning the word-order rules based on

concrete linear syntactic positions. These positions have to be specified when words that are directly subordinate to one component in a phrase are wedged in between words directly subordinate to another component. This phenomenon will be called wedging and two types can be distinguished: 1) wedging between a main operator and one of its operands; 2) wedging between the operands of a main operator. Depending on the order of the operands relative to their main operator the first type of wedging can occur either between the main operator and a preceding operand or between the main operator and a following operand. Unfortunately there is no space here to explore this topic, which will have to form the subject of a separate book.

To conclude this section the diagram below displays the correlations between the levels of representation of situations and the components of an applicational phenotype grammar.

| |  | |
|---|---|---|
| | 1 Deep-semantic level | I Semantic component (1–2) |
| II Morphological component (2–5) | 2 Surface-semantic level | |
| | 3 Deep-morphological level | |
| | 4 Surface-morphological level | |
| | 5 Deep-phonological level | III Phonological component (5–6) |
| | 6 Surface-phonological level | |

As shown by the diagram, the morphological component has three sub-components: one that maps the surface-semantic level into the deep-morphological level; a second that maps the deep-morphological level into the surface-morphological level; and a third that maps the surface-morphological level into the deep-phonological level.

## 2. A Fragment of an Applicational Grammar of Russian

The construction of applicational phenotype grammars has been discussed and it is now appropriate to examine such a grammar in operation. This will be done by means of a fragment of an applicational grammar of Russian.

The semantic component of this fragment generates synonymous sentences that constitute two phenotype semantic fields, the first being the field formed by sentences with predicates like *davat'* (give), the second being that formed by sentences with predicates like *govorit'* (speak), (i.e. with predicates of communication).

The first field is represented by sentences like:

(1) a) *Brat daet knigu sestre* (brother–gives–book–to sister)
b) *Kniga daetsja bratom sestre* (book–gives itself (is given)–by brother–to sister)
c) *Brat obespečivaet sestru knigoj* (brother–furnishes–sister–with book)

d) *Sestr obespečivaetsja bratom knigoj* (sister–is furnished–by brother–with book)

e) *Sestra polučaet knigu ot brata* (sister–receives–book–from–brother)

f) *Kniga polučaetsja sestroj ot brata* (book–is received–by sister–from–brother)

The second field is represented by sentences like:

(2) a) *Brat izlagaet fakty sestre* (brother–expounds–facts–to sister)

b) *Fakty izlagajutsja bratom sestre* (facts–are expounded–by brother–to sister)

c) *Brat uvedomljaet sestru o faktax* (brother–informs–sister–about–facts)

d) *Sestra uvedomljaetsja bratom o faktax* (sister–is informed–by brother–about–facts)

e) *Sestra uznaet fakty ot brata* (sister–finds out–facts–from–brother)

f) *Fakty uznajutsja sestroj ot brata* (facts–are found out–by sister–from–brother)

Semantic fields like those represented by the sentences in 1 and 2 consist of sentences with two types of three-place predicates. The first type includes predicates like *assignovat'* (allocate), *vručat'* (hand over), *davat'* (give), *darit'* (present), *dobyvat'* (obtain), *dostavat'* (deliver), *odalživat'* (lend), *platit'* (pay), *udeljat'* (devote). These are predicates like *davat'* (give) and belong to field 1. The second type includes predicates like *dokladyvat'* (report), *zajavljat'* (declare), *kričat'* (shout), *objavljat'* (declare), *pisat'* (write), *rasskazyvat'* (relate), *soobščat'* (communicate), *tverdit'* (repeat). These are predicates like *govorit'* (speak) and belong to field 2.

Before embarking on a formal account of the fragment of applicational grammar it is necessary to give an informal interpretation of the genotype processes by which are formed the genotype analogues of the two phenotype semantic fields.

The genotype semantic field corresponding to phenotype semantic field 1 is obtained by applying a series of semantic rules to the axiom:

(3) $R_{oa}(R_{lo}T_lT_o)T_a$

This genotype semantic field can be decomposed into four subfields, each subfield being associated with a particular set of semantic rules and a particular derivation. The derivations and their interpretation are given in 4, 6, 7 and 8:

(4)
1. $R_{oa}(R_{lo}T_lT_o)T_a$ (A)
2. $\mathbf{B}^2R_{oa}R_{lo}T_lT_oT_a$ ($\mathbf{B}^2$)
3. $R_{loa}T_lT_oT_a$ (fu2.2)
4. $\mathbf{C}_2R_{loa}T_lT_aT_o$ ($\mathbf{C}_2$)

The first line of the derivation is interpreted as a hypothetical sentence of Russian:

(5) **Brat kauziruet, čtoby kniga byla u sestry* (brother–causes–that–book–be–at–sister)

In the second line the combinator $\mathbf{B}^2$ brings together the predicates of the main and the embedded sentence, raising both arguments from the embedded sentence into the main one. In the third line the complex relator predicate $\mathbf{B}^2 R_{oa} R_{lo}$ is replaced by the three-place relator $R_{loa}$. This transformation models the reduction of a compound predicate like *kauziruet imet'* (causes–to have) to a simple predicate like *daet* (gives). The third line is interpreted as 1a. The fourth line shows the transfer of $T_o$ into theme position. The application of $\mathbf{C}_2$ models the transformation of a predicate like *daet* (gives) into one like *daetsja* (lit. 'gives itself', i.e. 'is given'), and the fourth line corresponds to 1b.

(6) 1. $R_{oa}(R_{lo} T_l T_o) T_a$ (A)
2. $\mathbf{B}^2 R_{oa} R_{lo} T_l T_o T_a$ ($\mathbf{B}^2$)
3. $R_{loa} T_l T_o T_a$ (fu2.2)
4. $\mathbf{C}_1 R_{loa} T_o T_l T_a$ ($\mathbf{C}_1$)

Derivations 4 and 6 are identical up to the third line. In the fourth line the permutator $\mathbf{C}_1$ permutes the first and second arguments. The complex relator predicate $\mathbf{C}_1 R_{lao}$ can be interpreted as a verb like *obespečivaet* (provides/furnishes) and the fourth line as a whole corresponds to 1c.

Since all the derivations associated with the first semantic field share the first three lines, only the final lines of the remaining derivations will be given:

(7) 3. $R_{loa} T_l T_o T_a$ (fu2.2)
4. $\mathbf{C}_{[2]} R_{loa} T_o T_a T_l$ ($\mathbf{C}_{[2]}$)

In the fourth line the predicate $\mathbf{C}_{[2]} R_{loa}$ is interpreted as a verb like *obespečivaetsja* (lit. 'provides itself', i.e. 'is provided') and the fourth line corresponds to 1d.

(8) 3. $R_{loa} T_l T_o T_a$ (fu2.2)
4. $\mathbf{C}^{[2]} R_{loa} T_a T_l T_o$ ($\mathbf{C}^{[2]}$)
5. $\mathbf{C}_2(\mathbf{C}^{[2]} R_{loa}) T_a T_o T_l$ ($\mathbf{C}_2$)

The permutator $\mathbf{C}^{[2]}$ moves $T_o$ into the position of theme and the predicate $\mathbf{C}^{[2]} R_{loa}$ is interpreted as a verb like *polučaetsja* (is received). The fourth line corresponds to 1f. In the fifth line the permutator $\mathbf{C}_2$ moves $T_l$ into theme position and the fifth line corresponds to 1e.

These genotype analogues of the first phenotype semantic field and the associated derivations can be set out in a tree-diagram, as in figure 29. The root of the tree is labelled with the number of the sentence that is taken as the axiom, the lines joining the nodes are labelled with the symbols for the appropriate semantic rules and opposite the nodes are the numbers of the phenotype sentences that have the nodes as their analogues.

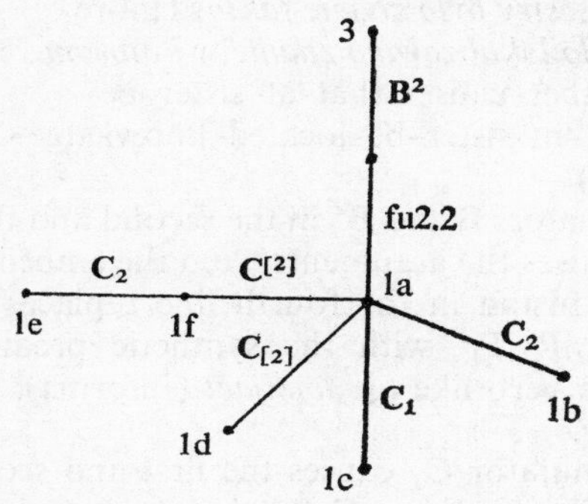


*Figure* 29

Note: the genotype semantic field in figure 29 also models the relation between other predicates that are the converse of each other syntactically. Such predicates are *gruzit'* (load), *zagružat'* (load), *naxodit'sja* (be located), *soderžat'* (contain), as in the following examples:

(9) a) *Oni gruzjat drova na baržu* (they–are loading–wood–on–barge)
b) *Drova gruzjatsja imi na baržu* (wood–is being loaded–by them–on–barge)
c) *Oni zagružajut baržu drovami* (they–are loading–barge–with wood)
d) *Barža zagružaetsja imi drovami* (barge–is being loaded–by them–with wood)
e) *Ovošči naxodjatsja v sumke* (vegetables–are located–in–bag)
f) *Sumka soderžit ovošči* (bag–contains–vegetables)

However, only the predicates like *davat'* (give) will be described in the fragment of the phenotype grammar.

The semantic field of verbs of communication consists of three subfields, each with its own derivation. All the derivations begin with the axiom:

(10) $R_{oa}(R_{ol}(R_{lo}T_l{}^1T_o)T_l)T_a$

The derivations are five or six steps in length. They are set out in 11, 13 and 14:

(11) 1. $R_{oa}(R_{ol}(R_{lo}T_l{}^1T_o)T_l)T_a$ (A)
2. $\mathbf{B}R_{oa}R_{ol}(R_{lo}T_l{}^1T_o)T_lT_a$ (**B**)
3. $\mathbf{B}^2(\mathbf{B}R_{oa}R_{ol})R_{lo}T_l{}^1T_oT_lT_a$ (**B**$^2$)

4. $P_{ola}T_oT_lT_a$ (fu1.15)
5. $C_1P_{ola}T_lT_oT_a$ ($C_1$)

Axiom 10 is interpreted as:

(12) **Brat kauziruet, čtoby u sestry bylo znanie faktov* (more exactly, *čtoby v sestre bylo lokalizovano znanie, v kotorom lokalizovany fakty*) (brother–causes–that–at–sister–be–knowledge–of facts (that–in–sister–be–located–knowledge–in–which–located–facts))

The application of the combinators **B** and $\mathbf{B}^2$ in the second and third lines of the derivation in 11 raises the arguments from the embedded sentences. The operation of fusion in the fourth line replaces the complex predicate $(\mathbf{B}^2R_{oa}R_{ol})R_{lo}T_l^{\ 1}$ with the synthetic predicate $P_{ola}$, which is interpreted as a verb like *uvedomljaet* (informs). The fourth line is interpreted as 2c.

In the fifth line the permutator $\mathbf{C}_1$ causes the first and second arguments to change roles. The predicate $\mathbf{C}_1P_{ola}$ is interpreted as a verb like *izlagaet* (explains) and the fifth line corresponds to 2a.

As the other derivations are identical with 11 up to the fourth line only their final lines will be given:

(13) 4. $P_{ola}T_oT_lT_a$ (fu1.15)
5. $\mathbf{C}_{[2]}P_{ola}T_lT_aT_o$ ($\mathbf{C}_{[2]}$)
6. $\mathbf{C}_1(\mathbf{C}_{[2]}P_{ola})T_aT_lT_o$ ($\mathbf{C}_1$)

In the fifth line of 13 the permutator $\mathbf{C}_{[2]}$ moves the first argument, $T_o$, into theme position. The predicate $\mathbf{C}_{[2]}P_{ola}$ can be interpreted as a verb like *izlagaetsja* (is explained) and the fifth line as a whole corresponds to 2b. In the sixth line the permutator $\mathbf{C}_1$ permutes the first and second arguments. The predicate $\mathbf{C}_1(\mathbf{C}_{[2]}P_{ola})$ can be interpreted as a verb like *uznaetsja* (is found out) and the sixth line corresponds to 2f.

The genotype analogues of the other two sentences in semantic field 2 are obtained via the derivation:

(14) 4. $P_{ola}T_oT_lT_a$ (fu1.15)
5. $\mathbf{C}_2P_{ola}T_oT_aT_l$ ($\mathbf{C}_2$)
6. $\mathbf{C}_1(\mathbf{C}_2P_{ola})T_aT_oT_l$ ($\mathbf{C}_1$)

In the fifth line the permutator $\mathbf{C}_2$ permutes the term in the locative and the term in the ablative, the former becoming the theme. The fifth line is interpreted as 2d, with the predicate corresponding to a verb like *uvedomljaetsja* (is informed). In the sixth line the permutator $\mathbf{C}_1$ permutes the term in the objective and the term in the ablative. The predicate corresponds to a verb like *uznaet* (finds out) and the whole line is interpreted as 2e.

The derivational tree for this semantic field is shown in figure 30. The tree is to be interpreted in the same way as the other derivational trees.

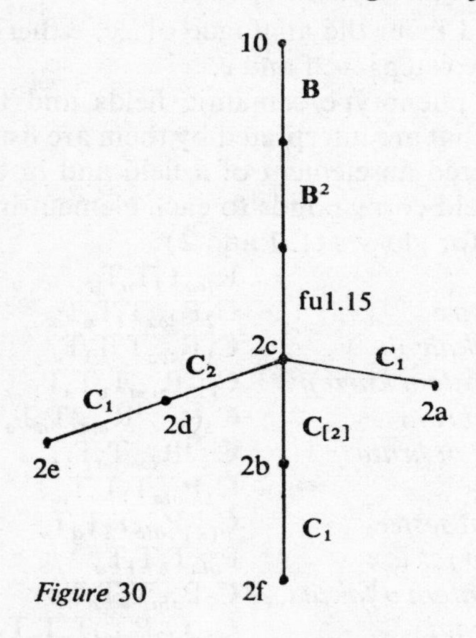


*Figure* 30

A comparison of the phenotype semantic fields 1 and 2 with their genotype analogues in figures 29 and 30 reveals a hierarchy of synonymous sentences that is not immediately obvious. In 1 and 2 the order in which the sentences are set out is determined by superficial, accidental features. Constructions without prepositions are given first and then constructions with prepositions. The latter constructions are organised with respect to whether they are active or passive, the active ones being ordered before the passive ones. This sort of organisation offers no clue as to their relative derivational simplicity or complexity, but the correlation of the phenotype semantic fields and their genotype analogues does reveal an underlying hierarchy and permits derivational relations to be established between the grammatical synonyms.

Thus, in both fields the simplest structure is the sentence of the primitive Russian language corresponding to the axiom, while the other sentences, corresponding to sentences of the expression Russian language, form a hierarchy of complexity, as is clear from figures 29 and 30. In the first phenotype field the simplest sentence is 1a, since its genotype analogue is obtained from the initial axiom in two steps. 1b, c, d and f are more complex, as their genotype analogues are obtained in three steps. In fact, they are obtained directly from the analogue of 1a. The most complex sentence is 1e, its analogue being obtained in the fourth step.

In the second field the simplest sentence is 2c, whose analogue is obtained on the third step. All the other sentences are more complex, since their analogues are derived from the analogue of 2c, either in one step—2a, b and d—or in two steps—2f and e.

The sentences in the two phenotype semantic fields and the sentences of the genotype fields that are interpreted by them are listed below. Each sentence is considered an element of a field and in the lists an element of a genotype field corresponds to each element in a phenotype field. Cf. 15 and 16 (for glosses cf. 1 and 2):

(15) a) *Brat daet knigu sestre* $R_{loa}T_lT_oT_a$
b) *Kniga daetsja bratom sestre* $\mathbf{C}_2R_{loa}T_lT_aT_o$
c) *Brat obespečivaet sestru knigoj* $\mathbf{C}_1R_{loa}T_oT_lT_a$
d) *Sestra obespečivaetsja bratom knigoj* $\mathbf{C}_{[2]}R_{loa}T_oT_aT_l$
e) *Sestra polučaet knigu ot brata* $\mathbf{C}_2(\mathbf{C}^{[2]}R_{loa})T_aT_oT_l$
f) *Kniga polučaetsja sestroj ot brata* $\mathbf{C}^{[2]}R_{loa}T_aT_lT_o$

(16) a) *Brat izlagaet fakty sestre* $\mathbf{C}_1P_{ola}T_lT_oT_a$
b) *Fakty izlagajutsja bratom sestre* $\mathbf{C}_{[2]}P_{ola}T_lT_aT_o$
c) *Brat uvedomljaet sestru o faktax* $P_{ola}T_oT_lT_a$
d) *Sestra uvedomljaetsja bratom o faktax* $\mathbf{C}_2P_{ola}T_oT_aT_l$
e) *Sestra uznaet fakty ot brata* $\mathbf{C}_1(\mathbf{C}_2P_{ola})T_aT_oT_l$
f) *Fakty uznaetsja sestroj ot brata* $\mathbf{C}_1(\mathbf{C}_{[2]}P_{ola})T_aT_lT_o$

It is generally the case that each element in a genotype semantic field can correspond to a sentence not just in one but in several classes of phenotype sentences. For example, $\mathbf{C}_1P_{ola}T_lT_oT_a$ corresponds to at least two classes of phenotype sentences. One class has predicates of the type *kto-to dokladyvaet/zajavljaet/kričit ... čto-to komu-to* (someone–reports/declares/shouts ... something–to someone) and the other class has predicates like *kto-ot zamalčivaet/obnaruživaet/osparivaet/priznaet/raskryvaet ... čto-to pered kem-to* (someone–keeps quiet about/reveals/disputes/admits/discloses ... something–before–someone). The phenotype predicates that are modelled by the genotype predicate $P_{ola}$ differ, as is obvious from the examples, with respect to which cases and prepositions are governed by the verb.

As another example consider the predicate $P_{ola}$ in the fourth line of the derivation of the second semantic field; the whole line is $P_{ola}T_oT_lT_a$. This predicate corresponds to at least five types of phenotype predicates, cf. the list in 17.

(17) a) *Kto-to dokladyvaet/donosit/zajavljaet/ob"javljaet/pišet ... komu-to o čem-to* (someone–reports/reports/declares/announces/writes ... to someone–about–something)
b) *Kto-to namekaet/otvečaet/ukazyvaet ... komu-to na čto-to* (someone–alludes/replies/shows ... to someone–to–something)
c) *Kto-to opoveščaet/sprašivaet/uvedomljaet ... kogo-to o*

*čem-to* (someone–notifies / asks / informs . . . someone–about –something)

d) *Kto-to izobličaet / ubeždaet / uverjaet . . . kogo-to v čem-to* (someone–exposes / convinces / assures . . . someone–in–something)

e) *Kto-to branit / pooščrjaet / rugaet / xvalit . . . kogo-to za čto-to* (someone–scolds / encourages / curses / praises . . . someone–for–something)

Not all genotype predicates correspond to more than one phenotype predicate. For instance, the predicate $\mathbf{C}_1 \mathrm{R}_{loa} \mathrm{T}_o \mathrm{T}_l \mathrm{T}_a$ in the fourth line of the derivation in 6 corresponds to only one type of phenotype predicate:

(18) *Kto-to žaluet / nagraždaet / nadeljaet / obespečivaet . . . kogo-to čem-to* (someone–grants / rewards / endows / provides . . . someone–with something)

The other elements in the field can generally be in a one-one or a one-many relation with phenotype objects. With respect to the above examples this type of correspondence can be represented in the schemas in 19–21. In these schemas P stands for predicate; subscripts are *D* for dative, *A* for accusative, *I* for instrumental (case), *N* for nominative, *P* for prepositional (case), and *pered, o, na, v* and *za* are the various prepositions that occur in 17:

(19) $\mathbf{C}_1 \mathrm{R}_{ola} \begin{cases} \mathrm{P}_{DAN} \\ \mathrm{P}_{peredIAN} \end{cases}$

(20) $\mathrm{P}_{ola} \begin{cases} \mathrm{P}_{oPDN} \\ \mathrm{P}_{naADN} \\ \mathrm{P}_{oPAN} \\ \mathrm{P}_{vPAN} \\ \mathrm{P}_{zaAAN} \end{cases}$

(21) $\mathbf{C}_1 \mathrm{R}_{loa} \quad \mathrm{P}_{IAN}$

In these schemas the phenotype predicates are denoted by P whether or not they correspond to genotype relator predicates or to genotype synthetic predicates.

The one-many correspondence established between elements of a genotype semantic field and phenotype structures leads to the conclusion that to one genotype semantic field there can correspond a whole class of phenotype semantic fields.

Phenotype fields containing sentences that are the converse of each other can not always be fully represented as containing six elements because for some predicates the impossibility of finding suitable combinations of lexical items limits the number of possible converse sentences.

For instance, *vozvraščat'* (return / give back) belongs to the same class as the predicates in *assignovat' / davat' / darit' / dobyvat'* . . . *čto-libo komu-libo* (allocate / give / present / obtain . . . something–to someone) but falls into a four-member semantic field, not a six-member one:

(22) a) *Kto-to vozvraščaet čto-to komu-to* $R_{loa}T_lT_oT_a$
(someone–returns–something–to someone)
b) *Čto-to vozvraščaetsja kem-to komu-to* $C_2R_{loa}T_lT_aT_o$
(something–is returned–by someone–to someone)
c) — $C_1R_{loa}T_oT_lT_a$
d) — $C_{[2]}R_{loa}T_oT_aT_l$
e) *Kto-to polučaet čto-to ot kogo-to* $C_2(C^{[2]}R_{loa})T_aT_oT_l$
(someone–receives–something–from–someone)
f) *Čto-to polučaetsja kem-to ot kogo-to* $C^{[2]}R_{loa}T_aT_lT_o$
(something–is received–by someone–from–someone)

The dashes indicate that there is no realisation of the corresponding genotype sentence. In this case the transformations yield sentences containing the predicates $C_1R_{loa}$ and $C_{[2]}R_{loa}$, for which there are no corresponding phenotype sentences containing forms of *vozvraščat'*. Interestingly, exactly the opposite holds for *odeljat'* (to present), which belongs to the same class as *žalovat'* (grant), *nagraždat'* (reward), *nadeljat'* (endow), *obespečivat'* (furnish), *odarivat'* (present) . . . *kogo-to čem-to* (someone–with something). For this verb it is only the genotype sentences 23c, d that *have* corresponding phenotype sentences:

(23) a) — $R_{loa}T_lT_oT_a$
b) — $C_2R_{loa}T_lT_aT_o$
c) *Kto-to odeljaet kogo-to čem-to* $C_1R_{loa}T_oT_lT_a$
(someone–presents–someone–with something)
d) *Kto-to odeljaetsja kem-to čem-to* $C_{[2]}R_{loa}T_oT_aT_l$
(someone–is presented–by someone–with something)
e) — $C_2(C^{[2]}R_{loa})T_aT_oT_l$
f) — $C^{[2]}R_{loa}T_aT_lT_o$

A comparison of the field in 15 and the fields in 22 and 23 shows that the latter two can be regarded as decompositions of the former. Phenotype predicates that do not have the full range of converse constructions will be asterisked. For example, *vozvraščat'* (return: $C_1R_{loa}T_oT_lT_a$, $C_{[2]}R_{loa}T_oT_aT_l$)*, *odeljat'* (present: $R_{loa}T_lT_oT_a$, $C_2R_{loa}T_lT_aT_o$, $C_2(C^{[2]}R_{loa})T_aT_oT_l$, $C^{[2]}R_{loa}T_aT_lT_o$)*.

It is time now to examine the rules governing the mapping of genotype objects into phenotype ones. As was shown in the preceding section, these rules should both parallel the processes that take place in the genotype language and enrich them with new phenotype processes. The parallel lies first and foremost in the use of rules of semantic derivation, the application of combinators, relators, the operation of fusion, etc., to phenotype objects, phenotype semions. The parallel is continued by the relation between genotype and phenotype axioms, which is analogous to that between genotype and phenotype derivations. Just as a genotype axiom is an axiom schema with respect to phenotype axioms, so a genotype derivation is a general schema with respect to phenotype derivations.

A further parallel is seen in the ubiquitous presence of the operator-operand relation between phenotype objects, right from the deep-semantic level to the phonological one. The relation even holds between newly generated phenotype objects, such as those that are generated when a surface-semantic representation is mapped into a morphological one, and when the latter is mapped into a phonological one. The application sign in such case will be $<$ or $>$. The formula $X > Y$ says that the operator X precedes the operand Y and the formula $Y < X$ says that the operand Y precedes the operator X.

Since a phenotype applicational grammar is a genotype applicational grammar enriched with special rules of phenotype derivation, a distinction must be drawn in the former between two major components, a genotype one consisting of rules of genotype semantic derivation and a phenotype one consisting of special phenotype rules. As the genotype semantic rules have already been discussed in chapter 3, I will concentrate here on the phenotype derivational rules. The interrelationship of the genotype derivational rules and the special phenotype ones will be obvious from the table of phenotype derivations at the end of the section. A systematic description of the special rules in a phenotype grammar is given below.

I. The Semantic Component

1. *Rules for the construction of deep situations*

These rules are divided into the following groups: assigning phenotype semantic features to elementary terms (R1); replacing relators with deep elementary phenotype semions (R2); replacing elementary terms with deep elementary phenotype semions (R3). The role and functioning of the rules will now be explained.

R1. *Assigning phenotype semantic features to elementary terms.* There are three categories of phenotype semantic features: a) features that are assigned to both predicates and terms; b) features that are assigned only to predicates; c) features that are assigned only to terms. Type a) includes gender and number; type b) includes tense, mood, aspect, voice and person; and type c) includes case, animacy, abstractness, countability and a few others.

The fragment of phenotype grammar deals with only some of these features. With respect to predicates only number and voice will be treated, the features of mood, aspect, tense and person being ignored (all examples will be present tense, third person singular, declarative mood, imperfective aspect forms). With respect to terms only case, number, gender and animacy will be taken into account. Features will be expressed in the form of indices below and to the right of predicates and terms. Phenotype cases will be denoted by capital letters: *N* (nominative), *P* (prepositional), *A* (accusative), *D* (dative), *I* (instrumental) and *G* (genitive). The features of voice will be denoted by *act* (active) and *pas* (passive), and number by *sg* (singular) and *pl* (plural). The letters *m* (masculine), *f* (feminine) and *n* (neuter) denote gender features, animacy being denoted by *an* (animate) and *inan* (inanimate). Gender will be denoted by the variables $G^1$, $G^2$, and $G^3$ and number will be denoted by the variables $N^1$, $N^2$, $N^3$. The different variables for the number and gender symbols ensure that for each term the value of the gender or number feature is independent of the value of the other feature. Elementary terms with identical genotype-case indices are assigned the same number variables no matter what sentence they are part of. Thus, in all instances, $T_a$ is rewritten as a term with the number index $N^3$, $T_l$ as a term with the number index $N^2$, and $T_o$ as a term with the number index $N^1$. Terms with identical variables must be linked so that in the phenotype semantic fields that are generated each word has the same number value. That is, only sentences like:

(24) *Brat darit knigi sestre* (brother–presents–books–to sister)
*Knigi darjatsja bratom sestre* (books–are presented–by brother–to sister)
*Brat odarjaet sestru knigami* (brother–presents–sister–with books)
*Sestra polučaet knigi ot brata* (sister–receives–books–from–brother)

etc., will be generated, and no sentences like:

(25) *Brat'ja darjat knigi sestre* (brothers–present–books–to sister)
*Sestry polučajut knigu ot brat'ev* (sisters–receive–book–from–brothers)

In our fragment of phenotype grammar the features of animacy and inanimacy will be assigned not as a variable but as a constant, since verbs of giving and verbs of communication are typically accompanied by an animate agent noun, an animate locative noun and an inanimate objective noun, as in 26:

(26) *Kto-to* (*a*) *daet čto-to* (*o*) *komu-to* (*l*) (someone (*a*)–gives–something (*o*)–to someone (*l*)).
*Kto-to* (*a*) *soobščaet komu-to* (*l*) *o čem-to* (*o*) (someone (*a*)–communicates–to someone (*l*)–about–something (*o*))

The nature of the semantic features and the objects to which they are assigned are determined by which component of the phenotype grammar is under consideration. For instance, on the level of deep situations phenotype semantic features are assigned only to elementary terms and the features are those of number, gender and animacy. Features are not assigned to two-place relator predicates. In fact, the phenotype features of number and voice are not assigned to predicates until after the operation of fusion and the derivation of many-place predicates. Phenotype-case features on nouns and features showing the phenotype-case government of predicates are assigned to semions during the transition from deep situations to surface ones.

The rules that assign phenotype semantic features to elementary terms are set out below.

R1.1.1. $T_l \rightarrow T_{l,N^1,G^1,an}$
R1.1.2. $T_l' \rightarrow T_{l,sg,n,inan}$
R1.2. $T_o \rightarrow T_{o,N^2,G^2,inan}$
R1.3. $T_a \rightarrow T_{a,N^3,G^3,an}$
R1.4. $N \rightarrow \{sg, pl\}$
R1.5. $G \rightarrow \{m, f, n\}$

Rules R1 are applied to the initial axiom. As was observed above, assigning elementary terms different number and gender variables ensures that these features are independent of each other when the R1 rules are applied to the whole genotype sentence.

N (number) is a cover symbol for $N^1$, $N^2$ and $N^3$, and in the same way G (gender) is a cover symbol for $G^1$, $G^2$, $G^3$.

If the R1 rules are applied to the axiom in (3), a whole class of sentences is obtained to which can be assigned a different set of phenotype semantic features, e.g.

(27) a) $R_{oa}(R_{lo}T_{l,pl,m,an}\ T_{o,pl,f,inan})T_{a,sg,f,an}$
b) $R_{oa}(R_{lo}T_{l,sg,f,an}\ T_{o,sg,m,inan})T_{a,sg,m,an}$
c) $R_{oa}(R_{lo}T_{l,sg,m,an}\ T_{o,sg,n,inan})T_{a,pl,m,an}$ and so on.

Rule R1.1.2 needs to be explained. This rule differs from the others in that the elementary term $T_l'$ is rewritten as a semion with constants and not variables as its phenotype semantic features. The reason for this is that $T_l'$, being in the most deeply embedded sentence in axiom 10 and being interpreted as the clearly defined class of words that includes *znanie* (knowledge), *poniženie* (reduction) and *predstavlenie* (representation), is assigned the features of singular number, neuter gender and inanimacy. If abstractness were included in the system of features it would also have to be assigned to $T_l'$. After the elementary terms have been assigned phenotype semantic features, the elementary relators and elementary terms can be replaced with deep elementary phenotype semions.

R2. *Replacing relators with deep elementary phenotype semions.* Deep elementary phenotype semions are meaning atoms. They are denoted either by the dictionary forms of words or by special symbols. It must be stressed that the dictionary forms of words have nothing to do with the usual concept of a word but are merely conventional labels for meaning atoms. The analysis of a situation into meaning atoms has nothing to do with the analysis of a sentence into words and the analysis of the words into morphs.

Deep elementary phenotype semions keep the phenotype semantic features that have been assigned to the corresponding genotype semions and they also keep the genotype-case index.

Since relator predicates are not assigned phenotype semantic features, the corresponding elementary phenotype semions also appear without extra indices.

R2.1. $R_{oa} \rightarrow kauzirovat'_{oa}$ (cause)
R2.2. $R_{lo} \rightarrow byt'_{lo}$ (be)
R2.3. $R_{ol} \rightarrow imet'_{ol}$ (have)

R.3. *Replacing elementary terms with deep elementary phenotype semions.* A deep elementary phenotype semion, corresponding to an elementary term, is a meaning atom embodied in the dictionary form of a Russian noun but still with the genotype-case index and the features of number and gender assigned to it by the R1 rules. The metasymbol C will stand for any genotype case. The number variable, as before, is N.

R3.1. $T_{C,N,m,an} \rightarrow brat_{C,N,m,an}$ (brother); $mal'\check{c}ik_{C,N,m,an}$ (boy); $master_{C,N,m,an}$ (foreman); $student_{C,N,m,an}$; $u\check{c}enik_{C,N,m,an}$ (pupil); etc.
R3.2. $T_{C,N,m,inan} \rightarrow karanda\check{s}_{C,N,m,inan}$ (pencil); $stakan_{C,N,m,inan}$ (glass); $strax_{C,N,m,inan}$ (fear); $fakt_{C,N,m,inan}$ (fact); etc.
R3.3. $T_{C,N,f,an} \rightarrow devo\check{c}ka_{C,N,f,an}$ (girl); $laborantka_{C,N,f,an}$ (lab. assistant); $sestra_{C,N,f,an}$ (sister); $studentka_{C,N,f,an}$ (woman student); $podruga_{C,N,f,an}$ (woman friend); etc.
R3.6.2 $T_{l,sg,n,inan} \rightarrow znanie_{l,sg,n,inan}$ (knowledge); $ponimanie_{l,sg,n,inan}$ (understanding); $predstavlenie_{l,sg,n,inan}$ (representation); etc.

The application of rules R2 and R3 yields the set of deep phenotype situations that are known as phenotype axioms:

(28) a) $Kauzirovat'_{oa}$ ($byt'_{lo}$ $student_{l,pl,m,an}$; $kniga_{o,pl,f,inan}$) $laborantka_{a,sg,f,an}$ (cause–be–student–book–lab. assistant)
b) $kauzirovat'_{oa}$ ($byt'_{lo}$ $studentka_{l,sg,f,an}$ $stakan_{o,sg,m,inan}$) $brat_{a,sg,m,an}$ (cause–be–woman student–glass–brother)

c) *kauzirovat'*$_{oa}$ (*byt'*$_{lo}$ *devočka*$_{l,sg,f,an}$; *bljudce*$_{o,sg,n,inan}$) *mal'čik*$_{a,sg,m,an}$ (cause–be–girl–saucer–boy) etc.

2. *Rules for the transition from deep phenotype situations to surface phenotype situations*

These rules are divided into genotype semantic rules and phenotype rules proper. Most of the former will not be discussed, because, as mentioned above, the operation of these rules on the phenotype level is in principle no different from their operation on the genotype level. There are, however, two rules that must be discussed, as their application on the phenotype level has certain peculiarities.

Once deep phenotype situations have been obtained via rules R1, R2 and R3 the rules that map these situations into surface phenotype situations come into play. This is done by applying the genotype semantic rules to the phenotype axioms, the semantic rules being, as was mentioned earlier, identical in form and function both in genotype and phenotype grammar. With respect to the two semantic fields that have been under consideration the corresponding steps in the derivation were discussed on pp. 131 and 133. No more will be said about the rules (**B**$^2$) in the derivation in 6—p. 132—nor about rules (**B**) and (**B**$^2$) in the derivation in 11, since their applications are completely identical in the genotype and phenotype derivations. I will, however, discuss the next two rules, which have some peculiarities in a phenotype grammar.

R4. *Fusion of phenotype predicates and the derivation of surface semions from deep semions.* The R4 rules parallel the genotype fusion rules: (fu2.2)—$\mathbf{B}^2 R_{oa} R_{lo} \rightarrow R_{loa}$; (fu1.15)—$\mathbf{B}^2(\mathbf{B} R_{oa} R_{ol}) R_{lo} T_l \rightarrow R_{ola}$; cf. p. 83.

In a phenotype grammar these rules are of the form:

R4.1. **B**$^2$ *kauzirovat'*$_{oa}$ *byt'*$_{lo}$ → DAVAT'$_{loa}$ (cause–be → give)

R4.2. **B**$^2$ (**B** *kauzirovat'*$_{oa}$ *imet'*$_{ol}$) *byt'*$_{lo}$ *znanie*$_{l,sg,n,inan}$ → GOVORIT'$_{ola}$ (cause–have–knowledge → speak)

As with the fusion of genotype predicates (fu1.00) and (fu2.00), a many-place predicate is obtained along with case-government indices which are transferred to it from the arguments that are released when the functions are collapsed.

The semions DAVAT'$_{loa}$ and GOVORIT'$_{ola}$ are general labels for classes of phenotype predicates with phenotype cases whose order corresponds to the order of the genotype cases, namely *loa* and *ola*. For example, DAVAT'$_{loa}$ stands not only for *davat' čto komu* (give–something–to someone) but also for *vozraščat' čto komu* (return–something–to someone), *darit' čto komu* (present–something–to someone), *dostavat' čto komu* (obtain–something–for someone), *naznačat' čto komu* (assign–something–to someone), *ostavljat' čto komu* (leave–something–to someone), etc. And GOVORIT$'_{ola}$ stands not just for *govorit' čto komu* (say–something–to someone) but also for *dokladyvat' komu o čem* (report–to someone–about–something), *zajavljat' komu o čem* (declare–to someone–about something), *namekat' komu na čto* (hint–to someone–about–something), *ukazyvat' komu na čto* (point out–to someone–to–something), *opoveščat' kogo o čem* (inform–someone–about–something), *izobličat' kogo v čem* (expose–someone–in–something, i.e. show someone to be something), *sprašivat' kogo o čem* (ask–someone–about–something), *ubeždat' kogo v čem* (convince–someone–of–something), etc.

These predicates are called surface semions because they are derived from deep semion-predicates by various steps in a derivation. To distinguish these surface semions from wordforms they are printed in small capitals, e.g. DAVAT', GOVORIT'.

R5. *Fusion of permutators with predicates*. The R5 rules, like the R4 rules, parallel the genotype semantic rules. The essential function of the R5 rules is to change the order of the case indices on the derived predicates. An essential feature of the R5 rules is that when the fusion takes place of permutators with predicates the permutation of the arguments is reflected in the changed order of the symbols in the case indices on the derived predicates. This changed order reproduces the order in which the case-index symbols occur when the arguments with which they are associated have been permuted.

These rules are known as (fu3). A complete list is given below, because they were not discussed in the section on the genotype semantic rules on account of their auxiliary nature.

(fu3.1) $\mathbf{C}_2\mathrm{R}_{loa} \rightarrow \mathrm{R}_{lao}$
(fu3.2) $\mathbf{C}_1\mathrm{R}_{loa} \rightarrow \mathrm{R}_{ola}$
(fu3.3) $\mathbf{C}_{[2]}\mathrm{R}_{loa} \rightarrow \mathrm{R}_{oal}$
(fu3.4) $\mathbf{C}^{[2]}\mathrm{R}_{loa} \rightarrow \mathrm{R}_{alo}$
(fu3.5) $\mathbf{C}_2(\mathbf{C}^{[2]}\mathrm{R}_{loa}) \rightarrow \mathrm{R}_{aol}$
(fu3.6) $\mathbf{C}_1\mathrm{P}_{ola} \rightarrow \mathrm{P}_{loa}$
(fu3.7) $\mathbf{C}_{[2]}\mathrm{P}_{ola} \rightarrow \mathrm{P}_{lao}$
(fu3.8) $\mathbf{C}_2\mathrm{P}_{ola} \rightarrow \mathrm{P}_{oal}$
(fu3.9) $\mathbf{C}_1(\mathbf{C}_2\mathrm{P}_{ola}) \rightarrow \mathrm{P}_{aol}$
(fu3.10) $\mathbf{C}_1(\mathbf{C}_{[2]}\mathrm{P}_{ola}) \rightarrow \mathrm{P}_{alo}$

The rules for the fusion of permutators with surface semions obtained via the R4 rules are an exact parallel of fu3.1–fu3.10. Cf. R5.1–R5.10.

R5.1. $\mathbf{C}_2$ DAVAT$'_{loa} \rightarrow$ DAVAT$'_{lao}$
R5.2. $\mathbf{C}_1$ DAVAT$'_{loa} \rightarrow$ DAVAT$'_{ola}$
R5.3. $\mathbf{C}_{[2]}$ DAVAT$'_{loa} \rightarrow$ DAVAT$'_{oal}$

R5.4. $\mathbf{C}^{[2]}$ DAVAT$'_{loa}$→DAVAT$'_{alo}$
R5.5. $\mathbf{C}_2(\mathbf{C}^{[2]}$ DAVAT$'_{loa}$)→DAVAT$'_{aol}$
R5.6. $\mathbf{C}_1$ GOVORIT$'_{ola}$→GOVORIT$'_{loa}$
R5.7. $\mathbf{C}_{[2]}$ GOVORIT$'_{ola}$→GOVORIT$'_{lao}$
R5.8. $\mathbf{C}_2$ GOVORIT$'_{ola}$→GOVORIT$'_{oal}$
R5.9. $\mathbf{C}_1(\mathbf{C}_2$ GOVORIT$'_{ola}$)→GOVORIT$'_{aol}$
R5.10. $\mathbf{C}_1(\mathbf{C}_{[2]}$ GOVORIT$'_{ola}$)→GOVORIT$'_{alo}$

The surface semions are general labels for classes of verbs whose associated cases correspond to a particular set of genotype cases in a particular order attached to the genotype predicates that model the verbs. When permutators are fused with the surface semions new surface semions are formed which differ from the initial DAVAT$'_{loa}$ and GOVORIT$'_{ola}$ in the order of the symbols in the case indices.

The linguistic significance of the alternating genotype cases is to be found in the corresponding change in the phenotype cases associated with verbs when there is a change of voice or when a verb from one semantic class is replaced by a verb from another. For example, DAVAT$'_{lao}$ corresponds to predicates like *daetsja čto kem komu* (is given–something–by someone–to someone), *vozvraščaetsja čto kem komu* (is returned– . . .), *daritsja čto kem komu* (is presented– . . .), *dostaetsja čto kem komu* (is obtained– . . .), *naznačaetsja čto kem komu* (is assigned– . . .), *ostavljaetsja čto kem komu* (is left– . . .), etc.

The surface predicate DAVAT$'_{ola}$ corresponds to verbs like *nagradit' kogo čem* (reward–someone–with something), *nadeljat' kogo čem* (endow– . . .), *obespečivat' kogo čem* (provide– . . .), *odarjat' kogo čem* (present– . . .), *snabžat' kogo čem* (equip– . . .), etc.

The surface predicate GOVORIT$'_{oal}$ corresponds to verbs like *govoritsja kem komu o čem* (is said–by someone–to someone–about–something), *dokladyvaetsja kem komu o čem* (is reported– . . .), *zajavljaetsja kem komu o čem* (is declared– . . .), *namekaetsja kem komu na čto* (is hinted– . . .), *ukazyvaetsja kem komu na čto* (is pointed out–by someone–to someone–to–something), *opoveščaetsja kto kem o čem* (is informed–someone–by someone–about–something), *sprašivaetsja kto kem o čem* (is asked– . . .), *izobličaetsja kto kem v čem* (is exposed–someone–by someone–in something), *ubeždaetsja kto kem v čem* (is convinced– . . .), etc.

The surface predicate GOVORIT$'_{aol}$ corresponds to verbs like *razvedyvat' čto u kogo* (find out–something–at–someone), *skryvat' čto ot kogo* (hide–something–from–someone), *slyšat' čto ot kogo* (hear–something–from–someone), *trebovat' čto u kogo* (demand– . . .), *uznavat' čto u kogo* (find out– . . .).

The correspondence between the order of genotype cases and the order of phenotype cases and the correspondence between surface word forms will be investigated in more detail when rules R7 and R8 are analysed.

II. The Morphological Component

The morphological component is a group of rules that transfer situations from the surface-semantic level of representation to the phonological level of representation. The unilateral units—semions—that make up a situation are transformed into bilateral units—deep wordforms. The deep wordforms are transformed into surface word-forms and surface wordforms are transformed into phonological representations of surface wordforms. Thus, between the surface semantic and the phonological levels of representation of situations there are two intermediate levels: the deep morphological level and the surface morphological level.

The following groups of rules make up the morphological component: transforming surface semions into deep wordforms (R6); mapping genotype case relations into phenotype case relations, and assigning voice to the verb (R7); transforming deep wordforms with a general lexical meaning into deep wordforms with a concrete lexical meaning (R8); the order of deep wordforms (R9); transforming deep wordform-verbs into surface wordform-verbs (R10); transforming deep wordform-nouns into surface wordform-nouns (R11); transforming verb inflexions into their phonological representation (R12); transforming nominal inflexions into their phonological representation (R13); transforming prepositions into their phonological representation (R14); transforming verb roots into their phonological representation (R15); transforming noun roots into their phonological representation (R16).

R6. *Transforming surface semions into deep wordforms.* The application of the R5 rules concludes the work of the semantic component of the grammar which transfers situations from the level of deep-semantic representation to the level of surface-semantic representation or, to be more concise, which maps deep situations into surface situations. When the R6 rule is being discussed below the boundaries between wordforms will be marked by the symbol $\#$.

Surface situations, like deep situations, are semions that consist of combinations of elementary semions.

Rules R1–R5 dealt with unilateral units (semions), i.e. they related only to the content plane. The transition from semions to deep wordforms, however, marks a transition from unilateral units to bilateral ones, since a deep wordform is a word that has not yet been split up into morphemes and since it has a signifiant and a signifié. The signifié is a complex of lexical and grammatical meanings that are in direct correspondence with the signifiant, which is a diffuse element not yet divided into phonemes. Combinations of deep wordforms constitute a sentence. Between the elementary semions and the deep wordforms there is in principle no one-one correspondence, as one elementary semion can correspond either to one deep wordform or to several, and as one deep wordform can correspond to more than one elementary semion. However, in the fragment of phenotype grammar that is presented here there is a partial instance of a one-one correspondence between elementary semions and deep wordforms.

Below each deep wordform is its position index. The following metasymbols denote both deep and surface wordforms: Nn, nominal wordform; Vb, verbal wordform; Pr, preposition. T denotes classes of phenotype semion-terms, and V denotes classes of phenotype semion-predicates. (This use of these symbols with these interpretations must be clearly distinguished from the use of these symbols in the genotype language to denote the corresponding elementary semions.) R6 is of the form:

R6. $PT^1T^2T^3 \quad \underset{00}{\#\mathrm{Vb}}\underset{010}{\#\mathrm{Pr}}\underset{011}{\#\mathrm{Nn}^1}\underset{02}{\#\mathrm{Nn}^2}\underset{03}{\#\mathrm{Nn}^3}\#$

R7. *Mapping genotype case relations into phenotype case relations, and assigning voice to the verb.* Deep wordforms differ from surface semions in that the genotype cases—locative, objective, ablative—are replaced by the phenotype cases *N*, *A*, *G*, *P*, *D*, *I*. If the phenotype cases are accompanied by a preposition then the phenotype-case index contains information about the preposition, e.g. $\mathrm{Vb}_{oPDN}$ ($o$ = 'about'). This formula represents verbs like *soobščil komu o čem* (communicated–to someone–about–something), *doložil komu o čem* (reported– . . .). Another example is $\mathrm{Vb}_{otGAN}$, which represents verbs like *polučil čto ot kogo* (received–something–from–someone), *uznal čto ot kogo* (learned– . . .).

In addition to a case index a deep wordform-verb is provided with an index of voice and number. The number index ensures that the verb in a sentence agrees in number with the subject noun, and voice is a morphological feature that is determined by the case index.

When attached to deep wordforms that are nouns, prepositions function as operators.

The R7 rules are of the following form:

R7.1. $\mathrm{DAVAT'}_{loa}\ \mathrm{T}_{l,\mathrm{N}^1,\mathrm{G}^1,an}\ \mathrm{T}_{o,\mathrm{N}^2,\mathrm{G}^2,inan}\ \mathrm{T}_{a,\mathrm{N}^3,\mathrm{G}^3,an}$

$\mathrm{DAVAT'}_{DAN,\mathrm{N}^3,act}\#\mathrm{Nn}_{D,\mathrm{N}^1,\mathrm{G}^1,an}\#\mathrm{Nn}_{A,\mathrm{N}^2,\mathrm{G}^2,inan}\#\mathrm{Nn}_{N,\mathrm{N}^3,\mathrm{G}^3,an}$

R7.2. $\mathrm{DAVAT'}_{lao}\ \mathrm{T}_{l,\mathrm{N}^1,\mathrm{G}^1,an}\ \mathrm{T}_{a,\mathrm{N}^3,\mathrm{G}^3,an}\ \mathrm{T}_{o,\mathrm{N}^2,\mathrm{G}^2,inan}$

$\mathrm{DAVAT'}_{DIN,\mathrm{N}^2,pas}\#\mathrm{Nn}_{D,\mathrm{N}^1,\mathrm{G}^1,an}\#\mathrm{Nn}_{I,\mathrm{N}^3,\mathrm{G}^3,an}\#\mathrm{Nn}_{N,\mathrm{N}^2,\mathrm{G}^2,inan}$

R7.3. $\mathrm{DAVAT'}_{ola}\ \mathrm{T}_{o,\mathrm{N}^2,\mathrm{G}^2,inan}\ \mathrm{T}_{l,\mathrm{N}^1,\mathrm{G}^1,an}\ \mathrm{T}_{a,\mathrm{N}^3,\mathrm{G}^3,an}$

$\mathrm{DAVAT'}_{IAN,\mathrm{N}^3,pas}\#\mathrm{Nn}_{I,\mathrm{N}^2,\mathrm{G}^2,inan}\#\mathrm{Nn}_{A.\mathrm{N}^1\ \mathrm{G}^1\ an}\#\mathrm{Nn}_{N,\mathrm{N}^3,\mathrm{G}^3,an}$

R7.4. $\text{DAVAT}'_{oal}\ \text{T}_{o,\text{N}^2,\text{G}^2,inan}\ \text{T}_{a,\text{N}^3,\text{G}^3,an}\ \text{T}_{l,\text{N}^1,\text{G}^1,an}$
$\text{DAVAT}'_{IIN,\text{N}^1,pas}\#\text{Nn}_{I,\text{N}^2,\text{G}^2,inan}\#\text{Nn}_{I,\text{N}^1,\text{G}^1,an}\#\text{Nn}_{I,\text{N}^3,\text{G}^3,an}$

R7.5. $\text{DAVAT}'_{alo}\ \text{T}_{a,\text{N}^3,\text{G}^3,an}\ \text{T}_{l,\text{N}^1,\text{G}^1,an}\ \text{T}_{o,\text{N}^2,\text{G}^2,inan}$
$\text{DAVAT}'_{otGIN,\text{N}^2,act}\#ot\#\text{Nn}_{G,\text{N}^3,\text{G}^3,an}\#\text{Nn}_{I,\text{N}^1,\text{G}^1,an}$
$\#\text{Nn}_{N,\text{N}^2,\text{G}^2,inan}$

R7.6. $\text{DAVAT}'_{aol}\ \text{T}_{a,\text{N}^3,\text{G}^3,an}\ \text{T}_{o,\text{N}^2,\text{G}^2,inan}\ \text{T}_{l,\text{N}^1,\text{G}^1,an}$
$\text{DAVAT}'_{otGAN,\text{N}^1,pas}\#ot\#\text{Nn}_{G,\text{N}^3,\text{G}^3,an}\#\text{Nn}_{A,\text{N}^2,\text{G}^2,inan}$
$\#\text{Nn}_{N,\text{N}^1,\text{G}^1,an}.$

Rules R7.1–R7.6 show that the parallel between the genotype and phenotype processes lies partly in the fact that the alternation of cases on the phenotype level corresponds to the permutation of case indices on the genotype level. The alternation of the phenotype cases depending on the position of the ablative, objective and locative in the case index on the predicate for the semantic field formed by verbs of giving is shown in table 2.

*Table* 2

| genotype case | place relative to predicate 1 | 2 | 3 |
|---|---|---|---|
| *a* | *G* | *I* | *N* |
| *o* | *I* | *A* | *N* |
| *l* | *D* | *I* | *N* |

The numbers 1, 2, 3 in the top line of table 2 represent the first, second and third place respectively in the sequence of noun-positions associated with a predicate. In the extreme left-hand column are the symbols of the case indices of the ablative, objective and locative on the corresponding terms (nouns). The cells in the table contain the labels of the phenotype cases on to which the genotype cases are mapped. The table shows that in the semantic field of verbs of giving in Russian the ablative typically corresponds to an alternation of the nominative, instrumental and genitive cases:

(29) a) Brat *daet knigu sestre* (brother (nominative)–gives–book–to sister)
b) *Kniga daetsja* bratom *sestre* (book–is given–by brother (instrumental)–to sister)
c) *Sestra polučaet knigu* ot brata (sister–receives–book–from–brother (genitive))

In the same field the objective typically corresponds to an alternation of the nominative, accusative and instrumental cases:

(30) a) Kniga *daetsja bratom sestre* (book (nominative)–is given–by brother–to sister)

b) *Brat daet* knigu *sestre* (brother–gives–book (accusative)–to sister)

c) *Brat obespečivaet sestru* knigoj (brother–provides–sister–with book (instrumental))

Finally, the locative typically corresponds to an alternation of the nominative, instrumental and dative cases:

(31) a) Sestra *polučaet knigu ot brata* (sister (nominative)–receives–book–from–brother)

b) Sestra *obespečivaetsja bratom knigoj* (sister (nominative)–is provided–by brother–with book)

c) *Kniga polučaetsja* sestroj *ot brata* (book–is received–by sister (instrumental)–from–brother)

d) *Brat daet knigu* sestre (brother–gives–book–to sister (dative))

Rules R7.1–R7.6 and table 2 also demonstrate how the realisation of one genotype case depends on the realisation of the others. For example, if the ablative is mapped into the nominative the objective can be mapped either into the accusative (29a) or the instrumental (30c), and the locative can be mapped either into the instrumental (31c) or the dative (31d). If the objective is mapped into the nominative case the ablative can be mapped either into the instrumental case (30a) or the genitive (29c), and the locative can be mapped either into the instrumental (31c) or into the dative (31d). If the locative is mapped into the nominative the ablative can be mapped either into the instrumental (31b) or the genitive (29c), and the objective can be mapped either into the accusative (29a) or the instrumental (31b).

I will now extend the list of rules for the mapping of genotype cases into phenotype ones and for the introduction of preposition-operators. Rules R7.7–R7.12 relate to the semantic field of verbs of communication:

R7.7. $\mathrm{GOVORIT}'_{ola}\mathrm{T}_{o,\mathrm{N}^2,\mathrm{G}^2,inan}\mathrm{T}_{l,\mathrm{N}^1,\mathrm{G}^1,an}\mathrm{T}_{a,\mathrm{N}^3,\mathrm{G}^3,an} \rightarrow$

$$\left\{\begin{array}{l}
\#\mathrm{GOVORIT}'_{oPDN,\mathrm{N}^2,act}\#o\#\mathrm{Nn}_{P,\mathrm{N}^2,\mathrm{G}^2,inan}\# \\
\qquad\qquad \mathrm{Nn}_{D,\mathrm{N}^1,\mathrm{G}^1,an}\#\mathrm{Nn}_{N,\mathrm{N}^3,\mathrm{G}^3,an}\# \\
\#\mathrm{GOVORIT}'_{naADN,\mathrm{N}^2,act}\#na\#\mathrm{Nn}_{A,\mathrm{N}^2,\mathrm{G}^2,inan}\# \\
\qquad\qquad \mathrm{Nn}_{D,\mathrm{N}^1,\mathrm{G}^1,an}\#\mathrm{Nn}_{N,\mathrm{N}^3,\mathrm{G}^3,an}\# \\
\#\mathrm{GOVORIT}'_{oPAN,\mathrm{N}^3,act}\#o\#\mathrm{Nn}_{P,\mathrm{N}^2,\mathrm{G}^2,inan}\# \\
\qquad\qquad \mathrm{Nn}_{A,\mathrm{N}^1,\mathrm{G}^1,an}\#\mathrm{Nn}_{N,\mathrm{N}^3,\mathrm{G}^3,an}\# \\
\#\mathrm{GOVORIT}'_{vPAN,\mathrm{N}^3,act}\#v\#\mathrm{Nn}_{P,\mathrm{N}^2,\mathrm{G}^2,inan}\# \\
\qquad\qquad \mathrm{Nn}_{A,\mathrm{N}^1,\mathrm{G}^1,an}\#\mathrm{Nn}_{N,\mathrm{N}^3,\mathrm{G}^3,an}\# \\
\#\mathrm{GOVORIT}'_{zaAAN,\mathrm{N}^3,act}\#za\#\mathrm{Nn}_{A,\mathrm{N}^2,\mathrm{G}^2,inan}\# \\
\qquad\qquad \mathrm{Nn}_{A,\mathrm{N}^1,\mathrm{G}^1,an}\#\mathrm{Nn}_{N,\mathrm{N}^3,\mathrm{G}^3,an}\#
\end{array}\right.$$

R7.8. $\text{GOVORIT}'_{loa}T_{l,N^1,G^1,an}T_{o,N^2,G^2,inan}T_{a,N^3,G^3,an}\rightarrow$

$$\left\{\begin{array}{l}\#\text{GOVORIT}'_{DAN,N^3,act}\#Nn_{D,N^3,G^3,an}\#Nn_{A,N^1,G^1,inan}\# \\ \qquad\qquad Nn_{N,N^2,G^2,an}\# \\ \#\text{GOVORIT}'_{peredIAN,N^3,act}\#\mathit{pered}\#Nn_{I,N^3,G^3,an}\# \\ \qquad\qquad Nn_{A,N^2,G^2,inan}\#Nn_{N,N^2,G^2,an}\end{array}\right.$$

R7.9. $\text{GOVORIT}'_{lao}T_{l,N^1,G^1,an}T_{a,N^3,G^3,an}T_{o,N^2,G^2,inan}\rightarrow$

$$\left\{\begin{array}{l}\#\text{GOVORIT}'_{DIN,N^2,act}\#Nn_{D,N^1,G^1,an}\#Nn_{I,N^3,G^3,an}\# \\ \qquad\qquad Nn_{N,N^2,G^2,inan}\# \\ \#\text{GOVORIT}'_{peredIIN,N^2,act}\#\mathit{pered}\#Nn_{I,N^1,G^1,an}\# \\ \qquad\qquad Nn_{I,N^3,G^3,an}\#Nn_{N,N^2,G^2,inan}\# \\ \#\text{GOVORIT}'_{oPID,N^1,pas}\#\mathit{o}\#Nn_{P,N^2,G^2,inan}\# \\ \qquad\qquad Nn_{I,N^3,G^3,an}\#Nn_{D,N^1,G^1,an}\# \\ \#\text{GOVORIT}'_{naAPD,N^1,pas}\#\mathit{na}\#Nn_{A,N^2,G^2,inan}\# \\ \qquad\qquad Nn_{P,N^3,G^3,an}\#Nn_{D,N^1,G^1,an}\#\end{array}\right.$$

R7.10. $\text{GOVORIT}'_{oal}T_{o,N^2,G^2,inan}T_{a,N^2,G^2,an}T_{l,N^1,G^1,an}\rightarrow$

$$\left\{\begin{array}{l}\#\text{GOVORIT}'_{oPIN,N^1,pas}\#\mathit{o}\#Nn_{P,N^2,G^2,inan}\# \\ \qquad\qquad Nn_{I,N^3,G^3,an}\#Nn_{N,N^1,G^1,an}\# \\ \#\text{GOVORIT}'_{vPIN,N^1,pas}\#\mathit{v}\#Nn_{P,N^2,G^2,inan}\# \\ \qquad\qquad Nn_{I,N^3,G^3,an}\#Nn_{N,N^1,G^1,an}\# \\ \#\text{GOVORIT}'_{zaAIN,N^1,pas}\#\mathit{za}\#Nn_{A,N^2,G^2,inan}\# \\ \qquad\qquad Nn_{I,N^3,G^3,an}\#Nn_{N,N^1,G^1,an}\#\end{array}\right.$$

R7.11. $\text{GOVORIT}'_{aol}T_{a,N^3,G^3,an}T_{o,N^2,G^2,inan}T_{l,N^1,G^1,an}\rightarrow$

$$\begin{array}{l}\#\text{GOVORIT}'_{otGAN,N^1,act}\#\mathit{ot}\#Nn_{G,N^3,G^3,an}\# \\ \qquad\qquad Nn_{A,N^2,G^2,inan}\#Nn_{N,N^1,G^1,an}\#\end{array}$$

R7.12. $\text{GOVORIT}'_{alo}T_{a,N^3,G^3,an}T_{l,N^1,G^1,inan}T_{o,N^2,G^2,inan}\rightarrow$

$$\begin{array}{l}\#\text{GOVORIT}'_{otGAN,N^2,pas}\#\mathit{ot}\#Nn_{G,N^3,G^3,an}\# \\ \qquad\qquad Nn_{I,N^1,G^1,inan}\#Nn_{N,N^2,G^2,inan}\end{array}$$

Rules R7.7–R7.12 display more complex alternations of phenotype cases than before, which is explained by the fact that the arrays of cases associated with verbs of communication are more varied than those associated with verbs of giving. For instance, compare the one case array with verbs of giving like *assignovat' / vozvraščat' / vručat' / davat' / darit' . . . čto-to komu-to* (allocate / return / hand / give / present–something–to someone) in R7.1 with the two case arrays that occur with verbs of communication: *vnušat' / vyskazyvat' / dokazyvat' / izlagat' / ob"jasnjat' . . . čto-to komu-to* (suggest / express / prove / expound / explain–something–to someone) and *obnaruživat' / osparivat' / raskryvat' . . . čto-to pered kem-to* (reveal / dispute / expose–something–to someone)—R7.8. In both sets of verbs the phenotype case array corresponds to the genotype sequence of cases: locative, objective, ablative.

Compare also the case arrays with verbs of giving like *nagraždat' / nadeljat' / obespečivat' / snabžat' / kogo-libo čem-libo* (reward / endow /

provide / equip–someone–with something) in R7.4 and the five case arrays with verbs of communication: *dokladyvat' / donosit' / zajavljat' / soobščat' . . . komu-libo o čem-libo* (report / inform / declare / communicate–to someone–about–something); *namekat' / otvečat' / ukazyvat' . . . komu-libo na čto-libo* (hint / reply / point out–to someone–to–something), *opoveščat' / sprašivat' / uvedomljat' . . . kogo-libo o čem-libo* (notify / ask / inform–someone–about–something); *izobličat' / ubeždat' / uverjat' . . . kogo-libo v čem-libo* (expose / convince / assure–someone–in–something); *branit' / poosčrjat' / rugat' / xvalit' kogo-libo za čto-libo* (scold / encourage / curse / praise – someone – for – something)—R7.7. The different case arrays both with the verbs of giving and the verbs of communication correspond to the same sequence of genotype cases: objective, locative, ablative.

With respect to the genotype predicate for the semantic field of verbs of communication, the alternation of phenotype cases as determined by the position of the ablative, objective and locative is displayed in table 3, which is set out in the same way as table 2.

*Table* 3

| genotype case | place relative to predicate 1 | 2 | 3 |
|---|---|---|---|
| *a* | *G* | *I* | *N* |
| *o* | *P, A* | *A* | *N* |
| *l* | *D, I* | *D, A, I* | *D, N* |

Rules R7.7–R7.12 and table 3 show that in the semantic field of verbs of communication the genotype ablative is realised as the genitive, the instrumental or the nominative depending on its position relative to the predicate:

(32) a) *Brat soobščaet sestre o faktax* (brother–informs–to sister–about–facts)

b) *Sestra soobščaetsja bratom o faktax* (sister–is informed–by brother–about–facts)

c) *Sestra uznaet fakty ot brata* (sister–learns–facts–from–brother)

If the genotype objective is the first argument it is realised as the prepositional or accusative case, if it is the second argument it is realised as the accusative case and if it is the third argument it is realised as the nominative:

(33) a) *Brat rasskazyvaet sestre o faktax* (brother–tells–to sister–about–facts (prepositional))

b) *Brat xvalit sestru za pravdu* (brother–praises–sister–for–truth (accusative))

c) *Brat izlagaet fakty sestre* (brother–expounds–facts (accusative)–to sister)

d) *Fakty izlagajutsja bratom sestre* (facts (nominative)–are expounded–by brother–to sister)

e) *Fakty uznajutsja sestroj ot brata* (facts (nominative)–are learned–by sister–from–brother)

The largest number of alternations in this field is correlated with the genotype locative. If it is the first argument it can be realised as the dative or the instrumental:

(34) a) *Brat dokazyvaet fakty sestre* (brother–proves–facts–to sister (dative))

b) *Brat raskryvaet fakty pered sestroj* (brother–reveals–facts–before–sister (instrumental))

c) *Fakty raskryvajutsja bratom pered sestroj* (facts–are–revealed–by brother–before–sister)

If the locative is the second argument it is realised as the dative, accusative or instrumental:

(35) a) *Brat zajavljaet sestre o faktax* (brother–declares–to sister (dative)–about–facts)

b) *Brat uprekaet sestru za lož'* (brother–reproaches–sister (accusative)–for–falsehood)

c) *Fakty uznajutsja sestroj ot brata* (facts–are learned–by sister (instrumental)–from–brother)

If the locative is the third argument it is realised either as the dative or the nominative:

(36) a) *Sestra uznaet fakty ot brata* (sister (nominative)–learns–facts–from–brother)

b) *Sestra uvedomljaetsja bratom o faktax* (sister–is informed–by brother–about–facts)

c) *Sestra poprekaetsja bratom za lož'* (sister–is reproached–by brother–for–falsehood)

d) *Sestre dokladyvaetsja bratom o faktax* (to sister (dative)–is reported–by brother–about–facts)

Rules R7.7–R7.12, like rules R7.1–R7.6, show how the realisation of one genotype case depends on the realisation of the others. Thus, if the ablative is realised as the genitive and is the first argument, then the objective is realised as the accusative (36a) if it is the second argument and as the nominative (33e) if it is the first argument. At the same time the locative is realised as the dative, the accusative or the instrumental if it is the second argument, cf. 33a, 33b, 35c; and as the dative or the nominative if it is the third argument, cf. 34a, 36a.

If the objective is the first argument and is realised as the prepositional or the accusative, the ablative, if it is the second argument, is realised as the instrumental, cf. 36b and 36c; and if it is the third argument the ablative is realised as the nominative, cf. 35a and 35b. At the same time the locative is realised as the dative or the accusative, cf. 33a and 33b, if it is the second argument, and if it is the third argument it is realised as the dative, cf. 36d, or the nominative, cf. 36a, b, c.

If the locative is the first argument and is realised as the dative or the instrumental, then the ablative, if it is the second argument, is realised as the instrumental, cf. 36d and 36c; and if it is the first argument it is realised as the nominative, as in 34a, b. At the same time the objective, if it is the second argument, is realised only as the accusative, as in 36a, but if it is the third argument it is realised only as the nominative, as in 33d and 34c.

R8. *Transforming deep wordforms with a general lexical meaning into deep wordforms with a concrete lexical meaning*. The application of the R7 rules yields deep wordform-verbs with phenotype case indices. Each such wordform is a general label for a set of wordform-verbs with identical case indices. The R8 rules, which are given below, show how these general units are realised in surface situations. The phenotype semantic features assigned to the surface semions by the R7 rules are preserved with the deep wordforms.

R8.1. DAVAT'$_{DAN,N,act}$ → *vozvraščat'*$_{DAN,N,act}$ (return);
*davat'*$_{DAN,N,act}$ (give);
*dostavat'*$_{DAN,N,act}$ (obtain)
*dostavljat'*$_{DAN,N,act}$ (deliver);
*prinosit'*$_{DAN,N,act}$ (bring); etc.

R8.2. DAVAT'$_{DIN,N,pas}$ → *vozraščat'*$_{DIN,N,pas}$;
*davat'*$_{DIN,N,pas}$;
*dostavat'*$_{DIN,N,pas}$;
*dostavljat'*$_{DIN,N,pas}$;
*prinosit'*$_{DIN,N,pas}$; etc.

R8.3. DAVAT'$_{IAN,N,act}$ → *žalovat'*$_{IAN,N,act}$ (grant);
*nagraždat'*$_{IAN,N,act}$ (reward);
*nadeljat'*$_{IAN,N,act}$ (endow);
*obespečivat'*$_{IAN,N,act}$ (provide);
*snabžat'*$_{IAN,N,act}$ (equip); etc.

R8.4. DAVAT'$_{IIN,N,pas}$ → *žalovat'*$_{IIN,N,pas}$;
*nagraždat'*$_{IIN,N,pas}$;
*nadeljat'*$_{IIN,N,pas}$;
*obespečivat'*$_{IIN,N,pas}$;
*snabžat'*$_{IIN,N,pas}$; etc.

R8.5. $\text{DAVAT}'_{otGAN,N,act}$ → *brat'*$_{otGAN,N,act}$ (take);
*dobyvat'*$_{otGAN,N,act}$ (obtain)
*dostavat'*$_{otGAN,N,act}$ (obtain);
*polučat'*$_{otGAN,N,act}$ (receive);
*prinimat'*$_{otGAN,N,act}$ (accept); etc.

R8.6. $\text{DAVAT}'_{otGIN,N,pas}$ → *brat'*$_{otGIN,N,pas}$;
*dobyvat'*$_{otGIN,N,pas}$;
*dostavat'*$_{otGIN,N,pas}$;
*polučat'*$_{otGIN,N,pas}$;
*prinimat'*$_{otGIN,N,pas}$; etc.

R8.7. $\text{GOVORIT}'_{DAN,N,act}$ → *vnušat'*$_{DAN,N,act}$ (suggest);
*vykladyvat'*$_{DAN,N,act}$ (reveal);
*vyskazyvat'*$_{DAN,N,act}$ (utter);
*govorit'*$_{DAN,N,act}$ (say);
*dokazyvat'*$_{DAN,N,act}$ (prove);
*dokladyvat'*$_{DAN,N,act}$ (report);

R8.8. $\text{GOVORIT}'_{DIN,N,pas}$ → *vnušat'*$_{DIN,N,pas}$;
*vykladyvat'*$_{DIN,N,pas}$;
*vyskazyvat'*$_{DIN,N,pas}$;
*govorit'*$_{DIN,N,pas}$;
*dokazyvat'*$_{DIN,N,pas}$;
*dokladyvat'*$_{DIN,N,pas}$; etc.

R8.9. $\text{GOVORIT}'_{peredIAN,N,act}$ → *zamalčivat'*$_{peredIAN,N,act}$ (be silent about);
*obnaruživat'*$_{peredIAN,N,act}$ (reveal);
*osparivat'*$_{peredIAN,N,act}$ (dispute);
*raskryvat'*$_{peredIAN,N,act}$ (disclose); etc.

R8.10. $\text{GOVORIT}'_{peredIIN,N,pas}$ → *zamalčivat'*$_{peredIIN,N,pas}$;
*obnaruživat'*$_{peredIIN,N,pas}$;
*osparivat'*$_{peredIIN,N,pas}$;
*raskryvat'*$_{peredIIN,N,pas}$; etc.

R8.11. $\text{GOVORIT}'_{oPDN,N,act}$ → *dokladyvat'*$_{oPDN,N,act}$ (report);
*donosit'*$_{oPDN,N,act}$ (inform);
*zajavljat'*$_{oPDN,N,act}$ (declare);
*kričat'*$_{oPDN,N,act}$ (shout);
*ob"javljat'*$_{oPDN,N,act}$ (announce);
*pisat'*$_{oPDN,N,act}$ (write); etc.

R8.12. $\text{GOVORIT}'_{oPID,N,pas}$ → *dokladyvat'*$_{oPID,N,pas}$;
*donosit'*$_{oPID,N,pas}$;
*zajavljat'*$_{oPID,N,pas}$;
*kričat'*$_{oPID,N,pas}$;
*ob"javljat'*$_{oPID,N,pas}$;
*pisat'*$_{oPID,N,pas}$; etc.

R8.13. GOVORIT$'_{naADN,N,act}$ → *namekat'*$_{naADN,N,act}$ (allude); *otvečat'*$_{naADN,N,act}$ (reply); *ukazyvat'*$_{naADN,N,act}$ (point out); etc.

R8.14. GOVORIT$'_{naAID,N,pas}$ → *namekat'*$_{naAID,N,pas}$; *otvečat'*$_{naAID,N,pas}$; *ukazyvat'*$_{naAID,N,pas}$; etc.

R8.15. GOVORIT$'_{oPAN,N,act}$ → *opoveščat'*$_{oPAN,N,act}$ (inform); *sprašivat'*$_{oPAN,N,act}$ (ask); *uvedomljat'*$_{oPAN,N,act}$ (notify); etc.

R8.16. GOVORIT$'_{oPIN,N,pas}$ → *opoveščat'*$_{oPIN,N,pas}$; *sprašivat'*$_{oPIN,N,pas}$; *uvedomljat'*$_{oPIN,N,pas}$; etc.

R8.17. GOVORIT$'_{vPAN,N,act}$ → *izobličat'*$_{vPAN,N,act}$ (show to be); *ubeždat'*$_{vPAN,N,act}$ (convince); *uverjat'*$_{vPAN,N,act}$ (assure); etc.

R8.18. GOVORIT$'_{vPIN,N,pas}$ → *izobličat'*$_{vPIN,N,pas}$; *ubeždat'*$_{vPIN,N,pas}$; *uverjat'*$_{vPIN,N,pas}$; etc.

R8.19. GOVORIT$'_{zaAAN,N,act}$ → *branit'*$_{zaAAN,N,act}$ (curse); *pooščrjat'*$_{zaAAN,N,act}$ (encourage); *rugat'*$_{zaAAN,N,act}$ (scold); *xvalit'*$_{zaAAN,N,act}$ (praise); etc.

R8.20. GOVORIT$'_{zaAIN,N,pas}$ → *branit'*$_{zaAIN,N,pas}$; *pooščrjat'*$_{zaAIN,N,pas}$; *rugat'*$_{zaAIN,N,pas}$; *xvalit'*$_{zaAIN,N,pas}$; etc.

R8.21. GOVORIT$'_{otGAN,N,act}$ → *razvedyvat'*$_{otGAN,N,act}$ (ascertain); *skryvat'*$_{otGAN,N,act}$ (hide); *slyšat'*$_{otGAN,N,act}$ (hear); *tait'*$_{otGAN,N,act}$ (conceal); *trebovat'*$_{otGAN,N,act}$ (demand); *uznavat'*$_{otGAN,N,act}$ (find out); etc.

R8.22. GOVORIT$'_{otGIN,N,pas}$ → *razvedyvat'*$_{otGIN,N,pas}$; *skryvat'*$_{otGIN,N,pas}$; *slyšat'*$_{otGIN,N,pas}$; *tait'*$_{otGIN,N,pas}$; *trebovat'*$_{otGIN,N,pas}$; *uznavat'*$_{otGIN,N,pas}$; etc.

R9. *The order of deep wordforms.* As the word order in Russian is free, almost any order of words is allowed on the surface level, even an order that is the same as that of the genotype semions. This means that if the words in a sentence are left in the order in which they occur after the application of the R6 rules the following steps in the derivation will yield completely grammatical sentences of Russian, as illustrated by 37, 38 and 39 on the one hand, and by 40, 41 and 42 on the other.

(37) $\#prinosit'_{DAN,sg,act}\#student_{D,pl,m,an}\#kniga_{A,pl,f,inan}\#laborantka_{N,sg,f,an}\#$
00 01 02 03

(bring–student–book–lab assistant)

(38) $\#polučat'_{otGAN,pl,pas}\#ot\#laborantka_{G,sg,f,an}\#student_{I,pl,m,an}\#kniga_{N,pl,f,inan}\#$
00 010 011 02 03

(receive–from–lab assistant–student–book)

(39) $\#soobščat'_{oPDN,sg,act}\#o\#zadanie_{P,sg,n,inan}\#soldat_{D,pl,m,an}\#komandir_{N,sg,m,an}$
00 010 011 02 03

(communicate–about–task–soldier–commander)

(40) *Prinosit studentam knigi laborantka* (brings–to students–books–lab assistant)

(41) *Polučeny ot laborantki studentami knigi* (received–from–lab assistant–by students–books)

(42) *Soobščaet o zadanii soldatam komandir* (communicates–about–task–to soldiers–commander)

37–40 are obtained by applying rules R1–R7. The order of word-forms is the same as the order of the semions which the sentences consisted of before the R6 rules were applied. 40–42 are Russian sentences that can be derived from 37–40 without changing the order of the lexemes, and they are grammatical because the non-neutral word order indicates that the speaker is focusing upon and emphasising a particular constituent.

If the order of the lexemes is changed in any possible way—and four elements yield twenty-four permutations—sentences are obtained of various degrees of correctness and emphatic colouring.

The following rule that orders deep wordforms ensures that the words are arranged in a neutral order, which can be called the normal one. The rule is:

R9.2. $\#Vb\#Pr\#N^1\#N^2\#N^3\# \rightarrow \#N^3\#Vb\#N^2\#Pr\#N^1\#$
00 010 011 02 03 → 03 00 02 010 011

The application of this rule to 37–49 yields the normal word order:

(43) *Laborantka prinosit knigi studentam* (lab assistant–brings–books–to students)

(44) *Knigi polučeny studentami ot laborantki* (books–received–by students–from–lab assistant)

R10. *Transforming deep wordform-verbs into surface wordform-verbs.* The essential function of the R10 rules is to transform into a sequence of morphemes the verb wordforms which are obtained by R8 and which have associated with them a set of semantic features—the cases they govern, number and voice. What is relevant to the expression plane of a morpheme is information about the conjugation of the verb (which in our fragment of grammar will be the first or the second) and the morphemic constituents. The division into morphemes is indicated by the application sign $<$ or $>$ (cf. p. 124). A morpheme that immediately follows the root is an operator and the root itself is an operand. The resulting sequence of two morphemes is itself an operand to which another morpheme can be applied as an operator and is enclosed in brackets. The metasymbol $Vb_{ca,N,vo}$ denotes any verb lexeme (*ca* is to be interpreted as 'case array', *vo* as voice and N as number). The morphemes are separated from each other by square brackets. The superscript index *i* with the verb-root morpheme indicates which conjugation the verb belongs to.

R10.1. $\#Vb_{ca,sg,act}\# \rightarrow \#[Vb_{ca}]^{i} < [sg, act]\#$

R10.2. $\#Vb_{ca,sg,pas}\# \rightarrow ([Vb_{ca}]^{i} < [sg]) < [pas]\#$

R10.3. $\#Vb_{ca,pl,act}\# \rightarrow [Vb_{ca}]^{i} < [pl, act]\#$

R10.4. $\#Vb_{ca,pl,pas}\# \rightarrow ([Vb_{ca}]^{i} < [pl]) < [pas]\#$

R10.5. $i \rightarrow \{1, 2\}$

Some examples of how the R10 rules apply are given below:

(45) $\#polu\check{c}at'_{otGIN,pl,pas}\# \rightarrow \#([polu\check{c}at']^{1} < [pl]) < [pas]\#$

(46) $\#prinosit'_{DAN,sg,act}\# \rightarrow \#[prinosit']^{2} < [sg, act]\#$

(47) $\#soob\check{s}\check{c}at'_{oPDN,sg,pas}\# \rightarrow \#([soob\check{s}\check{c}at']^{1} < [sg]) < [pas]$ etc.

R11. *Transforming deep wordform-nouns into surface wordform-nouns.* These rules apply to the deep wordform-nouns, which are obtained via the R6 rules and have associated with them a set of phenotype semantic features of case, number, gender and animacy, and transform them into a sequence of morphemes bound together by the operator-operand relation. The lexical morpheme has an index showing the declension of the noun. For simplicity the traditional classification into three declensions will be used, nouns like *put'* (road) and *vremja* (time) will be assigned to the third declension.

R11.1.1. $\#Nn_{N,sg,m,an}\# \rightarrow \#[Nn]^{j} < [N, sg, m, an]\#$

R11.1.2. $\#Nn_{N,sg,m,inan}\# \rightarrow \#[Nn]^{j} < [N, sg, m, inan]\#$

R11.1.3. $\#Nn_{N,sg,f,an}\# \rightarrow \#[Nn]^{j} < [N, sg, f, an]\#$

R11.1.4. $\#Nn_{N,sg,f,inan}\# \rightarrow \#[Nn]^{j} < [N, sg, f, inan]\#$

R11.1.5. $\#Nn_{N,sg,n,an}\# \rightarrow \#[Nn]^{j} < [N, sg, n, an]\#$

R11.1.6. $\#Nn_{N,sg,n,inan}\# \rightarrow \#[Nn]^{j} < [N, sg, n, inan]\#$

R11.1.7. $\#\mathrm{Nn}_{N,pl,m,an}\# \rightarrow \#[\mathrm{Nn}]^j < [N, pl, m, an]\#$
R11.1.8. $\#\mathrm{Nn}_{N,pl,m,inan}\# \rightarrow \#[\mathrm{Nn}]^j < [N, pl, m, inan]\#$
R11.1.9. $\#\mathrm{Nn}_{N,pl,f,an}\# \rightarrow \#[\mathrm{Nn}]^j < [N, pl, f, an]\#$
R11.1.10. $\#\mathrm{Nn}_{N,pl,f,inan}\# \rightarrow \#[\mathrm{Nn}]^j < [N, pl, f, inan]\#$
R11.1.11. $\#\mathrm{Nn}_{N,pl,n,an}\# \rightarrow \#[\mathrm{Nn}]^j < [N, pl, n, an]\#$
R11.1.12. $\#\mathrm{Nn}_{N,pl,n,inan}\# \rightarrow \#[\mathrm{Nn}]^j < [N, pl, n, inan]\#$
R11.2.1. $\#\mathrm{Nn}_{G,sg,m,an}\# \rightarrow \#[\mathrm{Nn}]^j < [G, sg, m, an]\#$
R11.2.2. $\#\mathrm{Nn}_{G,sg,m,inan}\# \rightarrow \#[\mathrm{Nn}]^j < [G, sg, m, inan]\#$
R11.2.3. $\#\mathrm{Nn}_{G,sg,f,an}\# \rightarrow \#[\mathrm{Nn}]^j < [G, sg, f, an]\#$
R11.2.4. $\#\mathrm{Nn}_{G,sg,f,inan}\# \rightarrow \#[\mathrm{Nn}]^j < [G, sg, f, inan]\#$
R11.2.5. $\#\mathrm{Nn}_{G,sg,n,an}\# \rightarrow \#[\mathrm{Nn}]^j < [G, sg, n, an]\#$
R11.2.6. $\#\mathrm{Nn}_{G,sg,n,inan}\# \rightarrow \#[\mathrm{Nn}]^j < [G, sg, n, inan]\#$
R11.2.7. $\#\mathrm{Nn}_{G,pl,m,an}\# \rightarrow \#[\mathrm{Nn}]^j < [G, pl, m, an]\#$
R11.2.8. $\#\mathrm{Nn}_{G,pl,m,inan}\# \rightarrow \#[\mathrm{Nn}]^j < [G, pl, m, inan]\#$
R11.2.9. $\#\mathrm{Nn}_{G,pl,f,an}\# \rightarrow \#[\mathrm{Nn}]^j < [G, pl, f, an]\#$
R11.2.10. $\#\mathrm{Nn}_{G,pl,f,inan}\# \rightarrow \#[\mathrm{Nn}]^j < [G, pl, f, inan]\#$
R11.2.11. $\#\mathrm{Nn}_{G,pl,n,an}\# \rightarrow \#[\mathrm{Nn}]^j < [G, pl, n, an]\#$
R11.2.12. $\#\mathrm{Nn}_{G,pl,n,inan}\# \rightarrow \#[\mathrm{Nn}]^j < [G, pl, n, inan]\#$
R11.3.1. $\#\mathrm{Nn}_{D,sg,m,an}\# \rightarrow \#[\mathrm{Nn}]^j < [D, sg, m, an]\#$
R11.3.2. $\#\mathrm{Nn}_{D,sg,m,inan}\# \rightarrow \#[\mathrm{Nn}]^j < [D, sg, m, inan]\#$
R11.3.3. $\#\mathrm{Nn}_{D,sg,f,an}\# \rightarrow \#[\mathrm{Nn}]^j < [D, sg, f, an]\#$
R11.3.4. $\#\mathrm{Nn}_{D,sg,f,inan}\# \rightarrow \#[\mathrm{Nn}]^j < [D, sg, f, inan]\#$
R11.3.5. $\#\mathrm{Nn}_{D,sg,n,an}\# \rightarrow \#[\mathrm{Nn}]^j < [D, sg, n, an]\#$
R11.3.6. $\#\mathrm{Nn}_{D,sg,n,inan}\# \rightarrow \#[\mathrm{Nn}]^j < [D, sg, n, inan]\#$
R11.3.7. $\#\mathrm{Nn}_{D,pl,m,an}\# \rightarrow \#[\mathrm{Nn}]^j < [D, pl, m, an]\#$
R11.3.8. $\#\mathrm{Nn}_{D,pl,m,inan}\# \rightarrow \#[\mathrm{Nn}]^j < [D, pl, m, inan]\#$
R11.3.9. $\#\mathrm{Nn}_{D,pl,f,an}\# \rightarrow \#[\mathrm{Nn}]^j < D, pl, f, an]\#$
R11.3.10. $\#\mathrm{Nn}_{D,pl,f,inan}\# \rightarrow \#[\mathrm{Nn}]^j < [D, pl, f, inan]\#$
R11.3.11. $\#\mathrm{Nn}_{D,pl,n,an}\# \rightarrow \#[\mathrm{Nn}]^j < [D, pl, n, an]\#$
R11.3.12. $\#\mathrm{Nn}_{D,pl,n,inan}\# \rightarrow \#[\mathrm{Nn}]^j < [D, pl, n, inan]\#$
R11.4.1. $\#\mathrm{Nn}_{A,sg,m,an}\# \rightarrow \#[\mathrm{Nn}]^j < [A, sg, m, an]\#$
R11.4.2. $\#\mathrm{Nn}_{A,sg,m,inan}\# \rightarrow \#[\mathrm{Nn}]^j < [A, sg, m, inan]\#$
R11.4.3. $\#\mathrm{Nn}_{A,sg,f,an}\# \rightarrow \#[\mathrm{Nn}]^j < [A, sg, f, an]\#$
R11.4.4. $\#\mathrm{Nn}_{A,sg,f,inan}\# \rightarrow \#[\mathrm{Nn}]^j < [A, sg, f, inan]\#$
R11.4.5. $\#\mathrm{Nn}_{A,sg,n,an}\# \rightarrow \#[\mathrm{Nn}]^j < [A, sg, n, an]\#$
R11.4.6. $\#\mathrm{Nn}_{A,sg,n,inan}\# \rightarrow \#[\mathrm{Nn}]^j < [A, sg, n, inan]\#$
R11.4.7. $\#\mathrm{Nn}_{A,pl,m,an}\# \rightarrow \#[\mathrm{Nn}]^j < [A, pl, m, an]\#$
R11.4.8. $\#\mathrm{Nn}_{A,pl,m,inan}\# \rightarrow \#[\mathrm{Nn}]^j < [A, pl, m, inan]\#$
R11.4.9. $\#\mathrm{Nn}_{A,pl,f,an}\# \rightarrow \#[\mathrm{Nn}]^j < [A, pl, f, an]\#$
R11.4.10. $\#\mathrm{Nn}_{A,pl,f,inan}\# \rightarrow \#[\mathrm{Nn}]^j < [A, pl, f, inan]\#$
R11.4.11. $\#\mathrm{Nn}_{A,pl,n,an}\# \rightarrow \#[\mathrm{Nn}]^j < [A, pl, n, an]\#$
R11.4.12. $\#\mathrm{Nn}_{A,pl,n,inan}\# \rightarrow \#[\mathrm{Nn}]^j < [A, pl, n, inan]\#$
R11.5.1. $\#\mathrm{Nn}_{I,sg,m,an}\# \rightarrow \#[\mathrm{Nn}]^j < [I, sg, m, an]\#$

R11.5.2. $\#\mathrm{Nn}_{I,sg,m,inan}\# \rightarrow \#[\mathrm{Nn}]^{j} < [I, sg, m, inan]\#$
R11.5.3. $\#\mathrm{Nn}_{I,sg,f,an}\# \rightarrow \#[\mathrm{Nn}]^{j} < [I, sg, f, an]\#$
R11.5.4. $\#\mathrm{Nn}_{I,sg,f,inan}\# \rightarrow \#[\mathrm{Nn}]^{j} < [I, sg, f, inan]\#$
R11.5.5. $\#\mathrm{Nn}_{I,sg,n,an}\# \rightarrow \#[\mathrm{Nn}]^{j} < [I, sg, n, an]\#$
R11.5.6. $\#\mathrm{Nn}_{I,sg,n,inan}\# \rightarrow \#[\mathrm{Nn}]^{j} < [I, sg, n, inan]\#$
R11.5.7. $\#\mathrm{Nn}_{I,pl,m,an}\# \rightarrow \#[\mathrm{Nn}]^{j} < [I, pl, m, an]\#$
R11.5.8. $\#\mathrm{Nn}_{I,pl,m,inan}\# \rightarrow \#[\mathrm{Nn}]^{j} < [I, pl, m, inan]\#$
R11.5.9. $\#\mathrm{Nn}_{I,pl,f,an}\# \rightarrow \#[\mathrm{Nn}]^{j} < [I, pl, f, an]\#$
R11.5.10. $\#\mathrm{Nn}_{I,pl,f,inan}\# \rightarrow \#[\mathrm{Nn}]^{j} < [I, pl, f, inan]\#$
R11.5.11. $\#\mathrm{Nn}_{I,pl,n,an}\# \rightarrow \#[\mathrm{Nn}]^{j} < [I, pl, n, an]\#$
R11.5.12. $\#\mathrm{Nn}_{I,pl,n,inan}\# \rightarrow \#[\mathrm{Nn}]^{j} < [I, pl, n, inan]\#$
R11.6.1. $\#\mathrm{Nn}_{P,sg,m,an}\# \rightarrow \#[\mathrm{Nn}]^{j} < [P, sg, m, an]\#$
R11.6.2. $\#\mathrm{Nn}_{P,sg,m,inan}\# \rightarrow \#[\mathrm{Nn}]^{j} < [P, sg, m, inan]\#$
R11.6.3. $\#\mathrm{Nn}_{P,sg,f,an}\# \rightarrow \#[\mathrm{Nn}]^{j} < [P, sg, f, an]\#$
R11.6.4. $\#\mathrm{Nn}_{P,sg,f,inan}\# \rightarrow \#[\mathrm{Nn}]^{j} < [P, sg, f, inan]\#$
R11.6.5. $\#\mathrm{Nn}_{P,sg,n,an}\# \rightarrow \#[\mathrm{Nn}]^{j} < [P, sg, n, an]\#$
R11.6.6. $\#\mathrm{Nn}_{P,sg,n,inan}\# \rightarrow \#[\mathrm{Nn}]^{j} < [P, sg, n, inan]\#$
R11.6.7. $\#\mathrm{Nn}_{P,pl,m,an}\# \rightarrow \#[\mathrm{Nn}]^{j} < [P, pl, m, an]\#$
R11.6.8. $\#\mathrm{Nn}_{P,pl,m,inan}\# \rightarrow \#[\mathrm{Nn}]^{j} < [P, pl, m, inan]\#$
R11.6.9. $\#\mathrm{Nn}_{P,pl,f,an}\# > \#[\mathrm{Nn}]^{j} < [P, pl, f, an]\#$
R11.6.10. $\#\mathrm{Nn}_{P,pl,f,inan}\# > \#[\mathrm{Nn}]^{j} < [P, pl, f, inan]\#$
R11.6.11. $\#\mathrm{Nn}_{P,pl,n,an}\# \rightarrow \#[\mathrm{Nn}]^{j} < [P, pl, n, an]\#$
R11.6.12. $\#\mathrm{Nn}_{P,pl,n,inan}\# \rightarrow \#[\mathrm{Nn}]^{j} < [P, pl, n, inan]\#$

48–50 illustrate the application of these rules:

(48) $\#kniga_{N,pl,f,inan}\# \rightarrow \#[kniga]^{1} < [N, pl, f, inan]\#$
(49) $\#student_{I,pl,m,an}\# \rightarrow \#[student]^{2} < [I, pl, m, an]\#$
(50) $\#laborantka_{G,sg,f,an}\# \rightarrow \#[laborantka]^{1} < [G, sg, f, an]\#$

The remaining rules transform wordforms into morphs, i.e. into their phonological representation.

R12. *Transforming verb inflections into their phonological representations.* These rules are context-sensitive and are written

(51) $X \rightarrow Y/A - B$

which is to be read: X is rewritten as Y if X has A immediately to the left of it and B immediately to the right of it. Either A or B may be null.

In the environment of a verb it is the conjugation-type that is crucial in the choice of a morph for a particular morpheme. As was observed earlier, an index that conveys this information is assigned to the verb root, and it is the verb root that constitutes the context that determines how a symbol is to be rewritten. Cf. R12.

R12.1. $[sg] \rightarrow et\#/\#[\mathrm{Vb}_{ca}]^{1}—$
R12.2. $[sg, act]\# \rightarrow et\#/\#[\mathrm{Vb}_{ca}]^{1}—$
R12.3. $[sg] \rightarrow it\#/\#[\mathrm{Vb}_{ca}]^{2}—$
R12.4. $[sg, act]\# \rightarrow it\#/\#[\mathrm{Vb}_{ca}]^{2}—$

R12.5. $[pl] \rightarrow ut\#/\#[Vb_{ca}]^1—$
R12.6. $[pl, act]\# \rightarrow ut\#/\#[Vb_{ca}]^1—$
R12.7. $[pl] \rightarrow at\#/\#[Vb_{ca}]^2—$
R12.8. $[pl, act]\# \rightarrow at\#/\#[Vb_{ca}]^2—$
R12.9. $[pas]\# \rightarrow sja\#$

In a fuller grammar of Russian the morphs *et*, *it*, *ut*, *at* would have to be represented as a combination of constituents with a different set of corresponding morphemes. The morphs *e*, *i*, *u*, and *a* would correspond to morphemes that included the semantic feature of present tense and the morph *t* would correspond to morphemes with the meaning of third person. However, these distinctions are not made here because we are abstracting away from tense and person (and also from aspect and mood). It is worthwhile repeating that all the sentences generated here are in the declarative mood and contain a present tense, imperfective aspect, third person verb form. Applications of the R12 rules are given below:

(52) $\#([polučat'_{otGIN}]^1 < [pl]) < [pas]\#$
$\rightarrow \#([polučat'_{otGIN}]^1 < ut) < sja\#$
(53) $\#[prinosit'_{DAN}]^2 < [sg, act]\# \rightarrow \#[prinosit'_{DAN}]^2 < it\#$
(54) $\#([soobščat'_{oPDN}]^1 < [sg]) < [pas]\#$
$\rightarrow \#([soobščat'_{oPDN}]^1 < ut) < sja\#$

R13. *Transforming nominal inflections into their phonological representations*. These rules are also context-sensitive. Since the choice of a morph for a particular morpheme is determined by the declension of the noun, it is the declension type that forms the context taken into account by the rules. The left hand side of the rule may contain one or several morphemes. In the latter case the various semantic features are separated by an oblique stroke. For example, the following four morphemes can be combined into one formula:

(55) $\left.\begin{array}{l} [N, pl, m, an] \\ [N, pl, f, an] \\ [N, pl, m, inan] \\ [N, pl, f, inan] \end{array}\right\} \rightarrow N, pl, m/f, an/inan$

A class of morphemes has a generalised representation if several morphemes are realised as phonologically identical morphs, as, for example, in 55—cf. also R13.1.7 in the list below. Setting up classes of morphs as is done for the R13 rules shortens the list of rules (cf. the complete list of morphemes in the R11 list).

R13.1.1. $[N, sg, m, an/inan]\# \rightarrow \emptyset\#/\#[Nn]^1$
R13.1.2. $[N, sg, m, an]\# \rightarrow a\#/\#[Nn]^1—$
R13.1.3. $[N, sg, f, an/inan]\# \rightarrow a\#/\#[Nn]^1—$
R13.1.4. $[N, sg, f, inan]\# \rightarrow \emptyset\#/\#[Nn]^3—$
R13.1.5. $[N, sg, n, an/inan]\# \rightarrow \emptyset\#/\#[Nn]^1—$

R13.1.6. [*N, pl, m/n, an/inan*]#→*a*#/#[Nn]$^1$—
R13.1.7. [*N, pl, m/f, an/inan*]#→*i*#/#{[Nn]$^1$, [Nn]$^2$}—
R13.1.8. [*N, pl, m/f, inan*]#→*i*#/#[Nn]$^3$—
R13.2.1. [*G, sg, m, an/inan*]#→*a*#/#[Nn]$^2$—
R13.2.2. [*G, sg, n, inan*]#→*a*#/#[Nn]$^2$—
R13.2.3. [*G, sg, f, an/inan*]#→*i*#/#[Nn]$^1$—
R13.2.4. [*G, sg, f, inan*]#→*i*#/#[Nn]$^3$—
R13.2.5. [*G, pl, m/n, an/inan*]#→*ej*#/#{[Nn]$^2$, [Nn]$^1$}—
R13.2.6. [*G, pl, m/f, inan*]#→*ej*#/#[Nn]$^3$—
R13.2.7. [*G, pl, m/f, an/inan*]#→∅#/#{[Nn]$^1$, [Nn]$^2$}—
R13.2.8. [*G, pl, n, inan*]#→∅#/#[Nn]$^2$—
R13.2.9. [*G, pl, m, an/inan*]#→*ov*#/#[Nn]$^2$—
R13.3.1. [*D, sg, m/n, an/inan*]#→*u*#/#[Nn]$^2$—
R13.3.2. [*D, sg, m/f, an/inan*]#→*i*#/#[Nn]$^1$—
R13.3.3. [*D, sg, m/n, inan*]#→*i*#/#[Nn]$^3$—
R13.3.4. [*D, pl, m/f/n, an/inan*]#→*am*#/#{[Nn]$^1$, [Nn]$^2$, [Nn]$^3$}—
R13.4.1. [*A, sg, m/f, inan*]#→∅#/#{[Nn]$^2$, [Nn]$^3$}—
R13.4.2. [*A, sg, m, an*]#→*a*#/#[Nn]$^2$—
R13.4.3. [*A, sg, f, an/inan*]#→*u*#/#[Nn]$^1$—
R13.4.4. [*A, sg, n/m, an/inan*]#→∅#/#[Nn]$^2$—
R13.4.5. [*A, pl, m/n, inan*]#→*a*#/#[Nn]$^2$—
R13.4.6. [*A, pl, m/f, inan*]#→*i*#/#[Nn]$^2$—
R13.4.7. [*A, pl, m, an*]#→*ej*#/#{[Nn]$^1$, [Nn]$^2$}—
R13.4.8. [*A, pl, f, an*]#→*ej*#/#[Nn]$^3$—
R13.4.9. [*A, pl, m, an*]#→*ov*#/#[Nn]$^2$—
R13.5.1. [*I, sg, m/n, an/inan*]#→*om*#/#[Nn]$^2$—
R13.5.2. [*I, sg, f, an/inan*]#→*ju*#/#[Nn]$^3$—
R13.5.3. [*I, sg, m/f, an/inan*]#→*oj*#/#[Nn]$^1$—
R13.5.4. [*I, pl, m/n, an/inan*]#→*ami*#/#{[Nn]$^1$, [Nn]$^2$, [Nn]$^3$}—
R13.6.1. [*P, sg, m/n, an/inan*]#→*e*#/#{[Nn]$^1$, [Nn]$^2$}—
R13.6.2. [*P, sg, m/f, an/inan*]#→*i*#/#[Nn]$^3$—
R13.6.3. [*P, pl, m/f/n, an/inan*]#→*ax*#/#{[Nn]$^1$, [Nn]$^2$, [Nn]$^3$}—

Some examples of the application of the rules are given below:

(56) #[*kniga*]$^1$ < [*N, pl, f, inan*]#→#[*kniga*]$^1$ < *i*#
(57) #[*student*]$^2$ < [*I, pl, m, an*]#→#[*student*]$^2$ < *ami*#
(58) #[*laborantka*]$^1$ < [*D, sg, f, an*]#→#[*laborantka*]$^1$ < *e*#
(59) #[*noč'*]$^3$ < [*A, sg, f, an*]#→#[*noč'*]$^3$ < ∅#

These examples show how grammatical morphemes associated with nouns are mapped into the appropriate morph-inflections.

R14. *Mapping prepositions into their phonological representations.* These rules are not of general application but have been specifically written for this fragment of grammar, which deals with only six prepositions:

R14.1. #[*o*]#→#*o*# (about)
R14.2. #[*v*]#→#*v*# (in)
R14.3. #[*na*]#→#*na*# (on)
R14.4. #[*za*]#→#*za*# (to behind)
R14.5. #[*ot*]#→#{*ot*, *u*}# (from, at)

The last rule requires an explanation. This rule is designed to handle the occurrence of either *ot* or *u* with the same set of nouns in the genitive case, e.g. *uznat' ot kogo* (find out–from–someone)/*uznat' u kogo* (find out–at–someone); *trebovat' ot kogo* (demand–from–someone)/*trebovat' u kogo* (demand–at–someone). In some cases only one of the two prepositions can occur, e.g. *tait' ot kogo* (conceal–from–someone), but *razvedat' u kogo* (ascertain–at–someone). Ignoring the complexities of the situation I will consider *ot* and *u* as free variants of the morpheme [*ot*].

When the phonological representation of grammatical morphemes and prepositions has been derived we can pass on to the rules that map lexical morphemes into their phonological representation. The order of the mapping rules is important—applying first to the grammatical, then to the lexical, morphemes—because the first set of rules is context-sensitive, the crucial part of the context being the conjugation- or declension-type of the root. Only when the grammatical morphemes have been mapped into morphs can the lexical morphemes, the roots, be mapped into morphs.

R15. *Mapping verb roots into their phonological representations.* These rules are context-free. There is a very great number of them because there are as many rules as there are lexemes in the lexicon. In fact, they are in principle infinite in number but only a limited number is needed for the present fragment of grammar.

R15.1. #[*vručat'*]$^1$→#*vručaj* (hand over)
R15.2. #[*davat'*]$^1$→#*daj* (give)
R15.3. #[*govorit'*]$^2$→#*govori* (speak/say)
R15.4. #[*dostavljat'*]$^1$#→*dostavljaj* (deliver)
R15.5. #[*izlagat'*]$^1$→#*izlagaj* (expound)
R15.6. #[*snabžat'*]$^1$→#*snabžaj* (equip)
R15.7. #[*polučat'*]$^1$→#*polučaj* (receive)
R15.8. #[*prinosit'*]$^2$→#*prinos* (bring)
R15.9. #[*rasskazyvat'*]$^1$→#*rasskazivaj* (relate)
R15.10. #[*uznavat'*]$^1$→#*uznaj* (find out)
. . . . . . . . . . . . . . . . . . . . . . . . . . . . . .

As a consequence of the decision to generate only present-tense verb forms only one variant of the verb root is given in each of the above examples, although in a full grammar both variants of the root would have to be provided and the R15 rules would have to be context-sensitive.

Examples illustrating the application of the R15 rules are set out below:

(60) #([polučat'$_{otGAN}$]$^{1}$<ut)<sja#→#(polučaj<ut)<sja#

(61) #[prinosit'$_{DAN}$]$^{2}$<it#→#prinos<it#

R16. *Mapping noun roots into their phonological representation.* Like the preceding group, these rules are context-free and there are as many rules as there nouns in the lexicon. Although in principle the rules are infinite in number, in this fragment only a few rules are needed.

R16.1. #[brat]$^{2}$→#brat
R16.2. #[devočka]$^{1}$→#devočka
R16.3. #[zadanie]$^{2}$→#zadani
R16.4. #[karandaš]$^{2}$→#karandaš
R16.5. #[kniga]$^{1}$→#knig
R16.6. #[komandir]$^{2}$→#komandir
R16.7. #[laborantka]$^{1}$→#laborantk
R16.8. #[sestra]$^{1}$→#sestr
R16.9. #[soldat]$^{2}$→#soldat
R16.10. #[student]$^{2}$#→student
R16.11. #[pero]$^{2}$→#per
R16.12. #[put']$^{3}$→#put'
R16.13. #[rešenie]$^{2}$→#rešeni
. . . . . . . . . . . . . . . . . . . . . . . .

The application of these rules is exemplified below

(62) #[student]$^{2}$<ami#→#student<ami# (by students: instrumental case)

(63) #ot#[laborantka]$^{1}$<i→#ot#laborantk<i# (from–lab assistant: genitive)

(64) #za#[ošibka]$^{1}$<u→#za#ošibk<u# (for–mistake: accusative)

These rules conclude the systematic description of the fragment of applicational grammar of Russian (for simplicity the phonological component has been left out). It must be borne in mind that many rules would have looked somewhat different if the fragment had been treated as part of a complete grammar, a unified formal system, but as it is it was necessary to simplify matters significantly and to describe the operation of the grammatical mechanism in the crudest terms. It must be said, however, that this fragment does afford an insight into the working of an applicational grammar and that this insight is in no way impaired by the simplifications.

The tables that follow exemplify the generation of semantic fields of synonymous sentences. The lines in the derivations are numbered, the number being in the leftmost column. On each line, in the rightmost column, is indicated the rule that has applied to yield the object on a particular line. The first line of each derivation contains an initial object, opposite which in the rightmost column is the symbol A, standing for 'initial axiom'.

One special feature of the rules in an applicational grammar is that groups of rules can be applied simultaneously to components of an object that is being generated. For example, the rules that derive grammatical morphs can apply simultaneously to the verb and to all three nouns in a sentence, as in line 11 of table 4. The rules that derive the phonological representation of lexical morphemes also apply simultaneously to verbs and nouns, as in line 12 of table 4.

The tables exemplify the generation of fragments from converse semantic fields with verbs of giving and verbs of communication.

*Table* 4

| | Derivation | Rule |
|---|---|---|
| 1. | $R_{oa}(R_{lo}T_lT_o)T_a$ | A |
| 2. | $R_{oa}(R_{lo}T_{l,pl,m,an}T_{o,pl,f,inan})T_{a,sg,f,an}$ | R1 |
| 3. | $kauzirovat'_{oa}\ (byt'_{lo}\ student_{l,pl,m,an}\ kniga_{o,pl,f,inan})\ laborantka_{a,pl,f,inan}$ | R2, R3 |
| 4. | $\mathbf{B}^2\ kauzirovat'_{oa}\ byt'_{lo}\ student_{l,pl,m,an}\ kniga_{o,pl,f,inan}\ laborantka_{a,sg,f,an}$ | $\mathbf{B}^2$ |
| 5. | $DAVAT'_{loa}\ student_{l,pl,m,an}\ kniga_{o,pl,f,inan}\ laborantka_{a,sg,f,an}$ | R4.1 |
| 6. | $DAVAT'_{DAN,sg,act}\ student_{D,pl,m,an}\ kniga_{A,pl,f,inan}\ laborantka_{N,sg,f,an}$ | R6,R7 |
| 7. | $prinosit'_{DAN,sg,act}\ student_{D,pl,m,an}\ kniga_{A,pl,f,inan}\ laborantka_{N,sg,f,an}$ | R8 |
| 8. | $prinosit'_{DAN,sg,act}\ student_{D,pl,m,an}\ kniga_{A,pl,f,inan}\ laborantka_{N,sg,f,an}$<br>00 01 02 03 | R9.1 |
| 9. | $\#laborantka_{N,sg,f,an}\#prinosit'_{DAN,sg,act}\#kniga_{A,pl,f,inan}\#student_{D,pl,m,an}\#$<br>03 00 02 01 | R9.2 |
| 10. | $\#[laborantka]^1<[N,sg,f,an]\#[prinosit'_{DAN}]^2<[sg,act]\#[kniga]^1<[A,pl,f,inan]\#[student]^2$<br>03 00 02 01<br>$<[D,pl,m,an]\#$ | R10, R11 |
| 11. | $\#[laborantka]^1<a\#[prinosit'_{DAN}]^2<it\#[kniga]^1<i\#[student]^2<am\#$<br>03 00 02 01 | R12, R13 |
| 12. | $\#laborantk<a\#prinos<it\#knig<i\#student<am\#$<br>03 00 02 01 | R15, R16 |

*Table 5*

| | Derivation | Rule |
|---|---|---|
| 1. | $R_{oa}(R_{lo}T_lT_o)T_a$ | A |
| 2. | $R_{oa}(R_{lo}T_{l,pl,m,an}T_{o,pl,f,inan})T_{a,sg,f,an}$ | R1 |
| 3. | $kauzirovat'_{oa}\ (byt'_{lo}\ student_{l,pl,m,an}\ kniga_{o,pl,f,inan})\ laborantka_{a,sg,f,an}$ | R2, R3 |
| 4. | $\mathbf{B}^2\ kauzirovat'_{oa}\ byt'_{lo}\ student_{l,pl,m,an}\ kniga_{o,pl,f,inan}\ laborantka_{a,sg,f,an}$ | $\mathbf{B}^2$ |
| 5. | $\mathrm{DAVAT}'_{loa}\ student_{l,pl,m,an}\ kniga_{o,pl,f,inan}\ laborantka_{a,sg,f,an}$ | R4.1 |
| 6. | $\mathbf{C}_1\ \mathrm{DAVAT}'_{loa}\ kniga_{o,pl,f,inan}\ student_{l,pl,m,an}\ laborantka_{a,sg,f,an}$ | $\mathbf{C}_1$ |
| 7. | $\mathrm{DAVAT}'_{ola}\ kniga_{o,pl,f,inan}\ student_{l,pl,m,an}\ laborantka_{a,sg,f,an}$ | R5 |
| 8. | $\mathrm{DAVAT}'_{IAN,pl,act}\ kniga_{I,pl,f,inan}\ student_{A,pl,m,an}\ laborantka_{N,sg,f,an}$ | R6, R7 |
| 9. | $snab\check{z}at'_{IAN,pl,act}\ kniga_{I,pl,f,inan}\ student_{A,pl,m,an}\ laborantka_{N,sg,f,an}$ | R8 |
| 10. | $\#\underset{00}{snab\check{z}at'_{IAN,pl,act}}\#\underset{01}{kniga_{I,pl,f,inan}}\#\underset{02}{student_{A,pl,m,an}}\#\underset{03}{laborantka_{N,sg,f,an}}\#$ | R9.1 |
| 11. | $\#\underset{03}{laborantka_{N,sg,f,an}}\#\underset{00}{snab\check{z}at'_{IAN,pl,act}}\#\underset{02}{student_{A,pl,m,an}}\#\underset{01}{kniga_{I,pl,f,inan}}\#$ | R9.2 |
| 12. | $\#\underset{03}{[laborantka]^1}<[N,sg,f,an]\#\underset{00}{[snab\check{z}at'_{IAN}]^1}<[pl,act]\#\underset{02}{[student]^2}<[A,pl,m,an]\#\underset{01}{[kniga]^1}$ $<[I,pl,f,inan]\#$ | R10, R11 |
| 13. | $\#\underset{03}{[laborantka]^1}<a\#\underset{00}{[snab\check{z}at'_{IAN}]^1}<et\#\underset{02}{[student]^2}<ov\#\underset{01}{[kniga]^1}<ami\#$ | R12, R13 |
| 14. | $\#laborantk<a\#snab\check{z}aj<et\#student<ov\#knig<ami\#$ | R15, R16 |

*Table* 6

| | Derivation | Rule |
|---|---|---|
| 1. | $R_{oa}(R_{lo}T_lT_o)T_a$ | A |
| 2. | $R_{oa}(R_{lo}T_{l,pl,m,an}T_{o,pl,f,inan})T_{a,sg,f,an}$ | R1 |
| 3. | $kauzirovat'_{oa}\ (byt'_{lo}\ student_{l,pl,m,an}\ kniga_{o,pl,f,inan})\ laborantka_{a,sg,f,an}$ | R2, R3 |
| 4. | $\mathbf{B}^2\ kauzirovat'_{oa}\ byt'_{lo}\ student_{l,pl,m,an}\ kniga_{o,pl,f,inan}\ laborantka_{a,sg,f,an}$ | $\mathbf{B}^2$ |
| 5. | $\text{DAVAT}'_{loa}\ student_{l,pl,m,an}\ kniga_{o,pl,f,inan}\ laborantka_{a,sg,f,an}$ | R4.1 |
| 6. | $\mathbf{C}^{[2]}\ \text{DAVAT}'_{loa}\ laborantka_{a,sg,f,an}\ student_{l,pl,m,an}\ kniga_{o,pl,f,inan}$ | $\mathbf{C}^{[2]}$ |
| 7. | $\text{DAVAT}'_{alo}\ laborantka_{a,sg,f,an}\ student_{l,pl,m,an}\ kniga_{o,pl,f,inan}$ | R5 |
| 8. | $\text{DAVAT}'_{otGIN,pl,pas}\ (ot\ laborantka_{G,sg,f,an})\ student_{I,pl,m,an}\ kniga_{N,pl,f,inan}$ | R6, R7 |
| 9. | $polučat'_{otGIN,pl,pas}\ (ot\ laborantka_{G,sg,f,an})\ student_{I,pl,m,an}\ kniga_{N,pl,f,inan}$ | R8 |
| 10. | $\#\underset{00}{polučat'_{otGIN,pl,pas}}\#\underset{010}{ot}\#\underset{011}{laborantka_{G,sg,f,an}}\#\underset{02}{student_{I,pl,m,an}}\#\underset{03}{kniga_{N,pl,f,inan}}\#$ | R9.1 |
| 11. | $\#\underset{03}{kniga_{N,pl,f,inan}}\#\underset{00}{polučat'_{otGIN,pl,pas}}\#\underset{02}{student_{I,pl,m,an}}\#\underset{010}{ot}\#\underset{011}{laborantka_{G,sg,f,an}}\#$ | R9.2 |
| 12. | $\#\underset{03}{[kniga]^1}<[N,pl,f,inan]\#(\underset{00}{[polučat'_{otGIN}]^1}<[pl])<[pas]\#\underset{02}{[student]^2}$ <br> $<[I,pl,m,an]\#\underset{010}{[ot]}\#\underset{011}{[laborantka]}<[G,sg,f,an]\#$ | R10, R11 |
| 13. | $\#\underset{03}{[kniga]^1}<i\#(\underset{00}{[polučat'_{otGIN}]^1}<ut)<sja\#\underset{02}{[student]^2}<ami\#\underset{010}{[ot]}\#\underset{011}{[laborantka]^1}<i\#$ | R12, R13 |
| 14. | $\#\underset{03}{knig}<i\#(\underset{00}{polučaj}<ut)<sja\#\underset{02}{student}<ami\#\underset{010}{u}\#\underset{011}{laborantk}<i\#$ | R14, R15, R16 |

*Table 7*

| | Derivation | Rule |
|---|---|---|
| 1. | $R_{oa}(R_{lo}T_lT_o)T_a$ | A |
| 2. | $R_{oa}(R_{lo}T_{l,pl,m,an}T_{o,pl,f,inan})T_{a,sg,f,an}$ | R1 |
| 3. | $kauzirovat'_{oa}\ (byt'_{lo}\ student_{l,pl,m,an}\ kniga_{o,pl,f,inan})\ laborantka_{a,sg,f,an}$ | R2, R3 |
| 4. | $\mathbf{B}^2\ kauzirovat'_{oa}\ byt'_{lo}\ student_{l,pl,m,an}\ kniga_{o,pl,f,inan}\ laborantka_{a,sg,f,an}$ | $\mathbf{B}^2$ |
| 5. | $\mathrm{DAVAT}'_{loa}\ student_{l,pl,m,an}\ kniga_{o,pl,f,inan}\ laborantka_{a,sg,f,an}$ | R4 |
| 6. | $\mathbf{C}_{[2]}\ \mathrm{DAVAT}'_{loa}\ laborantka_{a,sg,f,an}\ student_{l,pl,m,an}\ kniga_{o,pl,f,inan}$ | $\mathbf{C}_{[2]}$ |
| 7. | $\mathrm{DAVAT}'_{alo}\ laborantka_{a,sg,f,an}\ student_{l,pl,m,an}\ kniga_{o,pl,f,inan}$ | R5 |
| 8. | $\mathrm{DAVAT}'_{IDN,pl,pas}\ laborantka_{I,sg,f,an}\ student_{D,pl,m,an}\ kniga_{N,pl,f,inan}$ | R6, R7 |
| 9. | $prinosit'_{IDN,pl,pas}\ laborantka_{I,sg,f,an}\ student_{D,pl,m,an}\ kniga_{N,pl,f,inan}$ | R8 |
| 10. | $\#\underset{00}{prinosit'_{IDN,pl,pas}}\#\underset{01}{laborantka_{I,sg,f,an}}\#\underset{02}{student_{D,pl,m,an}}\#\underset{03}{kniga_{N,pl,f,inan}}\#$ | R9 |
| 11. | $\#\underset{03}{kniga_{N,pl,f,inan}}\#\underset{00}{prinosit'_{IDN,pl,pas}}\#\underset{02}{student_{D,pl,m,an}}\#\underset{01}{laborantka_{I,pl,f,an}}\#$ | R9 |
| 12. | $\#\underset{03}{[kniga]^1}<[N,pl,f,inan]\#(\underset{00}{[prinosit'_{IDN}]^2}<[pl])<[pas]\#\underset{02}{[student]^2}$ $<[D,pl,m,an]\#\underset{01}{[laborantka]^1}<[I,pl,f,an]\#$ | R10, R11 |
| 13. | $\#\underset{03}{[kniga]}<i\#(\underset{00}{[prinosit'_{IDN}]^2}<at)<sja\#\underset{02}{[student]^2}<am\#\underset{01}{[laborantka]^1}<oj\#$ | R12, R13 |
| 14. | $\#\underset{03}{knig}<i\#(\underset{00}{prinos}<at)<sja\#\underset{02}{student}<am\#\underset{01}{laborantk}<oj\#$ | R14, R15, R16 |

*Table* 8

| | Derivation | Rule |
|---|---|---|
| 1. | $R_{oa}(R_{ol}(R_{lo}T^{1}{}_{l}T_{o})T_{l})T_{a}$ | A |
| 2. | $R_{oa}(R_{ol}(R_{lo}T^{1}{}_{l,sg,n,inan}T_{o,sg,n,inan})T_{l,pl,m,an})T_{a,sg,m,an}$ | R1 |
| 3. | $kauzirovat'_{oa}\,(imet'_{ol}\,(byt'_{lo}\,ponimanie_{l,sg,n,inan}\,zadanie_{o,sg,n,inan})\,soldat_{l,pl,m,an})\,komandir_{a,sg,m,an}$ | R2, R3 |
| 4. | $\mathbf{B}\,kauzirovat'_{oa}\,imet'_{ol}\,(byt'_{lo}\,ponimanie_{l,sg,n,inan}\,zadanie_{o,sg,n,inan})\,soldat_{l,pl,m,an}\,komandir_{a,sg,m,an}$ | **B** |
| 5. | $\mathbf{B}^{2}(\mathbf{B}\,kauzirovat'_{oa}\,imet'_{ol})\,byt'_{lo}\,ponimanie_{l,sg,n,inan}\,zadanie_{o,sg,n,inan}\,soldat_{l,pl,m,an}\,komandir_{a,sg,m,an}$ | $\mathbf{B}^{2}$ |
| 6. | $\mathrm{GOVORIT}'_{ola}\,zadanie_{o,sg,n,inan}\,soldat_{l,pl,m,an}\,komandir_{a,sg,m,an}$ | R4.2 |
| 7. | $\mathrm{GOVORIT}'_{oPDN,sg,act}\,(o\;zadanie_{P,sg,n,inan})\,soldat_{D,pl,m,an}\,komandir_{N,sg,m,an}$ | R6, R7 |
| 8. | $soob\check{s}\check{c}at'_{oPDN,sg,act}\,(o\;zadanie_{P,sg,n,inan})\,soldat_{D,pl,m,an}\,komandir_{N,sg,m,an}$ | R8 |
| 9. | $\#\underset{00}{soob\check{s}\check{c}at'_{oPDN,sg,act}}\#\underset{010}{o}\#\underset{011}{zadanie_{P,sg,n,inan}}\#\underset{02}{soldat_{D,pl,m,an}}\#\underset{03}{komandir_{N,sg,m,an}}\#$ | R9.7 |
| 10. | $\#\underset{03}{komandir_{N,sg,m,an}}\#\underset{00}{soob\check{s}\check{c}at'_{oPDN,sg,act}}\#\underset{02}{soldat_{D,pl,m,an}}\#\underset{010}{o}\#\underset{011}{zadanie_{P,sg,n,inan}}\#$ | R9.2 |
| 11. | $\#\underset{03}{[komandir]^{2}}<[N,sg,m,an]\#\underset{00}{[soob\check{s}\check{c}at'_{oPDN}]^{1}}<[sg,act]\#\underset{02}{[soldat]^{2}}$ $<[D,pl,m,an]\#\underset{010}{o}\#\underset{011}{[zadanie]^{2}}<[P,sg,n,inan]\#$ | R10, R11 |
| 12. | $\#\underset{03}{[komandir]^{2}}<\emptyset\#\underset{00}{[soob\check{s}\check{c}at'_{oPDN}]}<et\#\underset{02}{[soldat]^{2}}<am\#\underset{010}{o}\#\underset{011}{[zadanie]^{2}}<i\#$ | R12, R13 |
| 13. | $\#\underset{03}{komandir}<\emptyset\#\underset{00}{soob\check{s}\check{c}aj}<et\#\underset{02}{soldat}<am\#\underset{010}{o}\#\underset{011}{zadani}<i\#$ | R14, R15, R16 |

*Table 9*

| | Derivation | Rule |
|---|---|---|
| 1. | $R_{oa}(R_{ol}(R_{lo}T_{l}T_{o})T^{1}{}_{l})T_{a}$ | A |
| 2. | $R_{oa}(R_{ol}(R_{lo}T_{l,sg,n,inan}T_{o,sg,n,inan})T^{1}{}_{l,pl,m,an})T_{a,sg,m,an}$ | R1 |
| 3. | $\mathit{kauzirovat'}_{oa}\ (\mathit{imet'}_{ol}\ (\mathit{byt'}_{lo}\ \mathit{ponimanie}_{l,sg,n,inan}\ \mathit{zadanie}_{o,sg,n,inan})\ \mathit{soldat}_{l,pl,m,an}\ \mathit{komandir}_{a,sg,m,an}$ | R2, R3 |
| 4. | $\mathbf{B}\ \mathit{kauzirovat'}_{oa}\ \mathit{imet'}_{ol}\ (\mathit{byt'}_{lo}\ \mathit{ponimanie}_{l,sg,n,inan}\ \mathit{zadanie}_{o,sg,n,inan})\ \mathit{soldat}_{l,pl,m,an}\ \mathit{komandir}_{a,sg,m,an}$ | **B** |
| 5. | $\mathbf{B}^{2}(\mathbf{B}\ \mathit{kauzirovat'}_{oa}\ \mathit{imet'}_{ol})\ \mathit{byt'}_{lo}\ \mathit{ponimanie}_{l,sg,n,inan}\ \mathit{zadanie}_{o,sg,n,inan}\ \mathit{soldat}_{l,pl,m,an}\ \mathit{komandir}_{a,sg,m,an}$ | $\mathbf{B}^2$ |
| 6. | $\mathrm{GOVORIT'}_{ola}\ \mathit{zadanie}_{o,sg,n,inan}\ \mathit{soldat}_{l,pl,m,an}\ \mathit{komandir}_{a,sg,m,an}$ | R4 |
| 7. | $\mathbf{C}_1\ \mathrm{GOVORIT'}_{ola}\ \mathit{soldat}_{l,pl,m,an}\ \mathit{zadanie}_{o,sg,n,inan}\ \mathit{komandir}_{a,sg,m,an}$ | $\mathbf{C}_1$ |
| 8. | $\mathrm{GOVORIT'}_{ola}\ \mathit{soldat}_{l,pl,m,an}\ \mathit{zadanie}_{o,sg,n,inan}\ \mathit{komandir}_{a,sg,m,an}$ | R5 |
| 9. | $\mathrm{GOVORIT'}_{DAN,sg,act}\ \mathit{soldat}_{D,pl,m,an}\ \mathit{zadanie}_{A,sg,n,inan}\ \mathit{komandir}_{N,sg,m,an}$ | R6, R7 |
| 10. | $\mathit{izlagat'}_{DAN,sg,act}\ \mathit{soldat}_{D,pl,m,an}\ \mathit{zadanie}_{A,sg,n,inan}\ \mathit{komandir}_{N,sg,m,an}$ | R8 |
| 11. | $\#\underset{00}{\mathit{izlagat'}_{DAN,sg,act}}\#\underset{01}{\mathit{soldat}_{D,pl,m,an}}\#\underset{02}{\mathit{zadanie}_{A,sg,n,inan}}\#\underset{03}{\mathit{komandir}_{N,sg,m,an}}\#$ | R9 |
| 12. | $\#\underset{03}{\mathit{komandir}_{N,sg,m,an}}\#\underset{00}{\mathit{izlagat'}_{DAN,sg,act}}\#\underset{02}{\mathit{zadanie}_{A,sg,n,inan}}\#\underset{01}{\mathit{soldat}_{D,pl,m,an}}\#$ | R9 |
| 13. | $\#\underset{03}{[\mathit{komandir}]^{2}}<[N,sg,m,an]\#\underset{00}{[\mathit{izlagat'}_{DAN}]^{1}}<[sg,act]\#\underset{02}{[\mathit{zadanie}]^{2}}<[A,sg,n,inan]\#\underset{01}{[\mathit{soldat}]^{2}}$ <br> $<[D,pl,m,an]\#$ | R10, R11 |
| 14. | $\#\underset{03}{[\mathit{komandir}]^{2}}<\emptyset\#\underset{00}{[\mathit{izlagat'}_{DAN}]^{1}}<\mathit{et}\#\underset{02}{[\mathit{zadanie}]^{2}}<\emptyset\#\underset{01}{[\mathit{soldat}]^{2}}<\mathit{am}\#$ | R12, R13 |
| 15. | $\#\underset{03}{\mathit{komandir}}<\emptyset\#\underset{00}{\mathit{izlagaj}}<\mathit{et}\#\underset{02}{\mathit{zadanie}}<\emptyset\#\underset{01}{\mathit{soldat}}<\mathit{am}\#$ | R14, R15, R16 |

*Table* 10

| | Derivation | Rule |
|---|---|---|
| 1. | $\mathrm{R}_{oa}(\mathrm{R}_{ol}(\mathrm{R}_{lo}\mathrm{T}^1{}_l\mathrm{T}_o)\mathrm{T}_l)\mathrm{T}_a$ | A |
| 2. | $\mathrm{R}_{oa}(\mathrm{R}_{ol}(\mathrm{R}_{lo}\mathrm{T}^1{}_{l,sg,n,inan}\mathrm{T}_{o,sg,n,inan})\mathrm{T}_{l,pl,m,an})\mathrm{T}_{a,sg,m,an}$ | R1 |
| 3. | $kauzirovat'_{oa}\ (imet'_{ol}\ (byt'_{lo}\ ponimanie_{l,sg,n,inan}\ zadanie_{o,sg,n,inan})\ soldat_{l,pl,m,an})\ komandir_{a,sg,m,an}$ | R2, R3 |
| 4. | $\mathbf{B}\ kauzirovat'_{oa}\ imet'_{ol}\ (byt'_{lo}\ ponimanie_{l,sg,n,inan}\ zadanie_{o,sg,n,inan})\ soldat_{l,pl,m,an}\ komandir_{a,sg,m,an}$ | **B** |
| 5. | $\mathbf{B}^2(\mathbf{B}\ kauzirovat'_{oa}\ imet'_{ol})\ byt'_{lo}\ ponimanie_{l,sg,n,inan}\ zadanie_{o,sg,n,inan}\ soldat_{l,pl,m,an}\ komandir_{a,sg,m,an}$ | $\mathbf{B}^2$ |
| 6. | $\mathrm{GOVORIT}'_{ola}\ zadanie_{o,sg,n,inan}\ soldat_{l,pl,m,an}\ komandir_{a,sg,m,an}$ | R4 |
| 7. | $\mathbf{C}_2\ \mathrm{GOVORIT}'_{ola}\ zadanie_{o,sg,n,inan}\ komandir_{a,sg,m,an}\ soldat_{l,pl,m,an}$ | $\mathbf{C}_2$ |
| 8. | $\mathbf{C}_1(\mathbf{C}_2\ \mathrm{GOVORIT}'_{ola})\ komandir_{a,sg,m,an}\ zadanie_{o,sg,n,inan}\ soldat_{l,pl,m,an}$ | $\mathbf{C}_1$ |
| 9. | $\mathrm{GOVORIT}'_{aol}\ komandir_{a,sg,m,an}\ zadanie_{o,sg,n,inan}\ soldat_{l,pl,m,an}$ | R5 |
| 10. | $\mathrm{GOVORIT}'_{otGAN,pl,act}\ [ot\ komandir_{G,sg,m,an}]\ zadanie_{A,sg,n,inan}\ soldat_{N,pl,m,an}$ | R7 |
| 11. | $uznavat'_{otGAN,pl,act}\ [ot\ komandir_{G,sg,m,an}]\ zadanie_{A,sg,n,inan}\ soldat_{N,pl,m,an}$ | R8 |
| 12. | $\#\underset{00}{uznavat'_{otGAN,pl,act}}\#\underset{010}{ot}\#\underset{011}{komandir_{G,sg,m,an}}\#\underset{02}{zadanie_{A,sg,n,inan}}\#\underset{03}{soldat_{N,pl,m,an}}\#$ | R9 |
| 13. | $\#\underset{03}{soldat_{N,pl,m,an}}\#\underset{00}{uznavat'_{otGAN,pl,act}}\#\underset{02}{zadanie_{A,sg,n,inan}}\#\underset{010}{ot}\#\underset{011}{komandir_{G,sg,m,an}}\#$ | R9 |
| 14. | $\#\underset{03}{[soldat]^2}<[N,pl,m,an]\#\underset{00}{[uznavat'_{otGAN}]^1}<ut\#\underset{02}{[zadanie]^2}<\emptyset\#\underset{010}{ot}\#\underset{011}{[komandir]^2}<a\#$ | R10, R11 |
| 15. | $\#\underset{03}{[soldat]^2}<i\#\underset{00}{[uznavat'_{otGAN}]^1}<ut\#\underset{02}{[zadanie]^2}<\emptyset\#\underset{010}{ot}\#\underset{011}{[komandir]^2}<\#$ | R12, R13 |
| 16. | $\#\underset{03}{soldat}<i\#\underset{00}{uznaj}<ut\#\underset{02}{zadanie}<\emptyset\#\underset{010}{ot}\#\underset{011}{komandir}<a\#$ | R14, R15, R16 |

*Table* 11

| | Derivation | Rule |
|---|---|---|
| 1. | $R_{oa}(R_{ol}(R_{lo}T^1{}_lT_o)T_l)T_a$ | A |
| 2. | $R_{oa}(R_{ol}(R_{lo}T^1{}_{l,sg,n,inan}T_{o,sg,n,inan})T_{l,pl,m,an})T_{a,sg,m,an}$ | R1 |
| 3. | $kauzirovat'_{oa}\ (imet'_{ol}\ (byt'_{lo}\ ponimanie_{l,sg,n,inan}\ zadanie_{o,sg,n,inan})\ soldat_{l,pl,m,an})\ komandir_{a,sg,m,an}$ | R2, R3 |
| 4. | $\mathbf{B}\ kauzirovat'_{oa}\ imet'_{ol}\ (byt'_{lo}\ ponimanie_{l,sg,n,inan}\ zadanie_{o,sg,n,inan})\ soldat_{l,pl,m,an}\ komandir_{a,sg,m,an}$ | **B** |
| 5. | $\mathbf{B}^2(\mathbf{B}\ kauzirovat'_{oa}\ imet'_{ol})\ byt'_{lo}\ ponimanie_{l,sg,n,inan}\ zadanie_{o,sg,n,inan}\ soldat_{l,pl,m,an}\ komandir_{a,sg,m,an}$ | $\mathbf{B}^2$ |
| 6. | $\text{GOVORIT}'_{ola}\ zadanie_{o,sg,n,inan}\ soldat_{l,pl,m,an}\ komandir_{a,sg,m,an}$ | R4 |
| 7. | $\mathbf{C}_{[2]}\ \text{GOVORIT}'_{ola}\ soldat_{l,pl,m,an}\ komandir_{a,sg,m,an}\ zadanie_{o,sg,n,inan}$ | $\mathbf{C}_{[2]}$ |
| 8. | $\mathbf{C}_1(\mathbf{C}_{[2]}\ \text{GOVORIT}'_{ola})\ komandir_{a,sg,m,an}\ soldat_{l,pl,m,an}\ zadanie_{o,sg,n,inan}$ | $\mathbf{C}_1$ |
| 9. | $\text{GOVORIT}'_{alo}\ komandir_{a,sg,m,an}\ soldat_{l,pl,m,an}\ zadanie_{o,sg,n,inan}$ | R5 |
| 10. | $\text{GOVORIT}'_{otGIN,sg,pas}\ (ot\ komandir_{G,sg,m,an})\ soldat_{I,pl,m,an}\ zadanie_{N,sg,n,inan}$ | R6, R7 |
| 11. | $uznavat'_{otGIN,sg,pas}\ (ot\ komandir_{G,sg,m,an})\ soldat_{I,pl,m,an}\ zadanie_{N,sg,n,inan}$ | R8 |
| 12. | $u\#\underset{00}{znavat'_{otGIN,sg,pas}}\#\underset{010}{ot}\#\underset{011}{komandir_{G,sg,m,an}}\#\underset{02}{soldat_{I,pl,m,an}}\#\underset{03}{zadanie_{N,sg,n,inan}}\#$ | R9 |
| 13. | $\#\underset{03}{zadanie_{N,sg,n,inan}}\#\underset{00}{uznavat'_{otGIN,sg,pas}}\#\underset{02}{soldat_{I,pl,m,an}}\#\underset{010}{ot}\#\underset{011}{komandir_{G,sg,m,an}}\#$ | R9 |
| 14. | $\#\underset{03}{[zadanie]^2}<[N,sg,n,inan]\#(\underset{00}{[uznavat'_{otGIN}]^1}<[sg])<[pas]\#\underset{02}{[soldat]^2}<[I,pl,m,an]\#\underset{010}{ot}\#$ $\underset{011}{[komandir]^2}<[G,sg,m,an]\#$ | R10, R11 |
| 15. | $\#\underset{03}{[zadanie]^2}<\emptyset\#(\underset{00}{[uznavat'_{otGIN}]^1}<et)<sja\#\underset{02}{[soldat]^2}<ami\#\underset{010}{ot}\#\underset{011}{[komandir]^2}<a\#$ | R12, R13 |
| 16. | $\#\underset{03}{zadanie}<\emptyset\#(\underset{00}{uznaj}<et)<sja\#\underset{02}{soldat}<ami\#\underset{010}{ot}\#\underset{011}{komandir}<a\#$ | R14, R15, R16 |

# Index